Service-Learning through Cultural Exchange and Expressive Arts Therapy

This book highlights various service-learning experiences that incorporate creative techniques such as art making and other expressive therapy practices. Utilizing service-learning provides students, faculty, and volunteers a chance to create an ethnorelativist world view, with the understanding that human beings are contextual in relationship to their culture. The use of expressive arts therapies is highlighted as a complementary way to build relationships with those who differ from one another and to increase students'/volunteers' cultural understanding and awareness. Chapters cover concepts such as cultural immersion, cultural exchange, transformational learning, and cultural competency in working with others. The focus of service within various cultures such as Nepal, South Africa, and the Cheyenne River Lakota Reservation in South Dakota are presented using anecdotal, narrative, and case vignettes.

Ideal for art therapists and art therapy students interested in engaging and/or providing service-learning experiences for others, this book is full of anecdotes from the author's personal experience, as well as cases that reflect cultural learning using various expressive arts techniques.

Katherine Jackson, PhD, LPAT, ATR-BC, RYT, is a professor of counseling and art therapy at Ursuline College in Ohio, USA. She also maintains an expressive arts therapy private practice working with children, teens, and adults.

"Based on her wide-reaching experiences, Dr. Katherine Jackson offers frameworks and examples to demonstrate how the heart of service-learning is mutual engagement. With examples from within the U.S. and around the globe, readers can appreciate many ways to integrate expressive arts with cultural arts for meaningful exchanges."

Jordan S. Potash, *PhD, REAT, LCPAT, ATR-BC,*
Associate Professor, Art Therapy Program,
The George Washington University

"Dr. Katherine Jackson's seminal work on service-learning utilizing expressive arts therapy brings an authentic and fresh perspective in the use of the creative arts to bridge human relationships. Dr. Jackson infuses discussion of applicable theory with practical insights gained from firsthand experiences not just facilitating service trips, but from her own personal experiences as a 'third culture kid' who grew up in Congo, making this a compelling and fascinating read. Her work not only focuses on bringing expressive arts, such as dance, music, and art making to those being served, it also highlights the cultural exchange that unifies and transforms diverse worldviews."

Rebecca D. Miller, *PhD, LPC, LPAT, ATR-BC, ATCS,*
PMH-C, Program Director and Associate Professor of Graduate
Counseling and Art Therapy, Ursuline College

"Dr. Katherine Jackson has written an engaging account of her service-learning work. I believe that her integration of expressive arts therapy is a powerful way to uplift and unify people. I hope that we can encourage and engage more students and practitioners in expressive arts therapy to participate in service-learning opportunities."

David Santulli, *founder of United Planet*

Service-Learning through Cultural Exchange and Expressive Arts Therapy

Katherine Jackson

Routledge
Taylor & Francis Group
NEW YORK AND LONDON

Designed cover image: Cover image of joyous children at the Samata School, Kathmandu, Nepal, supplied by Katherine Jackson

First published 2026
by Routledge
605 Third Avenue, New York, NY 10158

and by Routledge
4 Park Square, Milton Park, Abingdon, Oxon, OX14 4RN

Routledge is an imprint of the Taylor & Francis Group, an informa business

©2026 Katherine Jackson

The right of Katherine Jackson to be identified as author of this work has been asserted in accordance with sections 77 and 78 of the Copyright, Designs and Patents Act 1988.

All rights reserved. No part of this book may be reprinted or reproduced or utilized in any form or by any electronic, mechanical, or other means, now known or hereafter invented, including photocopying and recording, or in any information storage or retrieval system, without permission in writing from the publishers.

For Product Safety Concerns and Information please contact our EU representative GPSR@taylorandfrancis.com. Taylor & Francis Verlag GmbH, Kaufingerstraße 24, 80331 München, Germany.

Trademark notice: Product or corporate names may be trademarks or registered trademarks, and are used only for identification and explanation without intent to infringe.

Library of Congress Cataloging-in-Publication Data
Names: Jackson, Katherine (Art therapist) author
Title: Service learning through cultural exchange and expressive arts therapy / Katherine Jackson.
Identifiers: LCCN 2025049257 (print) | LCCN 2025049258 (ebook) | ISBN 9781041080398 hardback | ISBN 9781041080411 paperback | ISBN 9781003643432 ebook
Subjects: LCSH: Service learning | Art therapy | Cultural competence | LCGFT: Case studies
Classification: LCC LC220.5 .J34 2026 (print) | LCC LC220.5 (ebook)
LC record available at https://lccn.loc.gov/2025049257
LC ebook record available at https://lccn.loc.gov/2025049258

ISBN: 9781041080398 (hbk)
ISBN: 9781041080411 (pbk)
ISBN: 9781003643432 (ebk)

DOI: 10.4324/9781003643432

Typeset in Bembo
by KnowledgeWorks Global Ltd.

This book is dedicated to Sr. Kathleen Burke, founder of the Counseling and Art Therapy program at Ursuline College. With her guidance, love, and support, the service-learning program blossomed and flourished, and so did I.

Contents

	Acknowledgments	ix
	Author's Note	x
	About the Author	xii
	List of Contributors	xiii
	Preface	xiv
1	**What Is Service-Learning?**	1
2	**Utilizing Arts-Based Expressive Therapy within Service-Learning**	7
3	**Cultural Immersion**	23
4	**Cultural Exchange**	41
5	**Relationship Building** WITH CONTRIBUTIONS FROM MELISSA HLADEK	59
6	**Transformational Learning** BY MEGAN SEAMAN	77
7	**Cultural Competence**	101
8	**Social Justice and Service-Learning**	113

9	Indigenous Art-Making Practices as Connection	122
10	More Creative and Expressive Arts Practices	132
11	Planting the Seeds in Helping Professions: Service-Learning in Undergraduate Education BY HEATHER DENNING	139
12	Best Practices, Logistics, and Wisdom Learned from Service-Learning	159
13	Wisdom from Service Providers and Recipients: Interviews with Leaders, Volunteers, and Students	177
14	Epilogue: Gratitude, Humility, and Love	197
	Index	199

Acknowledgments

My gratitude is immense for all the girls, boys, women, and men who have allowed me to serve and who I have been reciprocally enriched by their love, care, kindness, and enthusiasm. Heartfelt appreciation for the service leaders and providers, including David Santulli at United Planet, Binita Adhikari at Antardristi, Raj Gyawali at Social Tours, Indira Ranamagar at PA Nepal, Julie Garreau at Cheyenne River Youth Project, graffiti artists from Red Can Graffiti Jam, Gideon and Jennifer Chishamba at Peniel Center, Zimbabwe, and Nick and Roxie Mould at United Through Sport, Gqeberha, South Africa. Thank you to my students and volunteers who made serving others possible.

I want to thank my loving husband, Jay Leitson, and my kind and open-hearted children, Max, Liam, and Haydn Palmer, and my bonus children, Jordan Leitson and Katie Gossen Leitson, and Rachael Leitson and Dan Zabludovsky, my faithful and loving parents, Marcia and Oscar Marvin, and Jim Krauss-Jackson and MJ Helms and Jane Krauss-Jackson, my brother Jonathan Jackson and his wife Jennifer for all their love and support over the years, grandparents and all my ancestors who came before me who unknowingly facilitated this journey to unfold and manifest into a book detailing my passion for service-learning.

I am also most grateful to my colleagues Heather Denning, Melissa Hladek, and Dr. Megan Seaman who not only share my passion for service-learning, but who I am honored to call my friends. These fearless, engaging, and bright women have contributed to this book in heartfelt and scholarly ways. My thanks to Ursuline College for allowing me the freedom to create the service-learning program. Special acknowledgment to the teachings of Saint Angela Merici, who inspired me through her own service work.

Author's Note

In January 2001, I got a telephone call from Catholic Charities' Migration Refugee Services. They were aware of my upbringing in Africa and my art therapy training, which prompted them to ask if I could work a few hours a week with the Lost Boys of Sudan, a refugee group of young men who had been displaced by rebels and war in Sudan. I jumped at this opportunity to be of service. It felt like I was going "home" to help my people, the people I had grown up with. This service to displaced Africans expanded to include many displaced persons from Afghanistan, Iran, Somalia, Congo, and Rwanda. Providing service in the form of creative expression and art therapy led to my establishing a service-learning program at Ursuline College.

Looking back on my early childhood, it occurred to me that one of the issues that haunted me was how people in the United States were ignorant or not informed of the devastation caused by colonizers in Africa, hardships in other countries as well as the toll of colonization, and widespread enslavement and genocide of African slaves and the Native American populations in the United States. In my work with displaced populations, I realized that human beings just want to be seen and heard, and that we are all interconnected. When someone in Africa hurts, we are all hurt (even if unconsciously and unknowingly), even if we cannot see the impact immediately.

In 2012, as a full-time associate professor in the Master of Counseling and Art Therapy department, I began a service-learning program through Ursuline College where students, alumni, and community members could travel to various locations to provide loving kindness, being seen and seeing other human beings, as well as providing heartfelt love and care for those in dire circumstances. Ursuline College is a small Catholic college in the greater Cleveland, Ohio area. Although the college has a Catholic identity, it remains open to all religious and non-religious backgrounds and has a spirit of progressive thinking and service traditions to all humankind. Ursuline College holds dear to Catholic social teachings and is led by its mission to be of service to others.

I was inspired by the Ursuline sisters, as they presented on their recent trip to Italy, following in the footsteps of St. Angela Merici, the foundress of the Ursuline sisters. St. Angela herself was a champion of young women and helped them find their calling by serving and teaching the underserved or neglected that were amidst the countryside and cities of northern Italy. I was awestruck at the narrative of St. Angela's serving, and also her ability to travel around parts of Italy to help others. In this moment, I had an epiphany of sorts and a strong urge to begin a service-learning program modeled after the teachings of St. Angela but from a lay person's rather than a religious perspective. During the faculty meeting, I quietly scribbled a note on a napkin and passed it to my program director to see if she might support a service-learning program, she said yes to my delight. I wanted the service-learning program to be secular and open to all diversities, ethnicities, and various religions. I set about proposing the program, met with administrators, and by the end of 2012 had a full-fledged service-learning program underway.

I wanted to create an opportunity for our students to become global helpers and healers, to be aware of their privilege, and to be able to see the world in a more realistic and holistic light. My hope was that the ability to get out of the United States comfort zone would help to create a mature and seasoned therapist in the world, who would have an increased sense of cultural competence and understand the concept that humans are all connected, part of the same human race, but with many differing and diverse backgrounds and viewpoints. To see and be seen are core needs in every human being's life. I was at the very least hoping to provide a lens of understanding and deep compassion for those in underserved countries by really "seeing" the essence of human suffering, courage, and resilience. Because my graduate students were soon to be art therapists and counselors, I also hoped that art making could be used as a common language, or at least an ice breaker of sorts, and that this would be of benefit for the expressive healing of art making and art psychotherapy to take hold.

To date, I have journeyed with students, alumni, community members, and faculty to South Dakota to work with Lakota Sioux, Nepal to work with orphans and sexually traumatized girls, Africa (South Africa and Zimbabwe) to work with underserved children and victims of AIDS, Peru, El Salvador, Ecuador, and Hungary. Currently, we have narrowed our focus to the Lakota Sioux in South Dakota, Nepal, and Africa, where our skills and unique approach are needed and requested. These are also communities that have taught my students and me the most valuable human lessons, of charity, generosity, love, and kindness.

About the Author

Katherine Jackson, PhD, LPAT, ATR-BC, RYT, has been a practicing expressive arts therapist for over 37 years. She holds a Masters in Expressive Therapy, and a PhD in Psychology. She is a board-certified art therapist, licensed professional art therapist, registered yoga teacher, and health coach. She teaches as a full-time professor at Ursuline College in the Master of Counseling and Art Therapy program. She started the service-learning program at Ursuline College in 2012, where she has taken students, alumni, and community members to Nepal, South Africa, Cheyenne River Reservation in South Dakota, Zimbabwe, Peru, El Salvador, Ecuador, and Hungary to volunteer with marginalized and unrepresented people.

Dr. Jackson maintains a private practice in Cleveland, Ohio, where she specializes in using expressive arts therapies, holistic health, and wellness approaches with a variety of people, including teens, adults, couples and families. She has presented nationally and internationally on various topics including multicultural competency, service-learning, expressive arts therapies, and holistic health and wellness.

List of Contributors

Heather J. Denning, MA, LPAT, LSW, ATR-BC, ATCS, is a licensed and board-certified art therapist and licensed social worker. She is the director of the undergraduate art therapy program and chair of the Art, Design, and Communication Department at Mercyhurst University in Erie, Pennsylvania. Her clinical experience in art therapy is working in community mental health primarily in group settings. Her previous publications focus on group work and undergraduate art therapy education.

Melissa Hladek, MA, LPCC-S, LPAT, ATR-BC, is a clinical mental health counselor, art therapist, clinical supervisor, counselor educator, and proud mother of three incredible daughters. Melissa has participated in service-learning since 2013 and has traveled to several parts of the world including Cheyenne River in South Dakota, Ecuador, Zimbabwe, South Africa, Hungary, and Nepal.

Megan M. Seaman, PhD, LPC, NCC, RYT, is a counseling and art therapy professor at Ursuline College. She acts as a co-leader for the Counseling and Art Therapy Program's service-learning program and has traveled around the world collaborating with global partners for social change and creative healing that support mental health. Dr. Seaman also maintains a private practice where she uses creative arts healing strategies with children, adults, and families to address concerns related to anxiety, mood disorders, trauma, and family cohesion.

Preface

After years of deliberating on how to share my experiences with cultural immersion, cultural exchange, transformational learning, and service-learning, I have created this book, part memoir, part reflections of service-learning experiences with students, and part scholarly research and best practices related to working with others in service-learning endeavors. My roots are those of a missionary granddaughter and daughter growing up in Congo, Africa.

In my current role as a therapist, this history is something that provides me with some joy and angst. On one hand, I feel proud of my lineage of do-gooders and helpers, but I also have a sense of contributing to colonization practices that may have kept African people unwittingly oppressed by white privileged people. I do know that my grandparents and parents certainly had no intention of doing harm, and that the time of my childhood in Africa the 1960s and early 1970s was a changing and transformational time. In history, we recognize that individuals are a product of their generation and whatever common cultural beliefs are present at the time guide actions and thoughts. It is because of my contrary feelings that I need to understand my history, my own part in the colonization practices as well as liberation of fellow human beings that led me to this journey. I will venture here to say, growing up in Congo, my first service-learning experience, had a lasting and profound effect on me and grew me into the person I have become and continue to become. It is what has motivated and inspired me to do this work and continues to be one of the invaluable gifts of learning in my life. I want to share this remarkable story here as a preface to the rest of this book.

As stated earlier, I come from a long line of helpers in my family, in fact two generations of Presbyterian missionaries who served as teachers, preachers, and nurses in the Democratic Republic of Congo (formerly known as the Belgian Congo). My grandparents James "Jimmy" Jackson and Alma

Headen met in Congo. Alma was one of the first women missionaries to go solo to what was referred to at the time as the "dark continent." As a southern woman from High Point, North Carolina, in 1923, going alone was unheard of, but my grandmother, who was 26 at the time, was fiercely independent and a true free spirit; in fact some would call her a tenacious go-getter. Her skill was in secretarial work, and through the help of a friendly cousin, Cecil Mariner, she was able to accept a post as secretary to a bush doctor already serving in the Belgian Congo, Africa. Meanwhile, my grandfather, in 1930 at the age of 29, was a shy and quiet southern gentleman from Augusta, Georgia, who prayed daily for God to show him the way. Being a newly minted pastor, he felt called to go to Congo as a missionary. My grandfather's parents were worried about their son's choice, but supported him, nonetheless. Around the year 1930, my grandparents met in Bulape, Congo; Jimmy fresh off the boat, and Alma who had been in Congo for seven years already. Within the first year of Jimmy's service, they were engaged and later married in 1932. Soon thereafter three sons were born, my father, James "Jim" Jackson being the first (Figure 0.1), then later William "Bill" and Cecil.

Figure 0.1 Alma Headen Jackson (grandmother) with my father, James Jackson, in Bulape Congo

Many years later, I recall my early childhood immersed in Congo, watching my parents help African folks who had been displaced and abused by years of colonization through King Leopold's dictatorship of the Congo for over 75 years. My parents had met in my grandfather's church in Jacksonville, Florida, both entranced with serving on the "mission field." My mother, Marcia Benefiel, had been preparing for some time to put her nursing skills to good use in Congo, and my father, also trained as a pastor, wanted to help in any way he could. My father ended up teaching school and my mother worked at a small clinic in Bulape, and later ran a clinic out of our home in Indesha, Congo. In essence both my grandparents and parents were helping the Congolese empower themselves from within, by providing healthcare and education opportunities. I was born en route to Congo, in Brussels, Belgium and had arrived at three months old, with my older brother, Jonathan ("Jon") in tow (Figure 0.2). The story goes that, once we had disembarked from our ocean liner ship at the mouth of the Congo River, the only passage to get to our waiting World War II type airplane was a raft down this crocodile-infested and wild rapids river. As my mother likes to explain, the raft was made of boards held up by empty oil barrels, used as a pontoon-like structure, no motor, and an oarsman in the back ready to lead us down this wild ride. With many prayers, my parents, my brother and I boarded the raft, with no guard rails, no seats, and no life jackets, which took us down the Congo River to our waiting transport. This early experience set the stage for my time in the Congo and surely created a more fearless version of myself, who later would be leading service-learning adventures. This humble, albeit rather exotic, risky, childhood contributed greatly to my intrinsic or possibly genetic need to be of service to others.

Growing up in Congo was a unique experience. From a very early age, I understood that Congolese had been mistreated by the Belgian government. I saw evidence of extreme poverty, infrastructure damage, and loss of sustainable jobs and agriculture. The Belgian government had destroyed large swaths of land, extracting valuable minerals and diamonds, leaving the land unable to be farmed. Large masses of land in Congo were rainforests, so this made agriculture challenging, once the pillaging of the diamond mines had wreaked havoc on what little agricultural land there was. By 1960 the Congolese were in a limbo time, the Belgian government having just been overthrown. The new government, which changed Congo's name to Zaire (briefly), had taken over, but in the 1990s lost control, and Congo reverted to its old name but now became known as the Democratic Republic of Congo, or DRC as folks commonly refer to it today.

From my childhood memory, people of Congo were kind, musical, artistic, creative, and resourceful. Congo was a collectivist culture, where everyone functioned in a community. All items were shared, whether it was food, clothing, housing, or child-rearing responsibilities. As a small child, I learned how to give, share, and be a part of this community. There was also a sense of distrust for persons with white skin, and we were white southerners, and very easy to spot in a crowd of brown-skinned Africans. This otherness was palpable and put us at risk of harm at times. Learned helplessness had also pervaded the Congolese, after years of harsh colonization under the Belgians, and it was hard for people to be motivated for change due to fear of oppressive regimes taking over. Despite these tumultuous times, I grew up as an African, learning to be in the company of fellow Africans and play alongside the village kids. I also realized that, although I felt African, there was another culture (which I did not know about in real life) of which my parents talked about. This was my first experience of otherness. I was not fully African, and I was not fully of the United States (Figure 0.2).

Imagine growing up in the 1960s and 1970s without electricity, television, radio, junk food, or restaurants, and having water that was pumped through a cistern for indoor use (water catchment system). Also imagine poisonous snakes in abundance, crocodiles in the lakes/streams, and small animals roving around. Contrary to popular belief, large game animals and other mammals steer clear of humans, so I never spotted an elephant, lion, water buffalo, or giraffe. In our yard, we had mango, avocado, and guava trees, as well as palm nuts, peanuts, and tubers. These foods were in high availability, but just about everything else was scarce.

Figure 0.2 The author with family in Congo, 1966. Jon (brother), Marcia (mother), Katherine, and Jim (father) Jackson

I write all of this to help the reader understand that I grew up with scarcity, even though my parents were from a privileged white background. I understood what it was to be hungry, and at the same time learned to share whatever I had, which seems contradictory, but growing up in Congo meant both. I also learned that I was what Pollock and Van Reken (2017) refer to as a third culture kid, having roots in one country, but growing up in another. This third culture is what arises when you are in no-persons land, and unable to fully fit in with either country. It is precisely this uncomfortableness that has spurred me forward to educate myself and want to help others within the framework of service-learning.

CHAPTER 1

What Is Service-Learning?

Service-learning has become a popular pedagogical learning approach among high school, college, and graduate students, combining classroom learning, community/civic engagement, and volunteer work at various locations in the United States and abroad. In this chapter, I seek to explain the concept of service-learning generally, as well as the theoretical underpinnings of service-learning in terms of intercultural sensitivity, postcolonial theory, and liberation philosophy. These key areas are important to understand what providing service-learning is all about.

In today's world, service-learning has spread to incorporate community members, retirees, gap year participants, and curious folks wanting to engage with the world through meaningful acts. In the field of mental health counseling and expressive arts therapy, service-learning has become a process of creating reciprocal knowledge between the social and personal, as well as objective and subjective experiences (Kolb, 1984). Utilizing service-learning provides students, faculty, and volunteers a chance to create an ethnorelativist worldview, which refers to understanding that human beings are contextual in relationship to their culture. Antiquated ideas of monoculturalism, ethnocentric, universalist, or melting pot approaches are not useful in understanding the diverse backgrounds of human beings that are served via service-learning endeavors (Bennett, 1998; Kapitan, 2015).

Although many definitions of service-learning exist, the best definition I have found was created by Jacoby (2015). She stated that,

> service learning is a form of experiential education in which students engage in activities that address human and community needs, together with structured opportunities for reflection designed to achieve desired learning outcomes. Reflection and reciprocity are key concepts of service learning.
> (*Jacoby,* 2015, p. 5)

Furco's (1996) balanced approach to experiential education suggests that service-learning is at the top of a pyramid of four other types of service: volunteerism, community service, field education, and internship experiences. The hallmark of service-learning is that there is equal benefit to the provider and the recipient of the service, as well as an equal focus on both the service being provided and the learning that occurs. Furco's (1996) approach, community service, field placement, internship, and volunteerism all have a role in the hierarchical continuum of service-learning. Many programs in universities around the United States do not differentiate between community service and other types of fieldwork, instead naming all of it service-learning. However, it can be noted that there are small details that create difference in these terms, most notably the fact that in service-learning there is an exchange and reciprocal learning between service-learning server and the served.

An important aspect of service-learning is reciprocity. Reciprocity is the shared learning and giving of the provider and the recipient engaged in a mutually beneficial relationship. The provider gives what the community or recipient requests, and in return is afforded an opportunity for growth and intrinsic reflection. As Sigmon (1994) states, "each participant is server and served, care giver and care acquirer, contributor and contributed to" (p. 4). To have the chance to witness and help alongside fellow human beings is a gift and honor that seems immeasurable and seeped in exceptional and profound experience.

Interestingly, the very phrase "service-learning" is made up of two words, service and learning, each word with the power to add value and transform (Porter-Honnet & Poulsen, 1989). The concept of service-learning does not imply learning just by providing service, but rather implies learning as the result of an experience and reflection on that experience (Furco, 1996). Types of service-learning endeavors are vast; however, the type that was used for the experiences in this book include understanding of social issues, understanding human differences and commonality, gaining awareness of self and other, and working together to solve community or collective problems (Jacoby, 2015).

Service-learning from an academic perspective is education that is grounded in experience. In essence, reflection through experience "stimulates learners to integrate experience and observations with existing knowledge, to examine theory in practice, and to analyze and question their assumptions and beliefs (Jacoby, 2015, p. 5). Dewey (1938, as cited in Jacoby, 2015), who is considered the early influencer of experiential education, believed that learning from experience is not enough, but that reflective thinking and expressing of the experience is formative. Reflecting on the experiences of the provider as well as the recipient is what creates the growth and transformational learning. From a clinical mental health perspective, service-learning is a philosophy of human growth and potential, creating meaning-making, as well as social justice opportunities and a deep reflective way of knowing the world and its people.

Reflective practice is integral to service-learning. Providing opportunities for participants to dialog with each other as well as keeping a daily journal have profound effects on transformational growth. Our identities as educators, students, and participants are in the process of becoming (Jacoby, 2015). Seeing the server as "in-process" of becoming allows for a more open-minded, constructing, and initiating way of being and seeing the served. Using reflective practice helps the practitioner create a contextually rich view of those being served, that places human beings within their place with differing customs and ways of being. It helps create "meaning schemes" that aid in critically re-looking and re-thinking old paradigms that may be culturally specific and unfitting for the new culture being learned and understood (Moon, 2013).

THEORY OF DEVELOPMENTAL MODEL OF INTERCULTURAL SENSITIVITY

In researching service-learning, I was introduced to the Developmental Model of Intercultural Sensitivity (DMIS) and the idea of ethnorelativism created by Milton Bennett (Bennett, 1998). He found that as people became more interculturally competent it seemed that there was a major change in the quality of their experience, which he called the move from ethnocentrism to ethnorelativism. Bennett used the term "ethnocentrism" to refer to the experience of one's own culture as "central to reality." Basically, the beliefs and behaviors that people receive in their primary socialization are unquestioned; they are experienced as "just the way things are." Bennett coined the term "ethnorelativism" to mean the opposite of ethnocentrism—the experience of one's own beliefs and behaviors as just one organization of reality among many viable possibilities" (Bennett, 2004, p. 62).

Ethnorelativism is a grounded theory that proposes that one's own culture is experienced in the context of other cultures. Acceptance of cultural difference is the state in which one's own culture is experienced as just one of a number of equally complex worldviews (Bennett, 2004). Bennett further adds, "By discriminating differences among cultures (including one's own), and by constructing a kind of self-reflexive perspective, people with this worldview are able to experience others as different from themselves, but equally human" (2004, p. 6).

More innovative approaches to service-learning include cultural code switching, examining biases and ethical choices, as well as providing opportunities for cultural competence and intercultural sensitivity (Kapitan, 2015).

In adopting a new lens based on ethnorelative theory, service-learning embodies an opportunity for experiential learning and meaning-making to support mental health counselors and expressive art therapists' development (Burnett, et. al., 2005).

POSTCOLONIAL THEORY

Colonization of less dominant countries/people by more dominant countries/people has happened repeatedly in history. The vestiges of this colonization have been made bare in Africa, island nations, Central and South America, as well as in the indigenous land of North America and Australia (to name a few). For centuries, the colonizer's attempted to educate people deemed barbarians and savages to help them become civilized and adopt the worldview of those more powerful and dominant. Another form of colonization was in teaching and helping from the perspective of the colonizer group, therefore discarding and invalidating traditional means of building, planting, religious worship, and child-rearing practices. The dominating group would implant their own worldviews as a superior way of living life (Kapitan, 2015; Moon, 2013).

Postcolonial theory refers to the historical legacy of control imposed on a culture or country by colonization practices (Moon, 2013). This can include inherited cultural traumas, institutional structures, and unequal distributions of social power and privilege (Norsworthy & Khuankaew, 2006). Remnants of colonization can be seen in a postcolonial country and culture when the dominant narratives, values, beliefs, and practices are still seen as superior. This can also be seen in trivializing indigenous practices, beliefs, and healing traditions as sub-par to more empirical and scientific ways of seeing the world (Moon, 2013). As Potash et al. (2017) states, "preparing to work from a culturally humble, decolonizing framework requires learning about the historical, political, economic and structural legacies of colonialism and White supremacy" (p. 76).

Thus, understanding colonization and Western people's participation (sometimes unknowingly) in the colonization process is imperative when attempting to provide service-learning experiences for others. Potash et al. (2017) urges service-learning volunteers to establish "collaborative, consultative relationships" to "decenter" the art therapist and/or counselor volunteer and foster "attunement to the hosts culture" (p. 76). Service-learning volunteers must be able to take responsibility and look at potential implicit biases, even if directly not responsible, for colonization practices of white European ancestors that are woven into the fabric of the United States and are very much at play in many underdeveloped countries. It is not the service-learner's role to hold superior worldviews or try to "save" those being served. The task at hand is to be open to other worldviews, other ways of being in a culture, and to set aside biases based on privilege.

LIBERATION THEORY

Lilla Watson (2007), an Aboriginal leader and teacher, said, "If you have come to help me you are wasting your time. If you have come because your liberation is bound up with mine, then let us work together." This quote sums up the essence of liberation philosophy and theory. To liberate, all must be free, but also striving for a just society and growing in transforming the oppressed and the oppressor. Freire (2000), in his seminal book *Pedagogy of the Oppressed*, states that, "the great humanistic and historical task of the oppressed: to liberate themselves and their oppressors as well" (p. 44). At the core of "helping" from a service-learning perspective is this idea, that in helping the oppressed we are also interested in helping the oppressor stop the oppression caused by colonization, caste systems, and other hierarchical power systems. Therefore, in service-learning, the reciprocal foundation of co-creating learning and growing together from a mutually beneficial project is paramount to my work in leading groups to various countries in need of help. More times than I can count, I have heard my students and other volunteers say to me that they have been deeply impacted and transformed by their service-learning experience more than those we helped. Taking the so-called "privileged" American into a so-called "third world" or developing country is just this concept. We must work to liberate the oppressed and those that have oppressed, whether wittingly or unwittingly, and have contributed to others' downturns. There is a popular adage in Nepal that says: "The ash that rises and flows from the Bagmati river after a cremation, eventually will flow to all countries and touch all people." This idea speaks to the interconnectedness of all beings and all life. When someone pollutes our world, the effects of this are many times found in other countries, without recognition by the "privileged" that this was caused by their actions.

With the groundwork set and the theoretical worldview clear, the next chapters in this book will highlight many experiences, lessons learned, case vignettes, and anecdotes gathered in working with others who some may say are oppressed. My role as leader of service-learning groups over the last 13 years has been to liberate us both from the view of the oppressed and oppressor, the have and have-nots, the privileged and unprivileged. My aim in providing service-learning experiences along with volunteers is to serve in showing up when asked, re-frame from my own views so that I may learn others' views, to work alongside my fellow human beings in the spirit of mutuality and shared common good.

REFERENCES

Bennett, M. (1998). *Basic concepts of intercultural communication*. Boston: Intercultural Press.

Bennett, M. (2004). Becoming interculturally competent. In J. Wurzel (ed.) *Toward multiculturalism: A reader in multicultural education*. (2nd ed. pp. 62–77). Newton, MA: Intercultural Resource Cooperation.

Freire, P. (2000). *Pedagogy of the oppressed*. New York: Bloomsbury Press.

Furco, A. (1996). Service-learning: A balanced approach to experiential education. In *Expanding boundaries: Service and learning*. Washington, DC: Corporation for Nation and Community Service.

Jacoby, B. (2015). *Service-learning essentials: Questions, answers, and lessons learned*. San Francisco, CA: Jossey-Bass.

Kolb, D. (1984). *Experiential learning: Experience as the source of learning and development*. Englewood Cliffs, NJ: Prentice Hall.

Kapitan, L. (2015). Social action in practice: Shifting ethnocentric lens in cross-cultural art therapy encounters, *Art Therapy*, 32 (2): 104–111, DOI: 10.1080/07421656.2015.1060403.

Moon, C. (2013). Developing therapeutic arts programs in Kenya and Tanzania: A collaborative consultation approach. In P. Howie, S. Prasad, & J. Kristel (eds.), *Using art therapy with diverse populations: Crossing cultures and abilities*. London, Jessica Kingsley.

Norsworthy, K.L., & Khuankaew, O. (2006). Bringing social justice to international practices of counseling psychology. In L.H. Toporek, L.H. Gerstein, N.A. Fouad, G. Roysircar, & T. Israel (eds.), *Handbook of social justice in counseling psychology: Leadership, vision, and action*. Thousand Oaks, CA: Sage.

Porter-Honnet, E., & Poulson, S.J. (1989). *Principles of good practice for combining service and learning*. Racine, WI: The Johnson Foundation.

Potash, J., Bardot, H., Moon, C.H., Napoli, M., Lyonsmith, A., & Hamilton, M. (2017). Ethical implications of cross-cultural international art therapy. *The Arts in Psychotherapy*, 56: 74–82.

Sigmon, R. (1994). Serving to learn, learning to serve. In *Linking service with learning*. Evergreen State University. Washington, DC: Council to Independent Colleges.

Watson, L. (2007). International Women's Network (2007). https://lillanetwork.wordpress.com/about/

CHAPTER 2

Utilizing Arts-Based Expressive Therapy within Service-Learning

At the start of every endeavor, it is important to ask, "Why am I doing this, and why do I want to do this and how is art making and/or expressive arts important? The "why" of any proposition is of the utmost importance; it forms the very backbone and foundation of any project. In my experience a "why" must be full of heartfelt desire and curiosity to explore or understand something of interest. In beginning this quest to create a service-learning program at Ursuline College, I had to understand the nature of what I was questing. In the service-learning program, I wanted to explore and help my graduate students, and understand other cultures by cultural immersion, cultural exchange, recognizing Indigenous art practices as art as therapy within the culture, and most importantly build lasting relationships with other folks around the world, to feel the interconnectedness of all beings, as well as the unique diversity within the human web of connection.

In addition, I was interested in teaching master's students how to be more culturally competent in breaking stigmas and understanding their own privilege as they helped in cultures different from their own. Creating a reciprocal learning environment where students were the providers and recipients of learning in and among other cultures was paramount. It was also important to help students become more ethnorelative, to understand that they have one perspective based on their own worldviews and inherent cultural biases.

DOI: 10.4324/9781003543432-2

ARTS-BASED THERAPY HISTORY

Because I teach in the master's program of Counseling and Art Therapy, I was more specifically interested to see if using art as therapy or simply art making could enhance deep intrinsic knowledge of oneself and the culture served. Art therapy has been in existence since the early 1940s. This field simultaneously had its roots in both the United Kingdom and the United States. In the US, early art therapy influencers were Margaret Naumburg, Edith Kramer, and Florence Cane, with a host of other early contributors. These early developers were simply putting a name to a type of creative expression that has been around for millennia. Human beings have existed in current form for about 200,000 years, and there is evidence dating as far back as 45,000 BCE that human beings were steeped in creative expression. Early humans drew on cave walls, crafted vessels and pottery, beautified their spaces, and left their indelible mark. These early cave paintings and vessels held meaning to the ancient people demonstrated by patterns and visual language in the form of symbols. Cathy Malchiodi (2022), in her book *Handbook of Expressive Therapy*, states that human beings

> have turned to various forms of arts-based expression when confronted by crisis, loss, disaster, or illness. As a species, we have been turning to the healing rhythms and synchrony of movement, gesture, sound, music, ritual, and ceremony to confront and resolved distress for thousands of years.
>
> (p. ix)

Art therapy today is not so different: art therapists help individuals to express themselves and find meaning in their life struggles. Of course, art therapy is more clinically oriented but ask any artist or art therapist about the pure healing power of creative arts. The very act of creating can be curative.

Hans Prinzhorn, a well-known psychiatrist and art historian of images created by individuals who were diagnosed with a severe mental illness, believed that all human beings have a creativity that needs expression. He was famous for collecting thousands of images of the mentally ill, which all seem to depict an expression of their inner and outer world. His contributions have been invaluable to the art therapy community, but also to the idea that human beings have an urge to create (Prinzhorn, 1922/1972). Art making helps human beings concretize experiences, discover meaning, and leave a legacy for future generations about their views of the world.

Viktor Lowenfeld, art educator and graphic development pioneer, looked at children's development through art making in his seminal book *Creative and Mental Growth* (1953). He created stages of artistic development and believed that all children, including those with special needs, followed a developmental sequence. There has been debate over the idea that Lowenfeld's graphic developmental indicators are culturally relevant and transferrable. Goodman et al. (2022), in their study of graphic indicators with Ugandan youth, found that Lowenfeld's stages did not align with their data samples. In fact, they discovered that art making had a lot to do with context within which the child making art resided and was culturally relevant to the image maker.

In Edith Kramer's work on the "third hand" (1986) she stresses that formed expression and inner consistency, which means the artwork is honest and authentic to the artist, are pivotal in art expression (in Henley, 2024). Kramer explained that economy of means should also be part of any art making, which simply indicates that no other additions to the art making are needed, it is just right the way it is. Lastly, Kramer believed that art making should have evocative and communicative power, in that art should move us in some way and have the ability to convey intention and meaning (1986). I have found Kramer's third hand approach to be the best fit for working cross-culturally. It is broad and does not rely on culture-bound developmental ideas as does Lowenfeld's stages.

Shaun McNiff (2015), art and expressive therapist, believes that the very act of expressing, whether it is through art making, dance, song, or movement, is deeply healing. He states that all people have the ability to be creative and express through creative means. According to McNiff (2015), "the arts in therapy has been grounded in personal experiences of how artistic expression transforms problems, brings relief and feelings of satisfaction. It is the most effective soul medicine" (p. 123). Likewise, Malchiodi (2022) explains that before human beings had a name for talking therapy/counseling humans used various forms of art-based expression when confronted with life's difficulties. Humans left their mark upon cliff faces, stone monuments, and caves as an act of expression of their lived experience.

SERVICE-LEARNING WITH EXPRESSIVE ARTS-BASED THERAPY

The use of expressive arts within the framework of service-learning is not well researched, but anecdotal evidence of providing creative outlets for those served has been written about. In Moon's (2013) work in Kenya and Tanzania, Kalmanowitz, Potash, and Chan s (2012) work in Asia, and Kapitan's work in Indigenous populations, we can see evidence of best practices.

In Moon's journey to Kenya and Tanzania to collaborate with the Global Alliance for Africa (GAA), a nonprofit that addresses the needs of orphans and other vulnerable children, she discovered multiple uses of creative arts therapies (2013). She has been working within the Therapeutic Arts Program (TAP), where children can use art materials to express feelings and trauma's that have occurred in their lives. Part of working within these nonprofit organizations is to train the trainer, which Moon has been actively doing. Kester (2011, as cited in Moon, 2013), suggests that the most successful art-based practices are characterized by "a pragmatic openness to site and situation, a willingness to engage with specific sites and communities in a creative and improvisational manner" (p. 125). Moon (2013) further adds that her collaborative model implemented by her team emphasizes "reflexivity, shared power, cultural relevance" and a general openness of mind and heart (p. 375).

Kalmanowitz et al. (2012), in their book *Art Therapy in Asia: To the Bone or Wrapped in Silk*, suggests that working cross-culturally needs to rely on cultural context of the country, not on Western ways or theories of art therapy. From their experience, people in Asia practicing mental health counseling and or expressive arts therapy include a more integrative approach considering traditional healing practices from Buddhism, Taoism, and Confucianism. Therefore, utilizing mindfulness, meditation, yogic practices and Ayurvedic medicine inform arts-based practices, creating a multi-dimensional and integrated type of expressive arts therapy.

Kapitan (2015), in her global work, emphasizes the need to practice art therapy enthnorelativism, which she defines as, "interacting with cultural differences while simultaneously engaging in guided critical reflection aimed at increasing self-reflexivity (i.e. the practice of examining the self-in-the-moment with particular attention to how one is actively constructing meaning)" (p. 109). When considering arts-based practices within other cultures, it is important to view the culture with openness and curiosity, while at the same time considering one's own viewpoint based on individual cultural context and worldview of the helper. In this way, one is able to culturally immerse without judgment, understanding that each culture has different ways of being, such as collectivistic standards or differing time perceptions.

ZIMBABWE

In our work in rural Bulawayo, Zimbabwe, we worked with children who were survivors of the AIDS epidemic. They were living in a residential center, called the Peniel Center. Most of the children were orphaned due to their parents' death from AIDS/HIV-related disease. In rural Africa, with no transportation to large cities and no money to buy or get medicine for AIDS, remission and treatment are nearly impossible. There is still an abundance of people dying from AIDS. This little-known fact is mostly obscured by the West with the majority of people believing that active AIDS is a disease of the past. Imagine if you were living in rural Africa, needing to walk about 5 miles to get clean water, and another 25-plus miles to get to a city, where life-giving medicine exists. Imagine that you had to make this trek daily for maintenance of your medicine. Would you walk a 50-plus-mile round trip daily for this? Most likely not, and hence the tragedy of failing health care measures in developing countries.

In 2015, Zimbabwe was still under militant control of dictator Robert Mugabe. We had decided to go to Zimbabwe, because one of our alumnus Rebecca Chilcote who had grown up there as a child and wanted to return to provide care for the orphans at the Peniel Center. Journeying to Zimbabwe was arduous and costly, therefore many of us came with few art materials, but with the hope that once we arrived we would utilize what was available in nature or what the small town of Bulawayo might have available for purchase. Once we arrived, we realized that the town had nothing except for some markets that had little food choices. In fact, Zimbabwe was a failing country, with 80% unemployment. Even with money for food, the choices were limited and many times out of date, rotten, or spoiled.

We were tasked with providing expressive arts for 15 children at the center. We noticed that the kids liked to play a stick game, where they would place a stick on the ground and then jump over it; each time a player jumped the stick was moved a little further away (Figure 2.1). The winner was chosen by the one who could jump the farthest without hitting the stick. In this instance, we used what Kapitan (2015) and Moon (2013) have written related to utilizing an ethnorelativistic lens, to be open to Zimbabwean culture, while at the same time understanding our own Western context. Of course, playing a game with a stick is probably as old as human evolution; however, until we were witness to the joy and fun that the kids were having, it did not occur to our over-complicated Western mindset.

Utilizing the brush, dried leaves, sundrenched weathered flora and fauna, we asked the children to gather these materials and create pictures in the dirt with these materials. This concept was novel to the kids, as they had never considered creating artwork with natural objects. Soon, the kids were all engaged and actively creating pictures, including their nature collage elements. This "urge to create," as dubbed by Prinzhorn (1922/1972), was indeed infectious and created a cacophony of sound as the children searched and giggled while assembling various twigs, rocks, and plants.

Figure 2.1 Girl playing stick-jumping game

Observing one's environment both in natural space as well as people's behaviors or habits can help inform us as to what method of creative engagement may work to create a relationship with others or help children learn about their own creativity and resourcefulness. Graduate students and volunteers can also learn flexibility, stepping outside their comfort zone and using the elements available to create an art-based session.

On another day in Zimbabwe, the children showed us how to get to the water pump station that was located about 2 miles from their village. As noted previously, clean water is scarce in rural Africa, thus water pumps have been installed outside of villages. In order to get clean ground water, a borehole has to be created using machinery. The hole can be anywhere from 50 to 280 feet deep. Many times, it takes multiple tries to tap into deep reservoirs below the earth's surface. Water is precious and is not wasted in these parts of Africa, where the climate is dry and arid. We walked the long path with our three girl companions, the girls carrying buckets on their heads to collect the water. The road to the water station was not much of a path, but a dusty, dry cut through sagebrush and other prickly plants, whose thorns attached to our clothing and skin. Once we arrived at the water, the girls made a singing and swinging game of the water pump apparatus. This small interlude of

Figure 2.2 Girls at the water pump singing

play turned into a song fest of expressive native folk songs and dancing, in which we were only too happy to join (Figure 2.2). We learned that music was imbued in this culture and created a nice diversion from hard menial tasks that needed to be completed. One of our greatest lessons was learned that day in that anything can be made into play, anything can be a meaningful moment, anything can create relationship if two parties are willing. The very act of walking to the watering hole with three girls created a bond and expression of self that could not have been made in other ways. In this moment the true spirit of service-learning was seen in the reciprocal nature of this interchange, the girls learned of our interest in them and their way of life, and we learned about the simple pleasure of being present in the moment.

Creating opportunities to express and create in rural Zimbabwe, although difficult at first, became relatively easy, once we stopped assessing events and situations with our Western minds. We learned to turn just about everything into expressive play, connection, or relationship building. Cooking was another creative expression outlet. As noted, food was a slim commodity in Zimbabwe. We had been asked by Gideon Chishamba, the director of the Peniel Center, to bring pizza-making ingredients with us in our suitcases. Having pizza was a rare occurrence in Zimbabwe, so

Figure 2.3 Women preparing vegetables

we sought to oblige our host. We carried flour, yeast, tomato paste, dried spices, and shelf-stable Parmesan cheese. When pizza day arrived, we were ready and engaged the help of the "women" to help prepare some veggies to go along with our pizza meal (Figure 2.3).

The only oven that existed was a wood-burning antique, which cooked with a wild variability, meaning that the dough was both raw and burnt in its final product. We found the kids actively watching and helping us as best they could. I am pretty sure that no pizza was ever made at the Peniel Center, based on the rapt excitement and intrigue the process brought. We had just enough for three pizzas which we divided amongst about 30 of us in total. Cooking is a form of expressive therapy if one pays close attention. So much was learned about our "kids" by the way they pitched in, held back, supported by words, or simply jumped in using their hands to assist. An endeavor like this one illuminated personalities, forged new connections. and solidified our place as helpful guests in their home.

HAND IMAGES ACROSS CULTURES

As mentioned earlier, since the beginning of time as we know it, human beings have left cave paintings, pottery, petroglyphs, and rock art as evidence that they existed. Little is known about these ancient civilizations dating back to 45,000–3,000 BCE. One of the most interesting and perplexing symbols left by our homo sapiens ancestors are handprints, mostly in the form of stencils. These hand stencils are found in Africa, South America, Australia, and Asia. One of the most famous sites is in Argentina, known as the "Cueva de la Manos" or "Cave of the Hands" dating back about 9,000 years ago. How is it that multiple human groups from diverse geographical areas all created handprints and/or hand stencils? I believe that leaving an image of one's hand was our ancestors' way of rooting themselves in collectivistic cultural history, of being a human being. Leaving a hand stencil denotes that one existed and was "here" on planet earth. I am reminded of street art, tagging, and graffiti arts as modern equivalents of this concept.

In our work with people from other cultures, we have found the concept of hand tracing to be a strong connector of humanity. To trace one's hand, to leave a mark that is uniquely yours, is empowering. In our work in Zimbabwe, South Africa, Nepal, and Cheyenne River Reservation, we have used hand tracing to facilitate communication and empowerment. We have created trees made out of everyone's stenciled decorated hands with construction paper. We have also used hand stencils to decorate walls, poles, outside areas, and individual bedroom spaces of kids we work with. In addition, we have used hands to list positive qualities, one per finger, and also as zentangle henna art type designs, just for fun. I like to think we are carrying on this ancient human tradition, transferred down through millennia across cultures, to signify that "we were here" together and in this space of creating and forming lasting relationships with those we serve.

In Nepal we created a stenciled hand tree utilizing a support pole that held up a metal corrugated roof top over an outside patio area. Each child we worked with created a hand stencil, added their name, and a few areas of interest or hobbies that they enjoyed. As each child finished their hand stencil, they were able to share what they had created and then affix their paper hand stencil to the pole using tape. Two of our community volunteers, both medical doctors, shared a moment with some children while the stenciled hand tree was in the process of being created (Figure 2.4).

Figure 2.4 Volunteers working with children to create hand stencils

SEEDS OF HOPE AND CONNECTION—NEPAL

Nepal has been referred to as the rooftop of the world due to the Himalayan mountain range that lines the northern border of this small country. Nepal is sandwiched between India to the south and China to the north. Lying east is Bhutan and west is Tibet. Nepal is mostly Hindu and Buddhist, lending itself to a peaceful and harmonious worldview. It is common in Nepal to be greeted by bowing and the customary palms together greeting of "Namaste." The term namaste roughly translates to "the light in me honors and sees the light in you" which sets the stage for understanding the importance of honoring the "other" first and then the self in Nepalese culture. Nepal has never been colonized or taken over fully by another nation or country, which puts it squarely in the minority of developing countries, whom have mostly been colonized by more developed countries, such as Britain's takeover of India and the United States' takeover of the indigenous America's.

Our work in Nepal has been ongoing for the last ten years. We have secured regular work within two nonprofit organizations, Antardristi, a safe house for girls and young women who have been sexually abused and traumatized, and Prisoner Assistance Nepal (PA Nepal) a residential facility for children whose mothers are incarcerated. Nepal is a country where there are people who live high in the mountains, where roads, access to modern conveniences, and modern ways of doing things does not exist. In the various Indigenous tribes living in the mountains of the Himalayan range, traditional ways of thinking are still in place. For example, a patriarchal system exists where girls are sub-par to their boy counterparts. Boys are given instruction in reading and writing, whereas girls rarely have access to education. Women are the custodians of the children, whereas men are hunters and gatherers, working in subsistence farming in order to provide for the family. In these rural and obscure parts of Nepal, traditional rice moonshine is distilled into a homebrew. Many adults have succumbed to alcoholism due to the reliance on this pure grain alcoholic drink which has become part of Nepalese culture. With subsistence farming which leads to extreme poverty, and many addicted to alcohol, young girls and women have become the victims of sexual abuse, sex trafficking, sold as child brides (mostly to China), and petty thievery to help support the family. Girls who are lucky enough to be rescued from these sex crimes sometimes end up at Antardristi, a safe house for girls as young as 5 up to age 18. Binita Adhikari started Antardristi in 2003, recognizing the objectification and oppression of young girls and women and the mistreatment in the form of sex abuse. Many women are sexually abused and then blamed for the abuse. She seeks to work with the young women by providing trauma therapy and support. She also attempts to engage family members in education and family therapy to prevent further sexual abuse from occurring.

In another tragic situation in Nepal, women who are caught stealing or found guilty of other petty crimes usually end up in prison outside of the capital Kathmandu. If the incarcerated women have children, their children are forced to go to prison with them. In rural Nepal child-rearing is a woman's job, and thus children follow the women. There is little legal representation for women imprisoned, and many times they stay in prison for years over a petty misdemeanor. PA Nepal headed by Indira Ranamagar, an educated attorney, attempts to free these women, and has founded a residential home for the displaced children of the imprisoned women. Indira herself was not allowed to attend school with her brothers as a child. She convinced her brothers to teach her what they were learning in school. She excelled in her learning and was able to test into university and later attended law school. Indira has seen firsthand what it is to be unprivileged in a traditionally patriarchal system. At this time, Indira has worked tirelessly to free women, save children from terrible prison conditions, and provide a safe environment for the children in her charge. All the children attend school and learn English as their second language.

Nepal, like Zimbabwe, has limited resources and scarcity of goods. In our work within the city of Kathmandu, we have tried to utilize creative arts goods found in local markets to engage the children in expressive arts activities. Nepal does seem to have a plethora of embroidery floss, beads, and fabric, as well as ceramic arts. In working at Antardristi, we saw that the girls had been involved in a sustainable garden project. We saw they were growing vegetables on their rooftop garden. Locating a local craftsman, we bought several large ceramic pots as well as small vegetable plants and rich soil ready for planting.

The girls at Antardristi were thrilled to use sidewalk chalk and pastels (which we also purchased at the market) to decorate their pots. The use of this expressive horticulture therapy had a symbolic meaning. First, I told a story about a little seedling plant that got lost and was found by a little girl who saved the plant and brought it back to life. This story was based on Wallas's (1985) book of therapeutic metaphors for various clinical issues. This book entitled *Stories for the Third Ear* is related to Kramer's original idea of the "third hand" technique which was borrowed from Theodore Reik's use of the metaphor of the third ear, used to intuitively understand what the psychiatric patient might need from the analyst.

The girls were totally engaged as I told a version of this story from my memory of Wallas's original story. They were given the directive to plant the vegetable plants and take good care of them, just as they need to take care of themselves. A frenzy of creative activity ensued once the girls were allowed to color and draw on the pots. Some of the girls had sharpie markers that they used to outline the shapes and images they created (Figures 2.5 and 2.6). One of the girls paid homage to my co-leader Dr. Megan Seaman in her portrait on the outside of this clay pot.

After ten years of providing service to the girls at Antardristi and their caregivers, a safe and trusting relationship has emerged. The girls know Dr. Megan Seaman and me very well, which does translate to more trust for the various graduate student volunteers change with each visit. The girls' portraits and writing of names of the volunteers and group leaders shows a connection and lifeline of sorts to people residing outside of Nepal who consistently show up every other year. Although many of the girls have left or graduated from the Antardristi center, there are still a

Figure 2.5 Nepalese girl drawing on a clay pot

Figure 2.6 Nepalese girl and student volunteers planting

few girls who have remained over the years, and who we feel close with. The sustainable nature of this program is the strength. We are not coming in as a one-and-done service trip, but a committed venture, filled with responsibility and intention to continue as long as we are able.

INVISIBLE STRING OF HEARTS CONNECTED

Meanwhile at PA Nepal, our other service-learning site, we have also planted seeds of hope by creating uplifting and meaningful art, play, and music projects with the kids, aged 2–18. On our last trip to PA Nepal, we found paper doily hearts that we decorated with the children. One little boy clearly enjoyed using detailed precision while decorating his heart

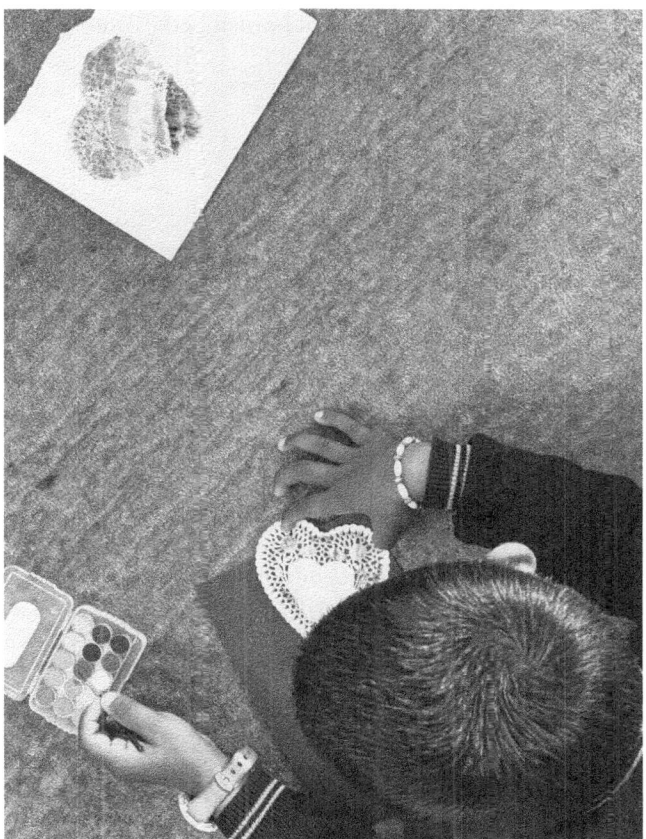

Figure 2.7 Boy at PA Nepal creating a paper heart

with donated mini-watercolor sets (Figure 2.7). We then used embroidery floss as string to string the hearts together and hang them across the ceiling of each classroom. We played pop music (Taylor Swift's "Invisible String") that was familiar to the kids and had an impromptu dance party under the paper hearts swaying in the breeze above our heads. We used a metaphor of tying an "invisible string" from our heart to their hearts. We later created a heart with our hands and passed our hearts to each other by bumping hand-hearts together as we sat in a circle. In this way, the kids and the volunteers symbolically shared their love for one another.

The symbolic gift of love and care is especially important for the kids at PA Nepal who do not have parents, due to absent fathers and mothers in prison. They are eager to share love and be loved. This is a testament to the resilience of the human spirit and of human beings' interconnectedness in the universal feeling of love.

REFERENCES

Goodman, G., Dent, V., Tuman, D., & Lee, S.Y. (2022). Drawings from a play-based intervention: Windows to the soul of rural Ugandan preschool children's artistic development. *The Arts in Psychotherapy*, 77 (4): 1–38.

Henley, D. (2024). *The Kramer method of art therapy: Exploring the third hand.* New York: Charles Thomas Publishing.

Kalmanowitz, D., Chan, S.M., & Potash, J. (2012). *Art therapy in Asia: To the bone or wrapped in silk.* London: Jessica Kingsley.

Kapitan, L. (2015). Social action in practice: Shifting ethnocentric lens in cross-cultural art therapy encounters. *Art Therapy*, 32 (2): 104–111. DOI: 10.1080/07421656.2015.1060403.

Kramer, E. (1986). The art therapist's third hand: Reflections on art, art therapy, and society at large. *American Journal of Art Therapy*, 24 (3), 71–86.

Lowenfeld, V. (1953). *Creative and mental growth.* New York: Macmillan.

Malchiodi, C. (2022). *The handbook of expressive arts therapy.* New York: The Guilford Press.

McNiff. S. (2015). *Imagination in action: Secrets for unleashing creative expression.* Boston, MA: Shambala Press.

Moon, C. (2013). "Developing therapeutic arts in programs in Kenya and Tanzania: A collaborative consultation approach." In P. Howie, S. Prasad, & J. Kristel (eds.), *Using art therapy with diverse populations: Crossing cultures and abilities.* London: Jessica Kingsley.

Prinzhom. H. (1922). *Eikdnereider Grisreskrunken.* Berlin: Veriag Julius Springer. (Also published in English, translated by Eric von Brockdorff as *Artistry of the Mentally Ill* in 1972. New York: Springer-Verlag.)

Wallas, L. (1985). *Stories for the third ear.* New York: Norton Press.

CHAPTER 3

Cultural Immersion

Cultural immersion is paramount to any global or more local service-learning experience. An essential characteristic of the immersive service-learning process is that it is reciprocal. As stated previously, service-learning programs tend to connect education and community service in a way that benefits both program participants and host communities. One of the significant underlying aspects of a service-learning program is the phenomenological or "lived" experience of the participant. Participants immerse themselves in the host community and work together on service projects alongside members of the host community (Onosu, 2021). Onosu (2021) states, "the immersion process creates opportunities for participants to engage in reflection activities that help them to connect the lived experience with the cultural, political, and social situations in the host community within a global context" (p. 2). The design of a global or local service-learning program varies as either cocurricular global service-learning, short-term global service-learning, course-embedded spring break global service-learning, or a curricular embedded global service-learning (García & Longo, 2017). Cultural immersive experiences include a short-term, medium-term, or long-term cultural immersion component. The short-term immersion experiences are generally between one and two weeks, the medium-term immersion is between six and eight weeks, and the long-term immersion is typically between 52 weeks and one academic year (Niehaus et al., 2017). The immersion experience allows students to encounter a new culture, while living within the culture. The service-learning encounters that are shared within this book are all short-term (two weeks) and participants have stayed in housing within the community.

PERSPECTIVE TRANSFORMATION THEORY

Mezirow's (2018) perspective transformation theory and Kiely's (2005) transformative service-learning model provide an outstanding theoretical lens to examine the transformation of self that occurs during cultural immersion. The perspective transformation theory explains that when people encounter an unknown situation, it pushes them to alter their regular pattern of thinking, and this experience might lead to the development of new perceptions. Mezirow (2018) found that people naturally function from a set of "habitual expectations" known as perspectives. Mezirow (2018) argues that people develop their perspectives through the lifelong process of interaction, communication, and socialization. These perspectives then become the frame or context that shapes beliefs, values, ideas, and viewpoints.

When a person encounters a disruptive, uncomfortable, or unknown event, it can trigger a transformative learning process and can create a new reference point, which may cause them to reflect on their beliefs, norms, values, ideas, and expectations (Onosu, 2021). Through this reflection process, human beings can then develop new perspectives that become the pivotal point of relating to self, others, and society (Mezirow, 2018). If an individual does not encounter or experience situations that challenge perspectives, their perspective will remain unchanged.

Illeris (2014) explains the process of transformative learning and the development of new self-identity; in other words, the way we see ourselves. He claimed that identity involves multiple personality layers which are formed by early experiences and cultural contexts, which make it difficult for people to alter their self-identity naturally. Illeris (2014) believes that it takes a strong reason, meaningful experience, disruption, and motivation to change self-identity. Illeris (2014) concludes that self-identity transformation can only happen when people experience a motivation that is strong enough to trigger transformative learning (Illeris, 2014).

Kiely's transformative service-learning model explains how transformation occurs during global service-learning experiences (2005). Kiely (2005) suggests that during global service-learning, transformative learning happens in five ways: contextual border crossing, dissonance, personalizing, processing, and connecting. The contextual border crossing describes the personal, structural, historical, and programmatic elements that can influence the learning process that promotes or deters transformative learning (Kiely, 2005). The dissonance illustrates the differences between previously held assumptions and the new experience. While personalizing represents how individuals respond to and learn from conflict. Finally, processing and connecting explain how reflective learning allows individuals to adequately understand, empathize, and transform the learning experience into actions during and after the service engagement (Kiely, 2005).

Mezirow's (2018) perspective transformation theory and Kiely's (2005) transformative service-learning model provide a unique theoretical lens to analyze the extent to which students experience the transformation of the perception of self and others during and after participation in cultural immersion, transformative learning, and self-identity studies show that often when students participate in immersion activities, such as global service-learning, the cultural exposure activates an awareness process that can lead to the reexamination of personal views of self and others (Elwood, 2017).

REMNANTS OF CONGO

Growing up in the Congo was a transformational immersive process; I was already culturally immersed in African traditions that existed in this region of the continent. Once my family returned to the United States, I was thrust into what one might call a cultural immersive experience but in the United States. My parents had of course spent time in the United States, and I knew that this was my home; however, I was not prepared for the "othering" experience that occurred once I was supposedly in my homeland, but not really my homeland. In their book, Van Reken and Pollock (2017) call these kids "third culture kids" which describes children whose parents are part of one culture, while the kids are raised or spend a significant amount of time in a different culture. He suggests this otherworldly experience can have both negative and positive effects on kids; namely, individuals can feel lost, isolated, confused, and othered, but can also have deep empathy and a unique perspective of both cultures. What Illeris (2014) refers to as a change in self-identity certainly happened to me upon my return to the United States. I was a school-aged child whose identity was still forming, thus this experience cut deep grooves in my developing sense of self.

One of the first experiences I had in the United States involved my feet, which were wide and calloused because I had grown up mostly barefoot, with flip-flops or jelly sandals as my shoe source. My feet were so wide that no shoes could fit me, so I was taken to a "special" store to buy humiliating corrective extra-wide shoes to somehow get my feet in a more culturally appropriate vice grip covered and slim width. The metaphor is not lost here; I literally needed to cram my wide feet into socio-culturally proper shoes to fit in. This was only the beginning of feeling out of place.

We were southerners, so there were tense race relationship struggles, the Vietnam War, television (which I did not have in Congo), air conditioning, heat, warm water, refrigeration, and all the social clothing styles, language, jargon, and new and confusing customs. My immersion was quick and painful, a blur of trying to understand social customs. When we had first returned to the United States, I saw a dark-brown-skinned person at the store and immediately started speaking to them in Chiluba, the dialect of the region of Congo I had just come from. My mother chastised me for not knowing that folks in the United States don't speak Chiluba, and the man looked at me unknowing. These early experiences of trying to understand culture were like swimming under water, only grasping snippets here and there with everything veiled in shadows. I look back and think of all the things I really did not understand and how this very seriously impacted me. I was forever not "getting it" and not able to carry on discourse with others due to my confusion.

These early experiences have stayed with me my entire life and career, and to this day I have a feeling I am somehow different than my fellow Americans. When I see someone clearly from another culture, or when I travel with my students, I am always aware of other cultures, how they experience the world based on upbringing and cultural traditions, and how my cultural ways of moving and being in the world may seem strange. When teaching my students about cultural immersion or ethnorelativism, I have found it best to dive in. It is important to live in similar conditions to the people we are serving, to eat similar foods, learn the language, and understand the nuances of culture as Mezirow (2018) has pointed out. It is also important to remember that each of us has our own cultural context where worldviews are created, but so do the people we serve.

THATCHED ROOF

Upon our arrival in Bulawayo, Zimbabwe, we had 15 graduate students, faculty, and my eldest son Max converging upon the Peniel Center and School where orphaned children lived and went to school. We arrived at the center and were ushered into our housing, which was a thatched roof building with holes in the roof and many birds roosting in the eaves. There was no running water and a toilet that was not functioning. Outside there were outhouses, and literally cows grazing right up to the window of our room. Nothing was watertight or rodent proof, and nothing was clean in terms of American standards. This was our first awareness into the plight of folks living in Zimbabwe, a country plagued by colonization by Britain and then left to fend for itself once independence was declared in 1980.

There is an adage, "You never miss what you never had," and thus our time in Zimbabwe illustrated this to all of us. As Americans, we missed the creature comforts of purified air and sanitary conditions. However, the kids and adults of Zimbabwe were quite content to live in more primitive structures and enjoy the fruits of their labors. They relished the beautiful weather, the day-to-day growth of crops in the garden, and the chickens milling about that granted an endless supply of eggs. The slower pace and ability to enjoy relationships by joining in song and dance was refreshing for our group. Circling back to Elwood's (2017) transformative learning that can provide deep awareness and real change once students are faced with differing cultures and ways of being in the world, one student gave up shopping for anything but food for an entire year once he returned to the United States. He was so moved by his new insights of Zimbabwe and how little the people had there. He acutely felt his privilege and, to this day, this particular student remains committed to not consuming more than he needs.

Sleeping with many other people in a thatched roof hut was an experience that provided some discomfort. In the United States, we honor sleeping alone or with a partner or sibling per one bedroom. In Zimbabwe, a collectivist culture, it is commonplace for kids and adults to sleep in a room together. This arrangement is just for sleeping, in that much of life happens outside in the gorgeous landscape, not in the huts. We all had to become accustomed to this different way of being in the world. One of the leaders, Dr. Megan Seaman, became agitated and irate that more information regarding the living situation was not shared upfront before we arrived at the Peniel Center. This simple idea is a Western way of thinking, that somehow things are organized and guest accommodations are planned ahead. In this case, we were just to sleep wherever we could and literally immerse ourselves. Some volunteers slept beside children who resided at Peniel, where other volunteers shared rooms with each other. At one moment, our host saw that we were uncomfortable and offered to draw a warm bath for me. I agreed to this, not realizing that to make a warm bath, gallons of water had to be boiled over an open fire, and then brought into the bathtub (which was not hooked up to plumbing). I remember feeling guilty that all this water was going toward a bath for me, but my hosts insisted. The amount of effort needed to take a warm bath far exceeded my wildest expectations.

How does any of this relate to expressive arts with kids? Unless one truly understands the rules, mores, worldview, scarcity, difficulty with clean water, etc., it is hard to know what type of expressive arts-based activities to do. Immersing fully into Zimbabwe culture was the only way to understand what types of media, what types of activities, and play the kids at Peniel Center might be engaged with.

As noted earlier, embroidery floss was an art material found in Zimbabwe culture, and we used friendship bracelet making to begin our first full day. No chairs or tables existed to sit on while we taught the kids how to braid and knot the embroidery floss, so we used the front stoop of the thatched roof houses, or the grass as our seats. The kids quickly learned how to tie the floss onto their big toe and use this as an anchor for their work. We explained to the kids that they could make the bracelets for each other or themselves. We hoped that this simple activity would create relationships between us. Another aspect of the friendship bracelet making was to "put a wish or intention" onto the bracelet and then, once it fell off, maybe the wish or intention would be granted. This idea is common practice in the United States, but here in Zimbabwe, which is mostly devoutly Christian, the idea did not go over well with the hosts and directors of the center. They forbid the kids from wearing the bracelets, because they thought it was the work of the devil. Faith (pseudonym), a young girl, created multiple bracelets, but opted just to hold onto them, not wear them, which was a good compromise between worldviews. This might appear shocking to readers, but this cultural difference, influenced by a strong Christian ideology, was something we upheld. Our job as volunteers and servers is to immerse into the culture, to practice open mindedness. Even if friendship bracelet wish making seems innocuous from a United States worldview, it is important to do what the culture prescribes.

To further illuminate this cultural immersion at times through culture shock, I am reminded of mealtimes in Bulawayo, Zimbabwe. As I have mentioned earlier, food was a scarcity and therefore sacred. We quickly learned the benefits of sadza, a corn maize mush, and chomolia, a wild spinach, that were easily acquired in Zimbabwe. We ate this food two to three times per day, with our hands. There were no knives, forks, or spoons available and the kids at the center delighted in teaching us how to use our three fingers as an eating utensil. Although this sounds simple, and maybe not so different, I can assure the reader that this was enough to throw many students off-kilter. Rebecca Chilcote, an alumnus of the Counseling and Art Therapy program at Ursuline, attempted to master the dinner with her hands (Figure 3.1). It is an important part of service-learning to immerse oneself in the culture of the people that you are serving.

This immersive experience is a form of experiential education, in that the volunteers are learning firsthand what it is to be in this culture. They are not staying in a fancy hotel or off site somewhere, but literally with the hosts that are providing the opportunity of service. Of course, all human beings eat and enjoy food, but the way food is eaten, shared, cooked, and presented are culturally specific. Food choices are dictated by availability and the common cuisine of the region. In Africa and also Nepal, the

Figure 3.1 Rebecca is eating sadsa with her hand

climate is warm and hot. Because spicy foods cause sweat, these are key ingredients in the diet to help people stay cool in the heat.

A TRIP TO EL SALVADOR—REMEMBERING DOROTHY KAZEL

Our first service trip was to El Salvador. We decided to go because of Ursuline College's connection to El Salvador through Sr. Dorothy Kazel. Sr. Dorothy and other church women had been working in El Salvador helping people deal with the atrocities of the civil war. She and three other women missionaries were viciously raped and murdered in 1980 as part of the horrific war that raged in El Salvador between the government and the liberation front from 1979 to 1992.

Getting to El Salvador from the United States is a relatively easy journey, but once there, things were not so easy. We were greeted by machine gun guards at the airport as well as a lottery system of bag checking, looking for contraband. In our case, we were traveling with some gifts and art materials to be delivered to St. Dominic school in Chiltiupán, a 45-minute drive from San Salvador. Gifts and art materials were considered contraband at the time, because El Salvador was trying to rebuild and wanted materials to be purchased within the country. Of course, we were unaware of this until afterwards. We had Sr. Kathleen Burke with us; she was the founder and former director of the graduate program at Ursuline College in Art Therapy. She was the person chosen by the lottery system to have a thorough search of her bags. Sr. Kathleen was a fierce lady, who did not speak Spanish, but did speak Latin. With all her grace, she made it known that she was a religious sister and spoke to the guards in Latin. They immediately waved her through, and we got to save the gifts that we had stowed in her baggage. This cultural immersion into a dangerous, militant, and not trusting governmental system was an eye opener for all of us. The students and I wondered what it must be like to grow up in a country with such a heavy military presence and suspicion for others.

While in El Salvador, we saw and learned about the culture and the strife inflicted by the civil war, as well as the continued fallout and destructive influences that were pervasive in 2013. We had been invited to work with the school children at St. Dominic (Santo Domingo). The school was run by Ursuline sisters and provided K-12 education to the local kids in Chiltiupán. This was our very first trip and we did not understand the nature of service-learning as we understand it today. At this time, we brought gifts of stuffed animals, many art materials, and art as therapy lesson plans to do with the kids. Of course, bringing lots of "stuff" that people may not want or need is a colonizer mentality, one that places the giver as superior to the receiver. This was a big "no-no" but we did not know this until later, after we gained more experience working with those served.

In bringing material possessions that were out of place in rural Chiltiupán, we were not culturally immersing ourselves. We believed that we were bringing gifts that would help and make the kids happy. What does one do with a stuffed animal when what is really needed is a school uniform or pencils and paper? This is a good question and one that I hate to answer. The truth is that the stuffed animals and kitschy art materials were not interesting to the kids. What was interesting was getting to know us and learn about our world as we learned of their world. What was interesting was going far into the mountains of El Salvador and visiting a remote school that no one ever visited. The teacher at this one-room schoolhouse proudly gave us a frozen mango on a stick, which was a delicacy for this part of El Salvador, first because electricity is scarce and second because mangos were not in season. She gave us her most treasured treat for our kindness in visiting her classroom.

The kids just wanted to connect, to be seen and heard. They wanted to engage in simple expressive arts, like forming a bowl out of clay, or drawing with a pencil or markers on a piece of paper. They wanted to share their dances and songs with us, to explain their way of life. This first trip was eye opening and changed the entire scope of how we practice service-learning. With cultural immersion or joining in with another culture, first we wait for the invitation to join, next we show up and share with others about ourselves and ask them to share about themselves, and lastly we never bring anything that was not asked for. We never make assumptions of what a particular culture needs or wants. In this way, we first immerse ourselves into the context and worldview of those being served to get an idea of how to form relationships and if any help is needed that we can somehow provide.

CHEYENNE RIVER RESERVATION

The Cheyenne River Lakota Sioux Reservation lies in the western part of South Dakota far away from large towns and cities. The reservation itself is vast with many small towns, such as Eagle Butte, dotted throughout. Over ten years ago on a quest to find a Native American Community that would accept us as volunteers, we stumbled upon the Cheyenne River Youth Program (CRYP) located in Eagle Butte, three hours north of Rapid City, South Dakota. I had been calling different Native groups and had gotten a rather "chilly" response by most, who stated they did not need our help. This is understandable in that Native persons have been the victims of lying and cheating Caucasian folks for generations; in fact no treaty has ever been kept in its totality between the Lakota Sioux nation and the United States government. Hence trustfulness is hard to come by. I had been given the name of CRYP by another Native group as a potential place we could provide service or help. Sure enough, the volunteer coordinator called me back and explained that at CRYP they had been trying to repair the hurt by building reciprocal relationship bridges. She said, in Lakota, the people believe that we are all each other's relations and that they have a Lakota phrase for this, *Mitákuye Oyás'iŋ*. Tammy explained that CRYP was trying to allow this old ideology of the Lakota to be extended to new folks as well.

Our first visit to the reservation was both difficult and rewarding. We had rented a large bus to drive 25 of us, a grueling 22 hours from Cleveland, Ohio to Eagle Butte, South Dakota. We drove straight through, only stopping for bathroom breaks and quick food stops. Our journey was long and vast. Once heading out of Chicago and into Wisconsin and Minnesota, the terrain became mostly large open swaths of prairie land. As we entered South Dakota, the rest stops and restaurants were few and far between. This was big open-sky country, where thunderstorms and other weather patterns could be seen miles away. I also noticed the yellow and muted green prairie grasses and gently rolling hills of this high desert. I remember thinking to myself, this reservation is extremely far out in the middle of nowhere. This is indeed true and part of the United States legacy of passive genocide to Indigenous persons. Native persons were pushed to the most barren and obscure corners of the United States, in this no-man's land, where crops have difficulty growing due to the environmental challenges and lack of rich agricultural land. What would it have been like so many years ago when Native people were forced to walk thousands of miles on the "trail of tears" only to arrive at this seemingly uninhabitable land and place?

Our cultural immersion and use of art-making materials was a gradual process of unfolding knowledge that was conveyed to us by Native elders, and the leaders of the CRYP. We were placed in a community room of the CRYP and laid out our sleeping bags in neat rows. We quickly learned that whatever ideas we had about helping were not useful or wanted. The volunteer coordinator, Tammy, took us to a supply building, where there were rows of blankets, pillows, toys, and all manner of supplies. She explained pointing to all the rows of supplies, "People feel badly for us and want to donate, old clothes, shoes, etc., but we don't need any of those things, we have them all." She went on to say that what is really needed is empowerment, mental health coping skills, relationship building, and networking for the kids. She said, "We don't want your stuff—we need your knowledge and care to help us help ourselves." Upon reflection, Tammy was correct. If non-Native people feel badly for Native people and give old worn-out donations, then this just continues the cycle of despair, that Native people aren't deserving of new clothes or better supply choices. What is needed most in Eagle Butte is spending time with elders, children, and community. To attempt to understand the Lakota way of life and strive to help the youth embrace their cultural heritage while at the same time building relationships with Caucasians and others who are different from them.

How does one begin to repair community and cultural relationships? We did it by offering ourselves as servant leaders and volunteers, agreeing to clean toilets, showers, and kitchen fryers, picking up garbage, vacuuming, mopping floors, washing dishes, and whatever else was needed. This was our way of making reparations, to give of ourselves, in a service-oriented way. Over time we have been able to work with Lakota youth and have built long-lasting relationships with the kids, leaders, and elders of this community.

One of the activities that the reservation does each year is the RedCan Graffiti Jam, where mostly Indigenous graffiti artists are invited by CRYP to graffiti the small town and art park in Eagle Butte. The street and graffiti art all have social justice and advocacy themes. Many of the paintings have Lakota words written on them as well, ensuring the continuation of the Lakota language which was almost entirely wiped out due to colonization, assimilation, and boarding school practices. Imagine if you were not allowed to speak or write your Native language and were punished if you did? This is what happened to countless Native groups; the United States government forbade Native language, dance, ceremonies, and religious beliefs to exist from about 1890 until the 1970s. This is a sure way to systematically annihilate a culture and civilization. Despite the federal government's actions, Native groups have continued to survive and thrive, in spite of reservations and harsh circumstances.

Founder of the Cheyenne River Youth Project Julie Garreau believes that the future lies in the kids reclaiming their Native ways and past, as well as incorporating modern ways of being in this world, a connection between the two. The CRYP has Lakota language and dance classes, as well as education about Lakota history. Youth are also encouraged to go to college, excel in whatever area of interest that draws them. Garreau has created a small community at CRYP within Eagle Butte where kids can get their daily needs met, such as free dinner programs, as well as activities, artist internships, and even the ability to run a small café onsite, called the Keya Café.

We have been to Cheyenne River Reservation ten times over the last ten years. We have become honorary friends and allies of the Lakota youth, community and elders. When we are there, we immerse ourselves in the culture of the Lakota, by helping with community meals, providing art-making opportunities for kids/teens, helping with mental health skills if asked, brainstorming innovative ideas, and just recently setting up an art therapy internship. Vanessa, the first art therapy intern from Ursuline College at Cheyenne River Reservation, enjoyed interacting with a Lakota girl, as they painted together at an outside mural wall art-making station (Figure 3.2).

Our role now is to help at the RedCan Graffiti Jam by providing art as therapy practices for the youth. We always ask CRYP what types of art projects they would like to see us do, and then create ideas based on their needs not our own. Waiting for an invitation to help and determining the needs of the community through community voice is important. I am not a Lakota tribe member, and I do not know what is needed or wanted by the Lakota

Figure 3.2 Vanessa and Lakota girl graffiti painting at Cheyenne River Reservation

youth and leaders, therefore I always wait for their feedback before offering any suggestions. My student volunteers and I are merely guests passing through every year, and thus we treat the Lakota with the utmost respect, honoring their sacred ways of being in this world. We put aside our expectations and ideas and begin each new visit with an open mind and heart.

CULTURAL IMMERSION VIA SACRED SITES

Not only does cultural immersion occur when integrating oneself into human connection and sharing, but it also occurs through visiting sacred/spiritual and tourist sites. Learning about a culture can be done by understanding what a culture values. There is no better way to do this than to observe cultural iconic sites that the culture reveres.

HINDU SACRED SITE: PASHUPATINATH TEMPLE

In Nepal there are primarily Hindu and Buddhist sites to visit and tour. These sacred and world heritage sites are revered not only by the Nepalese but by tourists as well. Pashupatinath temple is one of the most spiritual and sacred sites I have ever visited. This cluster of buildings, shrines, and temples encompasses about 500 acres of land built along the Bagmati River, a tributary of the Ganges River in India. The current temple structure dates to 400 CE, meaning that it is about 1600 years old. This sacred site was built to honor Shiva, one of the three main deities of Hinduism. Shiva is the good of life cycles, life, and death. The Pashupatinath Temple is a cremation temple, where families bring their deceased loved ones to be cremated on the banks of the Bagmati River. Eventually the cremated remains will wash into the larger Ganges River in India, a sacred river for all Hindus.

The circle of life and death is more accepted as a normal part of life in Hindu culture. Watching bodies be cremated is a sacred sight to behold, but also a part of the cycle of life, therefore all are welcome to watch as bodies are burned. Hindu people believe in reincarnation and thus want to practice loving kindness and good behavior in their lifetime with the hope that they will return to an even better life in their next incarnation. This is important information to understand the less noticeable materialism and personal ambition to get ahead, especially by hurting others. Nepal, with its mostly Hindu population, promotes peace, collectivity, and harmony with others. This is good Karma and is practiced daily by devout Hindu's.

It is important to dive into and deeply learn cultural practices, in order to more fully understand the culture. One of my student volunteers, Jodi (pseudonym), had a hard time watching Nepali people perform the death rituals on their deceased loved one. From her perspective, the ritual of washing the dead body, and then lighting the funeral pyre and watching the deceased body burn, was too public and not private. She felt like a voyeur in a macabre scene. This reaction speaks to being raised in the West, where death is sterile and clean. In the United States, when a person dies, they are taken from their homes or hospitals and cleaned by strangers at a funeral home, dressed nicely, and laid to rest in a coffin and then later buried or cremated. In the United States we are removed from the earthy and more personal aspects of a dead body. In Nepal and other Hindu collectivist cultures, the only people that can clean and take care of the deceased is the family. It would be unheard of for strangers to help with the death rituals. The concept of a public death ceremony and cremation is to remind the living that we all will die, that life is a cycle of living and dying. The public nature of the death ritual is also to garner support from the community in a family's bereavement. Interestingly, Jodi still had trouble with this explanation and needed to look away from the burning bodies. This reaction by Jodi is not an isolated incident. Many of my student volunteers have trouble visiting this sacred site, while others have a spiritual and uplifting experience. This variable reaction has to do with one's experience with death and loss, and openness to other realities of life and death. From my perspective, watching the eldest in the family, dressed in white, washing the deceased body in the waters of the Bagmati River is one of the most beautiful rituals I have experienced. There is such love, care, and compassion in readying the person for the next lifetime. In Nepal, the Hindu believe that water makes everything clean, hence even though the Bagmati River is less than "clean" by Western standards, it is still used to purify the body so that it can be purified again by fire, as the body is reduced to ashes that also go back into the river for a third purification. This is a sacred ritual to observe and be a part of, even as a bystander. This practice helps Western culture understand how and why people of Nepal are kind and compassionate most of the time, greeting each other and us with palms together, "namaste."

HINDU AND BUDDHIST SITE: SWAYAMBHUNATH TEMPLE (MONKEY TEMPLE)

Swayambhunath Temple, known as the Monkey Temple, is a world heritage site, honoring both Hindu and Buddhist people. The Monkey Temple has this nickname due to the hundreds of monkeys that make their home at this sacred site. It is a sight to behold the monkeys running, playing, grooming, eating, and resting in the midst of so many human visitors. For those of us from the United States, seeing all the monkeys is a thrill. The people of Nepal view all the monkeys as we might view the common squirrel in the United States, more of a common sight. The Monkey Temple is on the top of a hill and crowned with a stupa, a round building, that is encased by 108 prayer wheels. The idea is to walk around the stupa and spin each prayer wheel as one walks by; this signifies releasing or chanting the prayers or mantras that are written within each prayer wheel. The 108 number is a spiritual number that is said to connect the body with the cosmos, and to depict the interconnectedness of all beings. Thus, as one walks around and touches each wheel, the interconnectedness of all beings is manifested into the universe. Spinning the prayer wheel can facilitate your dharma, meaning your purpose of "right" way of being in this world. Volunteer Kate enjoyed walking around the stupa and spinning the wheels (Figure 3.3).

Figure 3.3 Volunteer Kate walks around the stupa touching each prayer wheel

ELEPHANT SANCTUARY

Elephants are revered in Nepal and Hindu culture. They are associated with the God Ganesha, who is revered as the "remover of obstacles." Elephants were used for work, in clearing forests and hauling heavy equipment, and for transporting heavy palette with up to six to eight human beings on their backs, but in recent years using elephants for human transport work is considered cruel. There are multiple elephant sanctuaries and safe spaces throughout Nepal. One place is inside Chitwan National Park. Within the grounds of Sapana Village, a local eco-friendly hotel, there is an elephant sanctuary, where overworked or abused elephants are rescued and live in a small herd. These elephants are never chained or used inhumanely. Each elephant has a handler, who stays with the elephant for life. One elephant, named Prema, which means unconditional love in Sanskrit, has been a favorite of mine over the years. Prema was used to carry heavy box saddles with up to six to eight humans riding upon her when she was too young to bear this weight. This left her legs bowing permanently and her spine disfigured. She was rescued about ten years ago from inhumane owners. Prema is now about 40 years old and is newly pregnant. Gestation will take about two years, just in time for our next visit!

The elephants are free to wander hundreds of acres in the Chitwan National Park. They are treated with dignity and respect, never hit, beaten, or hurt in any way. Nepal is a tiny country, with little resources; however, they are making an impact in sustainable practices. For example, animals are considered sacred, and individuals are encouraged not to harm them in any way. Once in Chitwan National Park, Sapana Village elephant sanctuary, visitors are allowed to interact respectfully with the elephants. Prema is pictured here with my student volunteer's hands on her trunk as she stands ready for her dinner (Figure 3.4). Sapana Village has introduced a "breakfast with the elephants" excursion, where volunteers feed elephants their breakfast, while the volunteers also have an open-air continental breakfast on the grasslands.

Figure 3.4 Volunteers touching Prema's trunk while she stands ready for her dinner

Being amongst people who revere elephants and have created sanctuaries, not zoos for these gorgeous giants of the animal kingdom, informs us of what is important to local Nepali people, and helps us get a glimpse into the values and ethics of modern Nepali life.

CANOES DOWN THE RAPTI RIVER

Another immersive excursion that we have participated in is dugout canoe rides down the Rapti River in Chitwan National Forest and Preserve, located in Southern Nepal. After our service work, we have a tradition of traveling the 90 miles to the southern region of Nepal known as Chitwan. Chitwan is known for its work in sustainability and animal preservation. The preserve hosts elephants tigers, sloths, black bears, many types of deer, monkeys, and other jungle animals. Chitwan is home to Indigenous people named the Tharu, who were at one time referred to as "forest dwellers" because of their history of relying on the forest for sustenance. In modern times, the Tharu hunt, fish, and grow small crops to support themselves.

The canoes are made from one tree trunk that is hollowed out into a canoe shape. The oarsman stand in the back of the canoe, and guides the direction with a long pole, similar to the gondolas of Venice, Italy. The canoes sit low in the water allowing a great view of many crocodile species, birds, small fish, and other waterfowl. Riding in this canoe helps us imagine what life must have been like for Indigenous Nepali people and also helps us explore the terrain like a local.

The wild jungle, grasslands, and waterways are under protection of the Nepalese government. The Nepali people are cleaning up litter, practicing sustainability, and reducing their footprint as best they can. Blue plastic bags (which we see often in the United States) have been outlawed. This is in an effort to keep Nepal clean and litter free. Reusable cloth bags are used instead. Nepal's global carbon footprint according to Worldometer (a reference website that reports on global statistics, including emissions across the globe) is 0.1% whereas the United States' is 12.6% of the world's greenhouse gas emissions. Nepal appears to be doing more to lower their contributions to global pollution, even though they are a tiny contributor, whereas the United States seems to be ever increasing its global carbon footprint. This information helps volunteers understand more clearly the culture of Nepal and the value placed on sustainability and reduction of pollution.

REFERENCES

Elwood, S.A., Johnson, R., Perales, C., Elwood, S.A., Johnson, R., & Perales, C. (2017). *The Vignette TaBLE: Team-based, blended learning experiences with classroom mentors and teacher candidates*. In Sagini Keengwe (ed.), *Handbook of Research on Mobile Learning, Constructivism, and Meaningful Learning* (pp. 259–279). Corpus Christi: IGI Global.

García, N., & Longo, N. V. (2017). Doing more with less: Civic practices for longer-term impact in global service learning. *Frontiers: The Interdisciplinary Journal of Study Abroad*, 29 (2): 35–50. https://doi.org/10.36366/frontiers.v29i2.391

Illeris, K. (2014). Transformative learning and identity. *Journal of Transformative Education*, 12 (2): 148–163. https://doi.org/10.1177/1541344614548423

Kiely. R. (2005) A transformative learning model for service-learning: A longitudinal case study. *Michigan Journal of Community Service Learning*, 12 (3), 5–22.

Mezirow, J. (2018). Transformative learning theory. In *Contemporary Theories of Learning* (pp. 114–128). Abingdon: Routledge.

Niehaus, E., Holder, C., Rivera, M., Garcia, C. E., Woodman, T. C., & Dierberger, J. (2017). Exploring integrative learning in service-based alternative breaks. *The Journal of Higher Education*, 88 (6): 922–946. https://doi.org/10.1080/00221546.2017.1313086

Onosu, G. (2021). The impact of cultural immersion experience on identity transformation process. *International Journal of Environmental Research and Public Health*, 18 (5): 2680. https://doi.org/10.3390/ijerph18052680

Van Reken, R., Pollock, M., & Pollock, D. (2017). *Third culture kids: Growing up among Worlds*. New York: Nicholas Brealey Publishing.

CHAPTER 4

Cultural Exchange

WHAT IS CULTURAL EXCHANGE?

Cultural exchange is where folks from one culture journey to another culture and cross-pollinate by sharing customs, mores, traditions, and worldviews (Bennett, 1998). Cultural exchange has been happening as long as human beings have been circumnavigating the globe. I am reminded of the spice routes, silk roads, and Viking expeditions that changed the face of the planet, by sharing or exchanging not only goods, but ways of living or being in this world. It is human nature to want to share cultures; it is also human nature to borrow or appropriate ideas from others. In the best sense of this idea from a service-learning perspective, it is to literally exchange and share and never to do any harm by imposing judgments or ideas onto the culture that is being served (Jacoby, 2015).

TRAVELING TO TAIWAN

In 1998, I had the pleasure of journeying to Taiwan to provide art therapy education to the Tai Pai Hospital and Palliative Care Center, and other various organizations that had interest. This trip was my first experience of visiting an Asian country and I was excited and nervous to learn more about Taiwan and its position in the Chinese landscape. After a rather exhausting 20-hour flight, I was greeted by a small group of very friendly Taiwanese women, who were to be my guides. Once seated in a very tiny car, we headed to our first stop, a McDonald's restaurant. Language was difficult, and this was before the day of Google Translate and international cell phone service. I had no ability to ask about this seemingly strange choice of restaurant to begin the day. I had been looking forward to some Chinese-Taiwanese cuisine and a full immersion into Taiwanese culture. My guides said, "We thought you might like a sandwich and Coca-Cola?" What my lovely trio of good meaning women did not know was that I was vegetarian and never ate McDonald's or drank Coca-Cola. They were assuming that because I was from the United States, I would prefer sandwiches and soft drinks. Attempting to be a gracious visitor and not wanting to show any hint of surprise, I attempted to eat a McDonald's apple turnover, the only vegetarian thing I could stomach at 8 a.m. in the morning! This experience was ultimately comical, but also an eye opener. I had spent weeks studying Taiwanese culture, full of stereotypes, and my guides had done the same in learning about United States culture. What is important to note here is that within sweeping generalizations about certain groups of folks there are many unique and individual differences. Once I became better acquainted with my hosts, we had an informative discussion about food, customs, and other stereotypes that each of our cultures had of the other.

This experience has left a lasting impression on me, and I have used it to help students, and other travelers put things into perspective. While many stereotypes can be generally true, there are always unique qualities and characteristics of groups of people that defy set expectations. I have made it a point to learn as much about a culture as possible, while remaining open minded to the culture being very different from whatever I have learned through literature and research.

Human beings over many thousands of years have acquired unique customs, food choices, mannerisms, gestures, and ways of being and acting in respective cultures. Culture is a social construction born out of ancestral stories, religious practices, language, and specific environmental and geographical limitations. People have created unique ways to flourish and function in our world. As the service-learning provider, it is of the utmost importance to be vigilant in learning the subtle nuances of each culture. To explore and at times measure this knowledge against our home culture can be deeply reflective and insightful.

CHAMPA DEVI: A SMALL HIKE

In every culture exists differing ideas of various activities; for example in Nepal, folks walk and hike everywhere. There are many villages and remote outcrops, where there are no roads or bridges to cross waterways, therefore the journey must be on foot. There are also folks living in very high altitude, who have acclimatized to this low oxygen existence, but this can play havoc on visitors climbing for the first time. Likewise, depending on geographical location, the very term hike, trek, and walk have different constructs. Arriving in Kathmandu, Nepal for the first time over ten years ago, we set out to hike a small mountain, considered the smallest mountain of the Himalayan range, a foothill really, according to the Nepalese.

The name of this mountain is Champa Devi, named after manifestations of the Hindu goddess Shakti. Champa Devi honors the goddesses Parvati and Durga. Parvati is worshipped for her maternal love and Durga is worshipped for her fierce warrior protectiveness. The shrine crowns this gorgeous mountainous vista, and many people hike the mountain to say prayers related to fertility and marital bliss. We were told by our guides that the hike was easy, and only about 6 miles. Upon our arrival, we were unprepared for what turned out to be a rather intense hike. Many students and I had inadequate footwear and clothing, but nevertheless we made the hike up to the summit of Champa Devi. We had guides with us, who literally ran up the mountain, with a tea service and snacks. Our group looked on in amazement that people can ascend at such a rate and also carry a heavy load. One needs to remember that this is the land of the sherpa, folks trained to scale high mountains, including Mount Everest, with relative ease and no need of oxygen tanks. We learned that the context in which a person grows and evolves creates the skill set needed to navigate the social and geographical landscape.

This hiking experience of conquering Champa Devi is one that we have returned to do on many visits to Nepal and one that gives me great joy, due to the sense of accomplishment in completing the hike, but also in understanding the landscape, the beauty, and wildness of Nepal. Over the years, in our trekking, we have encountered many people hiking Champa Devi for many reasons. As Americans, we are usually decked out in hiking gear, hiking sticks, appropriate shoes, hats, sunglasses, etc., but we have noticed the local Nepalese hike in whatever they happen to be wearing that day, whether it's a school uniform, flip-flops, or a traditional sari. The hike for Nepalese is a pilgrimage and any discomfort they may feel in making the trek is part of the process of striving. Once at the top of the mountain, there is a small outdoor shrine, which has a statue of the goddess, and red paste used to create a tika, or red dot, on the forehead between the eyebrows, to show devotion. Followers of Hinduism or Buddhism will kneel in supplication to the goddess, say their prayers, and then using their pinky finger dipped in the red paste apply the tika to their foreheads. Once this is complete, they rise up and make their way back down the mountain.

Many of our student volunteers have had difficulty ascending Champa Devi; due to unforeseen challenges. Students have had shortness of breath due to physical inactivity, asthma attacks, soreness, intense mosquito bites, and just general fear of heading into the unknown. These discomforts happen to some volunteers, but certainly no one has been in actual danger. The mind is a powerful force to reckon with, and I have found that students'/volunteers' lack of activity in the United States does not stack up to the tympical Nepali person, who walks and exercises on a daily basis. The challenges faced seem most likely brought on by the sheer incredulity of Champa Devi and the magnitude of this difficult trek. The students are clearly exhibiting what Keily (2005) has termed "dissonance" where previously held beliefs about the ability to hike, were not aligning with this new scenario. I always suggest we pause and breathe and have a conversation about the contextual construct of hiking and pushing oneself in a physical way. I have found counseling and art therapy students and volunteers to be quite adept at emotional and mental challenges, but not necessarily physical ones. Because of this, our minds can quickly go into fight or flight mode, which can create panic like symptoms. For other students, the challenge of ascending the shortest mountain (or hill as the Nepalese refer to Champa Devi) of the Himalayan range is exhilarating and they seem to lose their fear and inhibitions leaning into a peak experience. Many times, a new experience is fun and enjoyable, but often the new experience creates a fear response, or a "breaking open" in people, that allows for transformation and new growth to occur. In the end, students and other volunteers are encouraged to "lean into discomfort" to accept difficulties as learning experiences.

As one may imagine, there is conversation that naturally erupts between our group and local Nepalese making the trek. I have learned all of the things I have shared in conversation with the locals. When asked about sacred pilgrimage sites by the Nepalese travelers, I have struggled with finding an appropriate "similar experience" in the United States to share. What comes to mind is traveling to national parks, such as Yosemite. However, in my travels to national parks over the years, there is nothing quite like Champa Devi, where people come out of devotion or faith. Our geographical treasures are a destination or bucket list item to be checked off, not usually a spiritual experience meant to practice devotion or pray. Nepal is steeped in Hindu and Buddhist ideology; it is immersed in the culture. These religious practices are so interwoven that it is hard to determine what is a country celebration vs. religious tradition. The country and culture of Nepal are thousands of years old, and the rituals that exist are layered through the ages, dating back at least to 3,300 BCE. This history lines up with the origin of Hinduism, which can trace its roots to 3,000 BCE. Nevertheless, this is a multifaceted country that is not easily understood due to the many differing hill tribes and cultures that have unified into what we now know as Nepal.

SOUTH AFRICA: GQEBERHA

In the United States, it is hard to know sometimes what is happening in the outside world. It seems as if certain countries are reported on by the news and others are more forgotten about. In my opinion, much of Africa is put on the proverbial "back burner" of interest. In addition to our solo visit to Zimbabwe, we have been going to Gqeberha (formally Port Elizabeth) in South Africa for the last six years. South Africa has a unique history in that it was first colonized by the Dutch in the 1600s, and later by the British in the 1800s. It officially became an independent country in 1910 after the Boer Wars, but was still under British partial rule until 1961. Apartheid, which literally means "apart hood" and indicated forced segregation of whites and blacks in South Africa, was started in 1948 and officially ended in 1994, with the presidency of Nelson Mandela. The apartheid system had been in existence in more subtle ways for the last 400 years; however, it became official government policy for about 40 years.

Africa in the 1600s was an Indigenous continent that few knew much about. There was trade in northern parts of Africa, but not many people knew much about South Africa. The Portuguese explorer Bartolomeu Dias was the first person to sail around the horn of Africa, also known as the Cape of Good Hope in 1488. This journey around the very bottom of the African continent is deadly due to the currents that mark the Indian and Atlantic oceans as they converge causing extreme undertow and currents. Because of this dangerous terrain of ocean, sub-Saharan Africa and South Africa remained roughly unexplored for a long time by outside explorers. I set the stage here to highlight for readers how it was possible for Dutch explorers to so effortlessly establish a strong hold in South Africa. South Africans knew little of the outside world and had more rudimentary instruments and sailing vessels than their Dutch counterparts. From early on, the Dutch although few in number were able to rule the people of South Africa, because of their knowledge of the outside world and ability to use more technologically advanced weapons and transportation. This separation between black Africans and white Dutch remained. The Dutch created a new language called Afrikaans which has its roots in Dutch, but evolved to be a distinct language over the last 400 years. Afrikaans became the official language of South Africa for awhile, but now English and 12 indigenous African languages have been added such as Ndebele, Zulu, and Xhosa.

Language and skin color have become a particularly easy way to continue to segregate South Africa. In our service in South Africa, namely in the city of Gqeberha, we have noticed and were educated about the various schools and languages associated with each. There are three distinct school systems in the region that operate from a colorist perspective: black schools, colored schools, and white schools. The black schools are for those children who have dark skin and the language that is spoken is Xhosa or Ndebele. Afrikaans and English which are the primary languages used in commerce are not taught. The colored schools consist of mixed-race children, or lighter shades of brown, to include Indian and Asian immigrants. In the colored schools, Afrikaans and English are taught, thus making the colored school kids more able to obtain jobs and employment after high school. The white schools are taught English first and then Afrikaans, making those kids the most able to further their education abroad and compete in the global market.

What has struck me in looking at the South African education system ruled by colorism, segregation, and oppression is how closely aligned it seems to be with the United States systemic racism and oppression. There appears to be a lasting legacy in both cultures. In the United States, slavery existed for 300-plus years, and even after the abolition of slavery, modern-day slavery continued to happen with Jim Crow laws, mass incarceration, and implicit bias among the police, employment, character depictions on television and movies against black and brown-skinned persons. Likewise, South Africa, although different in some ways, is dealing with the fallout from the apartheid years, and colonization by white Europeans since the 1600s. In this cultural exchange, it has been both illuminating and jarring to see the aftereffects of oppression and segregation that seem consistent in both cultures.

This important insight helps the reader understand the context in which the South African black children have grown, and the context in which the faculty and student volunteers providing service-learning have come from. It is easy to think that with the ending of slavery and apartheid that things will return to some equality, but as we have seen in history, it takes a long time to undo the damage of oppressive and unjust systems.

My student Abby noted that the colorist segregation in the schools in Gqeberha seem to follow the trends in the United States, during the first half of the 20th century, where much of the country was living segregated. What does this kind of othering or minority status do to a child growing up with the lens of oppression? What must it be like to go through the world always thinking of how one's skin color may or may not affect day-to-day interactions or privileges acquired?

Gqeberha, which was formerly called Port Elizabeth (a name given by the English colonizers), created a new name for itself to honor heritage in 2021. Gqeberha is a Xhosa word meaning Baakens River which runs through the town. Xhosa is one of 11 distinct languages that are spoken in South Africa and the native language of the honorable peace leader Nelson

Mandela. It is a clicking language, which operates using a series of complicated clicks and guttural sounds. To actually pronounce Gqeberha, one has to first click with the mouth, which constitutes the first three letters, then pronounce the rest of the word "ber-ha" with a guttural sound. My students and I spent hours trying to get this seemingly simple pronunciation mastered. Using clicks is extremely foreign to Western language speakers, but especially satisfying once accomplished. When native Gqeberhans hear us using the clicks, they beam with pride and joy that us foreigners are indeed trying. I believe that attempting language learning and speaking is a way of cultural exchange. We learn from the kids how to speak Xhosa, and they sharpen their English-speaking skills by having conversations with us. It is always amazing how diverse and unique languages are, and how language creates cultures. Certain concepts are sometimes not applicable in a specific language; therefore, certain concepts technically may not exist. An example of this is the more unified and collectivist culture built into Xhosa language that suggests a collectivist culture, which is contrary to English language where language is geared to the individual. Just this simple emphasis of "we" vs. "I" changes the cultural ideals.

Showing up for the first time in Gqeberha was an eye-opening experience. We were quickly oriented to the colorist system of segregation in the school system and then began our work at a "colored" school and a "black" school. Just using the term "colored" is jarring in that the United States does not use this terminology any longer. The differences between the two schools were staggeringly unjust. The kids at the colored school have nicer desks and chairs, adequate space, paper, pencils, and teachers who seem educated and caring. The kids at the black school are crammed into small classrooms, there is a smell of urine and other foul odors that linger in hallways, there is very little paper or writing implements, and the teachers, although some very caring, are at times not present or lacking in adequate education themselves to teach the students properly. From my Western lens of awareness of inequality and practicing anti-racism as best I can, I have been appalled and outraged by this blatant oppression, but this is the way in Gqeberha, I cannot change the system, but I can provide loving care and opportunities for both school's children. I have been told by locals that they know it is unjust, but the fact that the kids are actually attending school overcomes the injustice here. There was a time when many black and colored children were not able to go to school at all. It was not until the 1990s that children were mandated to attend school. In historical context this is a very new regime of education and, despite my own shock, the system is slowly becoming more equal and just, but it is a slow process.

While in Gqeberha, we rotate between the two schools, one in the morning, and one in the afternoon. Our focus is on enhancing their education by relationship building and providing art making, yoga, reading, games, and playing. The task is simple in that we just want to make sure the kids feel loved and cared about, and if they happen to learn a few things about themselves or are able to share a little about their lives, that is a bonus.

In Africa, mask making is a common and well-practiced craft. Masks are created for ceremonial and spiritual purposes, but also to honor cultural traditions and ancestors. We have found that the kids love creating animal or creature masks. Once masks are made, the kids role play and interact with each other as whatever animal or make-believe creature they have become. Making masks is empowering, because the children can pretend to be their favorite animal or make-believe person. They can leave their personal struggles behind, just for a few moments and play and have fun with this new person. One of the girls at the black school created this cat mask using paper plates, markers, and string (Figure 4.1). These materials

Figure 4.1 Little girl with cat mask

were found at the local "crazy store" similar to a dollar store in the United States. The children have access to these simple materials, and that is why we chose them.

While in Gqeberha, we dropped in at a local colored preschool, which provides education and day care to children ages 3–5. This particular preschool is full of joyful teachers and students, and is in a more affluent part of the city. We set about making masks with these small kids, using Kramer's third hand intervention to facilitate the animal mask making. This group of eager kids wanted to wear their masks all together and pretend to be jungle animals. In both mask-making ventures, it provided an opportunity to share various animal favorites and determine which animals are native to Africa, and have conversations about which animals reside in the United States. The kids in both schools loved to hear stories of various cats and dogs and how they are the same in Africa as they are in the United States. As volunteers we like to join in with the play and let the animal-masked kids chase us and pretend to scare us.

The universality of animals and the love of animals by children is a way to connect and make a bridge between cultures. The children can envision animals in the United States, and also tell us about their own cultural animals. This simple communication creates a bond and a relationship between the servers and the service recipients. The kids take away their masks, but also knowledge about the United States and us as a group, thus creating a reciprocal learning experience. It is with stories that kids make associations and also memories of events.

DANCE AS CONNECTION: SOUTH AFRICA

In our work with South African children and teens in Gqeberha, dance is a unifying element between cultures. It is commonly believed that Africa was the birthplace of human civilization and that for at least 100,000 years human beings resided all over the continent of Africa in small bands and tribes of people. Although we have no exact evidence of early dance or creative expression until about 35,000 years ago, it is safe to assume that creating art and dance were part of human culture from the earliest beginnings. I am always amazed at how children of Africa have the innate ability to move through dance. Dance is a highly expressive modality that can form a bridge of cultural understanding. Hip hop has its roots in African dance, borrowing from rhythm, cadence, and storytelling that is still widely seen in modern African culture. In the United States, an African American man named Earl Tucker, also known as "Snake Hips," used slides, loose hip movements, and cadence in his dance, being dubbed the first to bring early "hip hop" moves into the music and dance genres in the United States. These movements were steeped in his history of dance passed down through African American history and Pentecostal spiritual practices (Siebert, 2019).

In Gqeberha, there is a teen girls' empowerment program that meets after school a few days a week. This special program is designed to help young women think and dream about their future careers and aspirations. Within this program, teens are assisted in career choice, dressing for success, hair styles, and hygiene as well as general advice about child rearing and marriage. The aim is to help teen girls be successful in navigating choices for their own life. This program started due to high pregnancy and dropout rates of girls in high school. To date, the girls enrolled in the after-school program have been successfully navigating college and/or trade school after high school. Upon our last visit, the teens were excited to share that one of their older peers who had been in the empowerment group just became a doctor.

Upon our first visit to the girls' empowerment program many years ago, I was enchanted by the dancing and "hip hop" moves that the girls liked to do. As part of our learning about each other's cultures, the girls were excited to share with us some dance moves. The ability to move within the dance with an effortless cool vibe was extraordinary. These girls seemed to have dancing in their genes, which is quite possibly true after thousands of years of cultural dance practices in ritual and ceremony. The following image (Figure 4.2), taken from a video of the girls grooving to a techno beat, helps to grasp the intricacies and importance of dance. Some of the girls were leaders in the dance, others joined in, while a few looked on at the enthusiastic dance group.

We were mesmerized by the dancing and how all the girls seemed to know the dances, or if they did not know they quickly tuned in and learned. The girls wondered about dancing in the United States and if we had a dance to show them. When we were first in South Africa, all we could teach were line dances like the macarena, or electric slide. However, over the last several years, we have worked with professional dancers, my stepson Jordan Leitson and his wife Katie Gossen, to choreograph a simple dance that we could show the girls. Our students and volunteers must lean into their discomfort zone in learning and then be able to teach a dance. Of course, the dance is all in good fun and a bridge to connect, and the African girls like to laugh and tease us as we try to show them a dance. Our volunteer group and the African girls quite enjoyed doing the "shimmy" dance move as part of a line dance.

CULTURAL EXCHANGE   51

Figure 4.2 Girls engaged in African "hip hop" in the after-school program

Dance provides movement, freedom, joy, and a sense of mastery for my volunteers and the kids we serve. Dance has been an integral part of most cultures around the world, and therefore we can understand cultural context more easily when studying dance and meanings of movement. With dancing we have created long-lasting relationships and memories, and the girls do not let us forget that each time we visit, they teach us, and we teach them a dance from our respective cultures. This allows for something to look forward to on both ends, and a continuity of care that transcends the spoken word.

A BOY NAMED JUSTICE

Also, in Gqeberha, I had the pleasure of spending some one-on-one time with a boy, who I will call Justice. Justice was 13 years old, grew up in the townships of Gqeberha, with no running water and electricity. His family belonged to a group of "squatters" who built homes in highway medians, or other common city-owned spaces. These homes were built using plywood, corrugated sheet metal, plastic tarps, and other found objects to secure a roof overhead. These local people who had no land or ability to afford housing, claimed whatever "non-usable" land they could find. Sometimes, they would tie to an electrical line and illegally rig electricity to their homes, until the authorities demand that they stop. The people in these squatter villages were also ready to move at a moment's notice if the local police upended their encampment.

Justice came to school in the one uniform that he owned, which was quite small on him, and his pants had holes in the crotch, knees, and thighs. His shirt was also falling apart with rips around the elbows and collar. Nevertheless, he wore a tie and a sweater vest proudly. In our conversations, which were challenging because Justice only spoke a little English and I did not speak Xhosa at all, he shared with me his hopes and dreams to visit the United States or United Kingdom and to get a better education. He idolized Western culture and believed that if he could get out of South Africa, he might have a chance at success. It is from Justice that I learned of the hardships of being a black person in Gqeberha, not to have access to better education, not to learn English, for his father not to be employed due to racist and oppressive practices. He lived on the fringe of what we might call civilization. He and his family had been the unlucky ones, when apartheid was finally ended. They had no home and nowhere to go, and although they had applied for governmental support in the form of subsidized housing, they were on a 10–20-year waiting list. I shared about the United States problems with materialism and greed, and how we sometimes lack community, which surprised him. Together we brainstormed different ways Justice could increase his educational opportunities, which felt nonexistent. After two hours of conversation, and no resolutions for a way forward, we decided to listen to music on my iPhone, to which he excitedly downloaded some of his favorite African musical groups. Together we created a dance party for two and laughed and cried with sadness and joy.

I have never seen Justice again and I wonder what happened to him. I do know that spending a few hours in the present moment with him on a beautiful sunny day was life changing for me. I realized that we both had a sort of idealized version of each other's countries, which were not 100% accurate. I also realized the power of hope. Human beings need to be able to dream and hope about their future, about their difficult times, and about what may happen to them in their lives. So many times, there seems to be no meaning in people's suffering, and I am reminded of Viktor Frankl (1959/2006), a Holocaust survivor and psychologist, in his book *Man's Search for Meaning*, where he extols the reader to find the meaning in difficulties because we cannot make meaning out of such great tragedies of the human condition.

LEARNING THE LAKOTA WAY

Earlier, I mentioned that it was both difficult and rewarding learning about the Lakota. In this moment of remembering our experiences, I believe we are now in what the Lakota call "right relations" within the Cheyenne River Reservation, which means we have been accepted as in a relationship within this community. We have graciously been included in many ceremonies and sacred dances and feel as if we have become adopted members of this tribe. Cultural exchange is simply just an awareness and openness to others' ways of being in this world. In the spirit of service-learning, I believe we have created a reciprocal relationship and collective efficacy for Ursuline College volunteers as well as the Lakota Sioux tribe. It is in times like these when I wonder who is the served and who is the service provider, as we both exist in a dance like an infinity symbol, wrapping around each other with no end and the inability to determine who is providing what to whom anymore. We are a community, we are together in this experience of the celebration of the arts.

One of the most moving experiences we have had on the reservation is the participation in the sacred drum circle that meets in the morning and the evening (Figure 4.3). During this drum circle, the elders play the

Figure 4.3 Lakota Sioux elders at a drum circle

drums, the community and volunteers circle the drummers, and burning sage (smudge) is passed around to cleanse oneself from the energy of the day. One of our student volunteers, Malick, identified himself as a mixed-race individual with Black and Native American ancestry. It had been Malick's dream to attend our volunteer experience, and commune with like relations. He experienced what I will call an "aha" moment, where he finally felt at home and embraced by his Native family. The elders were moved by Malick's show of emotion and kinship and allowed him to carry the sage, which was cradled in an abalone shell bowl. He proudly brought the sage/smudge to each member of the collective drum circle. He slowly circled with the smudge bowl, holding it while volunteers and Lakota community members used their arms to wave the sage smoke around the body in a cleansing ritual.

GRAFFITI ARTS: CHEYENNE RIVER YOUTH PROJECT

Working on the reservation has also provided an entrée into working with professional graffiti artists, most of whom are Indigenous themselves. The graffiti artists come from all over the United States and other countries, as far away as New Zealand. They come to this invitational RedCan Graffiti Jam out of a calling to be with the land and its people, to create images that stand for social justice and human rights. They also come to help the Lakota youth reclaim their ancestral selves by creating traditional Native artwork as well as incorporating Lakota words into their art creations. As volunteers we get to partner with the artists and learn graffiti and street art painting. This also creates a bridge between graffiti artists and volunteer (most often a volunteer student in art therapy). The artists bring wisdom and new ways of seeing the world to the student volunteers. The last several years, student volunteers have been able to create their own graffiti walls in honor of the Lakota.

Seattle-based Latina graffiti artist Angelina Villalobos Soto, known as "179," has been attending the RedCan Graffiti Jam as an invited artist for several years. Her story is unique in that she tries to bring community together and give a voice to folks that don't otherwise have a voice, through her compelling graffiti artwork. Angelina is one of the only women graffiti artists who has risen to such notoriety. She humbly creates her art, in hopes that people can find meaning and transformation by viewing her vibrant pieces, even amid urban places people reside in. Angelina, a person of color, brings hope to the Lakota youth who watch and help with her murals. She is a role model, for the youth but also for my volunteers in creating beauty and meaning in a sometimes meaningless and

Figure 4.4 Angelina, "179," creating a mythic horse graffiti piece at Cheyenne River Reservation

socially decaying world. In her art pieces, she embodies anime characters, fantasy, and nature elements that evoke mindfulness, thought, and delight (Figure 4.4). Communing with and helping graffiti artists is a novel experience for most of my volunteers, which makes this service project unique and offers opportunities to be introspective about community, sense of place, and social justice for underserved people.

Angelina, "179," has been a role model and mentor for many of the Ursuline College volunteers. Not only has her presence as one of few women been invaluable in representation, but also her willingness to talk and educate us about her craft.

Another graffiti artist, and art professor at the Institute for Native American Arts in Santa Fe, New Mexico, Hoka Skenandore, who goes by "Hoka," is a veteran of the RedCan Graffiti Jam. He is a member of the Oneida and Lakota tribes and tries to incorporate native murals and meanings in his art making. Hoka shared about a young child named Antonio. He said,

> My first mural at RedCan was a visual of hands doing sign language. Then this little guy rides up on his bike, puts his hand on the hands of my mural and says, "this is me." It was a profound moment—a touching experience that he saw himself in the art I was creating for the community. How do you put a price on that? Later on, I was taking art interns to DC and one

of those interns, Antonio, was that kid that rode up on that bike. To think of that fateful moment—that turning point that changed the course of his path——it is momentous. It touches the heart—gets me on multiple levels. That is the power of art.

(Personal communication, 7/12/25)

Hoka deeply cares about the kids on the Cheyenne River Reservation and hopes that his artwork can continue to inspire and show the youth that there are viable opportunities in the arts world, and that creativity can prevail and become a transferable skill for later endeavors. Hoka shared that he struggled as a young Native person with traditional schooling and found art making to be his coping skill. By creating art pieces from childhood, Hoka developed the fortitude to continue on his academic path and eventually became a faculty member at an arts college. Many of the graffiti artists have similar stories to share, and all come to the RedCan to donate their time and expertise to help create bridges, networking opportunities, and basic hope for the Lakota youth.

RAISING THE TIPI

Inspiration and team work also come in the form of community effort of raising a tipi, a traditional Native American dwelling used in time immemorial. The tipi was traditionally built by women, and careful steps and attention have always been given in the assembly process. Tipis are meant to be portable, as early Native persons were nomadic and would travel to different areas within a geographical region so as not to over-hunt, over-fish, or grow crops in the same areas for too long. Raising and securing a tipi is no small feat and requires careful precision and strength. In today's modern world, men are used to helping the women put the tipi in place. The volunteers and other community helpers assemble in the large field outside of the Cheyenne River Youth Center, and the hand-painted tipi canvases are unfurled and laid on the ground. Next, large aspen tree trunk poles (about 25 feet tall), which have been carved into slender support sticks, are brought out to the field. Three poles are assembled first with leather ropes securing the top to make a triangle (Figure 4.5). By lassoing the leather rope around the support poles and then using the rope to circle the tipi, it is secure enough to add the other poles (usually 13 in total representing 13 different peoples of mother earth). Lastly the canvas cover is hoisted up on to the poles and secured with leather rope. The volunteers and I learned quite a bit about the meaning behind a tipi; for example, the symbols and pictures painted on the outside of the tipi's canvas all have

Figure 4.5 Lakota tribe members and volunteers hoisting the tipi poles into a triangle position

special significance to the Lakota tribe. We have also learned the care and thoughtfulness behind this process, and the back-breaking work it takes to assemble. Each year, we have worked together to assemble four tipis, which is also a sacred number in the Native American tradition. The use of the number four represents the four directions of the earth: east (represent new beginnings—the sunrise), south (represents youth and the full sun—fullness of life), west (represents the harvest and ending of life—the sunset), and north (represents the cold harsh weather and ancestors). Therefore, it is also a number of completion and captures the entire life cycle.

The very act of setting up a tipi has become a spiritual experience, steeped in thousands of years of history and ritual. It is important for the volunteers to join with the Lakota community as novice helpers, and to be led through this experience by others who know the traditional ways of doing things. I am reminded in this process that we are guests of the Lakota and asked via invitation to help with the sacred tipi, an honor and great joy. At times however, this can be a difficult task, not only physically setting up the tipi but psychologically understanding the spiritual sacred traditions that the original Indigenous Native persons practiced. It is a returning to the roots of the United States, when it was called "Turtle Island" by native people. It is a new way of viewing and seeing the world. In this way it is a cultural immersion and exchange of thoughts, ideas, and ways of celebrating fellow humans as well as the ebb and flow of the life cycles.

REFERENCES

Bennett, M. (1998). *Basic concepts of intercultural communication.* Boston, MA: Intercultural Press.

Frankl, V. (1959/2006). *Man's search for meaning* (5th ed.) (I. Lasch, trans.). Boston, MA: Beacon Press.

Jacoby, B. (2015). *Service-learning essentials: Questions, answers, and lessons learned.* San Francisco, CA: Jossey-Bass.

Keily. R. (2005) A transformative learning model for service-learning: A longitudinal case study. *Michigan Journal of Community Service Learning,* 12 (3), 5–22.

Seibert, B. (2019, December 23). Overlooked no more: Earl Tucker, a dancer known as 'Snakehips.' *The New York Times.* https://www.nytimes.com/2019/12/18/obituaries/earl-tucker-overlooked.html

CHAPTER 5

Relationship Building

*With Contributions from
Melissa Hladek*

In my work with others, I have found at the core of any connection is relationship. How do we as human beings connect with others? How do we form, provide, and exchange meaningful relationships with those who are different from us? One of the premises of my approach to service-learning is to "see and be seen," thus just showing up and seeing folks as they are authentically, practicing cultural humility and a sense of curiosity not judgment forms the basis for successful relationships. Further, relationships exist in a state of reciprocity which is also the framework for service-learning. It is this mutuality that creates and maintains relationships with others. Jordan et al. (1991, 2004) developed relational-cultural theory (RCT), which is a popular and well-researched state of being with others in the world.

RELATIONAL-CULTURAL THEORY

Jordan et al.'s (1991, 2004) relational-cultural theory (RCT), grew out of the self-in-relation theory (Jordan, 2004; Surrey, 1997). Self-in-relation theory is understanding that we know ourselves partly by how others respond and interpret us. Important tenets of the RCT are that growth-fostering relationships are a basic need throughout one's life and that disconnections between people are the primary source of psychological problems (Miller & Stiver, 1997). In addition, Miller and Stiver found that relationships were highly defined by the cultural context. For example, the reality view, based on early upbringing and culture, shapes people's perceptions.

Key concepts in RCT include mutual empathy, mutual empowerment, authenticity, and movement toward connection or mutuality (Miller & Stiver, 1997). Miller and Stiver define mutual empathy as, "joining together based on authentic thoughts and feelings of all the participants in a relationship" (p. 29). Mutual empathy also created, "Something more because each person can receive and then respond to the feelings and thoughts of the other, each is able to enlarge both her own feelings and thoughts, and the feelings and thoughts of the other person" (Miller & Stiver, 1997, p. 29).

Mutual empowerment is a step further in that it consists of a dynamic process that functions as a central tenet for psychological growth, and, therefore, naturally grows out of mutual empathy (Jordan, 2004; Miller & Stiver, 1997). Mutual empowerment consists of "five good things" which are "zest, action, clarity, sense of worth, and sense of more connection" (Miller & Stiver, 1997, pp. 31–32). Authenticity is the ability to represent oneself more fully and honestly in a relationship (Jordan, 2004; Miller & Stiver, 1997). Movement toward mutuality or connection is the by-product of the first three concepts. With mutual empathy, mutual empowerment, and authenticity present, there is an increased desire for connection with another person (Jordan, 2004; Miller & Stiver, 1997).

CULTURAL DIFFERENCES IN RELATIONAL-CULTURAL THEORY

Writings from The Stone Center, in Wellesley, Massachusetts, suggested that RCT was applicable across cultures, but possibly in a more complicated manner and with more difficulty in expression. In studies with Western non-American women, such as women from Puerto Rico, African American, and Jewish cultures, Coll, Cook-Nobles, and Surrey (1997) found that minority differences created a deeper, and sometimes below the surface, struggle for mutuality. They described ongoing efforts to sustain friendships and mutually empowering relationships by the quality of their "relating and real dialogue" (p. 177). Although striving for relational ways of being, people from other cultures who have been oppressed by colonization practices, or other forms of oppression, many times experience disconnection because of the collective history and political social environment. Specifically, women of other cultures may have experienced a harder time with mutual empowerment because of the subversive and unseen prejudice that exists in any majority culture and many times targets women due to outdated patriarchal standards and practices (Coll et al., 1997).

In cultures of the East, the idea of RCT also exists, but in a different, or possibly opposite, light. Jordan (1997a) wrote,

> In American culture, there is an imperative in socializing children to wean the helpless and dependent infant toward greater self-sufficiency and independence; so engrained is this bias that it is hard for most of

us to appreciate that other cultures may in fact perceive the infant born independent and needing acculturation toward dependency.

(p. 10)

In the models promulgated in the East, there is found the communal self, the interdependent self, the familial self, the spiritual self, and the independent self (Roland, 1989). In Roland's popular book *In Search of Self in India and Japan*, he identified the Eastern self as more familial or "we-self" oriented (p. 7). In the East, ego boundaries appear more permeable, with more shared sense of self in the context of the family. Roland viewed Eastern cultures as more accepting of the self-in-relation or being-in-relation ideology. This view supports exploration of the question, how do individuals from the East or other non-Western cultures view "being-in-relation" and mutuality based on the we–self societal learning?

A possible gift of the East is in its positing the contextual nature of self as embedded in relationship with family and others. Jordan (1997a) wrote that, in American or Western culture, self is de-contextualized and seen as existing as a separate entity rather than as "being as a contextual, interactional process" (p. 16). She further explored a new paradigm of self:

> If on the other hand, self is conceived of as contextual and relational, with the capacity to form gratifying connections, with creative action becoming possible through connection, and a greater sense of clarity and confidence arising within relationship, others will be perceived as participating in relational growth in a particular way that contributes to the connected sense of self.
>
> (Jordan, 1997a, p. 17)

The need to objectify and "it-ify" or render our existence into "thing-dom" is powerful in the very language that is used in Western psychological theory (Jordan, 1997a, p 19). The Western tendency to "do" or "have," instead of honoring the state of "being," stresses the self as separate. Jordan proposed a need to shift from the terminology of self-knowing to that of relational-knowing. Self-in-relation looks beyond polarities of self versus other, and embraces the and/both of self and other.

Cady et al. (1986) focused on women and people of color being fully "accepted as equals within their own species" as a first step toward connection or oneness (p. 5). They suggested that oneness that may be sought through connection is not merging or losing self in another, it is "differentiated connectedness, a connectedness precisely because of our separation from one another. In this sense interdependence is the opposite of fusion" (p. 5). This is the diversity model of today: we are all separate but also connected in the great web of life.

As Miller and Stiver (1997) proposed about the role of relationships in self-growth for women and men,

> Our fundamental notions of who we are are not formed in the process of separation from others, but within the mutual interplay of relationships with others. In short, the goal is not for the individual to grow out of relationships, but to grow into them. As the relationships grow, so grows the individual. Participating in growth-fostering relationships is both the source and the goal of development.
>
> (p. 22)

Human beings' sense of self is intricately tied to and grounded in the ability to create and maintain relationships. As Miller (1976) wrote specifically about women, "women stay with, build on, and develop in a context of attachment and affiliation with others" (p. 83). Miller and Stiver (1997) reported that an inner "sense of connection to others is the central organizing feature of women's development" (p. 16). I concur with the authors and would also suggest that a sense of connection and affiliation is also important to men, but this idea of relatedness has been socialized out of men raised in Western and/or patriarchal societies. Men have been unable to have clear ways of relating that aren't construed as "feminine," and instead have been socialized to complete tasks, problem solve or maintain systems.

In terms of service-learning, the research on RCT is on point, and can inform best practices in working with others from diverse cultures. Relationships are created in mutuality, where both parties come together with a common goal, to learn, understand, appreciate, and garner insight into each other's worldview and context. Coming from a place of reciprocity and open mindedness can set the stage for relationships to grow.

ANTARDRISTI: SAFE HOUSE FOR GIRLS

In our work with the girls from Antardristi, the safe house in Kathmandu, Nepal, we have been acutely aware of the need to foster relationship growth in the most loving and compassionate way. The girls in the safe house have been sexually abused and mistreated, therefore mistrust and wariness of strangers is present. We have learned to just "show up" and use authenticity, mutual empathy, and empowerment, as RCT suggests.

To be authentic means that one must be authentic with oneself first. A first step in being authentic is to be open and honest with biases and preconceived notions that one might hold about the group of people you are working with. It is important to set aside stereotypes and get to know people as human beings, not, for example, as girls who have been traumatized. Being able to be authentic is hard work, in that there is a good deal of internal confrontation and reflection of one's inner thoughts and feelings about any given situation, environment, or group of people.

Making friendship bracelets out of embroidery floss is a popular activity to do with the girls at Antardristi. The teaching, creating, and making bracelets is therapeutic in that the girls are busy using their hands to create, which frees up their conversation. The bracelet making is a low-stress and fun way to connect with the girls. They have free choice as to what colors they choose and also how intricate or complicated they want the specific weaving of the bracelet to be. The younger girls can do something as simple as braiding, whereas some of the older girls can create detailed chevron patterns using multiple colors. This exercise in itself provides the opportunity for mutual empowerment, where the girls have free choice with the help of the volunteers to create whatever they would like. During the bracelet making, there is a lot of conversation, laughter, and joy in successfully completing the process. Once the bracelets are complete, the girls can gift their bracelet or keep it. As volunteers, we make bracelets alongside the girls with the intention of giving the bracelet we have created to the girl we were working with. This gifting of the bracelet is a metaphor for a relational bond. Each volunteer ties their bracelet onto the wrist of the girl, with the idea of object permanence (Figure 5.1). The girls can remember our time with them, by looking at the bracelet, knowing that we will return. Over the last many years of going to Nepal, some of the girls still have their bracelets. On our last visit, one girl's bracelets from our previous visit was still tied onto her wrist two years later!

BUILDING A RELATIONSHIP ACROSS THE YEARS

On our last trip to Nepal to work with the kids at PA Nepal, I was so pleased to see many of the same young children whom I recognized from our last visit. In the spirit of relational-cultural theory about being separated but connected through bonds of mutual empathy, I stumbled upon a small child, named Sameep (pseudonym), who I had held and loved as a toddler two years previously. Sameep was a special child in that he was the youngest boy at PA Nepal and was mothered by almost everyone there. He was precocious but full of love with a mischievous grin and twinkle in his eye. I had quite simply developed an affection toward this small imp of a kid. I was unsure if I would see him on this current trip, but upon our first day at PA Nepal, Sameep remembered me and immediately took my hand and we continued on with our mutually affectionate relationship as if two years had not divided

Figure 5.1 Service-learning volunteer tying a friendship bracelet onto a young girl

us. Here on the outskirts of Kathmandu, with little outside influences, this little one seemed to remember me or at least had a sense of remembrance with me. This relationship with little Sameep picked up where it left off, and I was reminded that although separate we are connected through a loving bond. Forming relationships with the people we serve is an intentional and hopeful byproduct of providing service-learning to others. In any therapeutic encounter, it is the relationship that heals and facilitates the healing process. For each one of us, it is important to have loving care and support. Sameep is a good example of the relationship that can form so quickly but seems to have lasting power. Relationships with others help everyone and help us feel interconnected with each other.

IN SERVICE-LEARNING: CONNECTION AND GROWTH BY MELISSA HLADEK

As a student in the Counseling and Art Therapy program in 2013, I was introduced to service-learning; an opportunity to travel, lead with my creative and therapeutic skills, and make art with others. This idea of service-learning resonated so loud in my heart, I knew immediately I wanted to participate as much and as often as I could. Since that introduction, I have volunteered in various schools, programs, and communities in Quito, Ecuador (2014), Bulawayo Zimbabwe (2015), Eagle Butte, South Dakota (2015), Kathmandu, Nepal (2016, 2018, 2023, 2025), Ozd, Hungary (2017), and Port Elizabeth and Cape Town, South Africa (2019).

Over the years of participating in service-learning I have volunteered in different roles including student, group leader, and community member. The most special part of doing this work was the opportunities to travel and learn with my family. Similar to my varying roles, I have also volunteered in different groupings of my family including participating as an independent woman, as a couple with my husband, as a family with my husband and daughter, and as a mother–daughter duo. Through these endeavors my family and I have had the privilege of making connections and building relationships with folks around the world.

The rest of this chapter is compiled of my stories and experiences of building and maintaining global relationships. I will share the ways my family and I have been able to "see and be seen" as well as stories that highlight our growth in authenticity, mutual empathy, and mutual empowerment (Jordan, 2004; Miller & Stiver, 1997). When I reflect on these experiences, I can't help but think of the vast parallel processes of learning and growing that have impacted my family both in the moments and everlasting. Service-learning as a family has shaped our values and strongly impacted the way we parent, communicate, view the world, exist in relationships, and most importantly love each other.

Leeches

This is a story of vulnerability and learning about being authentically me. On my first trip to Nepal in 2016, I was volunteering at Prisoner Assistance Nepal (PA Nepal). PA Nepal is a refuge and school for children whose mothers are incarcerated. It is located in the mountainside just outside of the city of Kathmandu. One of the days we finished the activities early and instead of playing and dancing in the courtyard the kids wanted to take us on a hike up the mountain to a small pond. I later learned that most of the year that area on the mountain is completely dried up, but that particular time was shortly after the rainy season and a small pond had gathered about 20 feet wide and about 1 foot deep. The kids were so excited to have this body of water nearby and couldn't wait to share it with us.

In the spirit of *being* with others in the world as Jordan et al. (1991, 2004) discussed, I embraced the joy exuding from the children and walked with them around the pond. I watched as they ran right into the water, quick to splash themselves and each other. I too splashed the kids with my hands and walked in the water just deep enough to cover my Keens shoes. It was a beautiful moment full of joy and laughter.

On the walk back down the mountain, I started to notice what felt like a pebble in my shoe. After a while of trying to remove the pebble by kicking and banging my foot on the ground, I needed to stop to get it out. Much to my surprise after removing my shoe, I realized there was not a pebble in my shoe, but rather multiple leeches on my foot. Now, in that moment my startled and frightened brain turned three black creatures on my foot into one hundred leeches all over my body and created one hundred more suddenly falling from the trees onto my head. Panicking, I screamed, covered my head, and ran back down the mountain with one shoe on. Unknowing the source of my screams, the kids and the other volunteers also started screaming and ran with me down the mountain, back to the courtyard.

On the stoop of the doorway of one of the main gathering rooms, I quickly removed my other shoe and inspected the rest of my body. Shocked by the blood on my foot, I was slightly terrified, yet desperate to remove the leeches. At this point the kids and other volunteers were gathering around me questioning what happened. Looking for mutual empathy, I showed the group the leeches on my foot. Rather than offering me empathy, they laughed at me! One of the kids reached down and in the most casual and nonchalant way he picked the leeches off my foot. It was as if he was removing a piece of fuzz from my sweater. The kids continued to laugh at my big reaction and could not believe my screams came from a common creature, like how an American would view a fly.

After calming down, I was able to join the kids in their laughter. I was given high fives and friendly body bumps for getting the leeches. In that moment, I felt the epitome of *being* with others in the world. I had a true Nepali experience, and it was as if I had reached a milestone in service-learning if there is such a thing. Even in my big reaction, I felt seen as one with my fellow Nepali friends.

I've thought about this experience many times since it happened and while it is funny to look back on and laugh, I also see this experience as a turning point in developing authenticity. As stated previously, authenticity is the ability to represent oneself more fully and honestly in a relationship

(Jordan, 2004; Miller & Stiver, 1997). This was an experience that gave me permission to be more genuinely me, and to be content with being genuinely me, in relation to others, specifically those who I am building relationships with. Part of that learning and developing authenticity was learning about my emotional and behavioral reactions through the reactions and responses of the kids and volunteers. The essence of self-relation theory is gaining a deeper understanding of ourselves by how others respond and interpret us (Jordan, 2004; Surrey, 1997). Building those relationships in that service-learning experience taught me more about the person I was and gave insight into the person I wanted to be. It also taught me not to dip my toes in any bodies of water in the mountains of Nepal.

Cactus

One of the shortest, and yet one of the most impactful, connections I have made while doing service-learning was during my time in Bulawayo, Zimbabwe. I was volunteering at a residential center called the Peniel Center which offered hospitality to children and young adults of the village who had been orphaned due to their parents' death from AIDS/HIV-related diseases. The Peniel Center was located in a remote location outside of the closest city of Bulawayo, often referred to by the locals as *the brush*. The brush translates to a natural habitat or wild vegetation area that is mostly made up of low grass fields and wild animals. Needless to say, the resources, specifically food and water, were scarce at the Peniel Center.

One afternoon, a small group of volunteers had just finished an activity with some of the kids using a few sets of watercolor paints and white computer paper that had been torn in half to make sure we had enough for everyone. The kids and volunteers had transitioned to the next location, and I stayed behind to clean up the materials. While the owners and residents at Peniel took pride in their home and what little belongings they had, they also had an amazing practice of non-attachment. Because of this, after the kids were finished with their activity, the image or piece that they created seemed to stay right where it was created.

As I was helping to clean up after the group, one of the older women at the center came outside and approached me with an equal sense of shyness and curiosity. In her limited English, she asked to try the watercolor paints. I sat down next to her on a red brick pathway and gave her a quick tutorial of how to use the paint. She shared with me, she had never seen watercolors before and she was amazed that it was activated by the water. She appeared a little timid to try the paint for herself but eventually was able to put the brush to paper. In our conversation of hand gestures, pointing, and broken English, I was able to gather she had looked out the kitchen window at a very tall and overgrown cactus plant. In her own way she stated, "I've stared at it for so long I can picture it with my eyes closed." I encouraged her to paint the cactus. With a little assistance using the water and paint, she was able to recreate the very cactus she had looked at every day. She looked at her completed image and began to softly cry. She sat for a moment in silence, looking between her image and the cactus plant in awe of what she had just created. She eventually leaned over and gave me the biggest hug I think I have ever received and thanked me for that moment. I later saw her showing her image to some of the other women in the village, talking through a full smile of pride.

I never saw her after that and I don't even know her name, but similar to her ability to close her eyes and see that cactus, I can close mine and bring myself right back to that moment. I can feel her hug and I feel the connection we made through the cactus and the watercolors. I remember that moment often, and when I think about relationships built through service-learning, hers is one that is very present for me.

Invisible Strings

The Invisible String Theory is a spiritual and symbolic belief that connects people who are not in close physical proximity. The Invisible String Theory is believed to originate from an ancient Chinese concept, the Red Thread of Marriage, that has similar roots and beliefs in various Eastern Asian cultures. The roots of this belief are more focused around a romantic connection, similar to a soulmate, where two people are connected by an invisible red string who are destined to meet. This concept and tradition have been shared for centuries and recently retold by author Lyn Liao Butler (2022) who talks about this concept in her novel *Red Thread of Fate*, a story about a distant family connected by a delicate thread.

Another author, Patrice Karst (2018), wrote a children's book about this concept called *The Invisible String*. She talked about her motivation for writing this book as a single mother when navigating the struggles of dropping her son off at daycare and operating from a strategy to help create comfort for her and her son while they were apart. She adopted the concept of the invisible string and metaphorically tied an end of the string to each of their hearts. The Invisible String concept grew in popularity in recent years through social media and the 2020 song "Invisible Strings" by Taylor Swift.

Modern interpretation expands beyond romantic relationships and includes all meaningful connections including friendships and family relationships. The modern theory suggests deeper concepts of comfort and hope, in that an unseen bond exists between two or more people even when they are separated (Karst, 2018). The belief further suggests that one is not

Figure 5.2 Decorated heart doilies tied to a clear string at FA Nepal

alone and one is always connected to a loved one regardless of distance or circumstance which can lead to a stronger sense of belonging (Karst, 2018).

The invisible string concept has been used many times in my ventures with service-learning, but more intentionally during a return trip to PA Nepal in 2025. I read the kids at PA Nepal the book *Invisible Strings*, and talked to them about our deep heart connection to them. We shared that several of the volunteers from our group had returned to PA Nepal four or five times, and it was because of the invisible strings that kept us connected and it is the very thing that keeps us coming back. Each child and volunteer decorated a paper heart with a special symbol about their invisible string. We then strung all our hearts on clear fishing wire (Figure 5.2) as a symbolic way of connecting all of our hearts on an invisible string.

Suman

This chapter of the book would not be complete if I did not include one of the strongest invisible strings I have made while participating in service-learning. This is a story about a young man named Suman. Upon arriving in Nepal for the first time in 2016 we were greeted by several members of an organization called Social Tours, who were supporting us with our volunteer work while in Nepal. One of the Social Tours employees was a young man who couldn't be happier to meet us and work with us. He walked with a joyous pep in his step, and he smiled from ear to ear every time he talked.

I was introduced to Suman when dividing into small groups. Most of the group were going to the Samata School and a very small group of us were going to PA Nepal. I felt lucky to be part of that group, and I was excited to work alongside Suman. Suman was our guide and translator and traveled with us from Kathmandu to the mountainside every day.

We were driving along a very bumpy road when it suddenly seemed to end. We all got out, confused, looking for our destination. Suman, very humbly, escorted us the rest of the way on foot. We traveled up the mountain, over a small river that had 50lb bags of rice as a makeshift dam, and across a large field to get to PA Nepal. Suman was very patient as we walked like it was the end of the earth knowing he could probably make this walk twice as fast and blindfolded.

Suman is about ten years younger than me; however, our friendship was instant and has been one of those bonds that feels like we have known each other for a lifetime. We quickly skipped the small talk and got to know each other in a more meaningful way. We talked, joked, laughed, and shared stories about each of our lives. By day two of hiking up that mountain the polite patience turned into friendly banter, which quickly turned into friendship that felt more like family (Figure 5.3).

Figure 5.3 Melissa and Suman celebrating Holi at PA Nepal

Suman moved to PA Nepal when he was a young boy. He has lived there and stayed there off and on for most of his life. He is very well loved by the kids who live there currently, who refer to him as Suman dāi, which translates to elder brother. Suman continued to visit and volunteer at PA Nepal as often as he could until he was hired by PA Nepal in 2024. He works part-time in the admin office as well as part-time developing programming for the kids. Although, with the number of pictures he shares of him and the kids having fun, I'm not sure how much admin work he is getting done!

Suman and I have remained friends over the years, and we message on social media about once a week. Through financial hardships, terrible weather and flooding, lack of technology or access to internet, an 11-hour time difference and about 8000 miles, Suman and I have maintained an invisible string that keeps us connected. On social media, we share updates on our lives and families, and we celebrate each other's special moments. Although our lives are very different, we look forward to seeing each other every other year. Suman maintains a contract with social tours where he rejoins the company every two years just to work with our group.

Sustained Family Impact

Similar to the concept of ethnorelativism discussed earlier in this book, which suggests that one's own culture is experienced in the context of other cultures (Bennett, 1998), I propose that one's own family is experienced, and found, in the context of other cultures. One of my biggest gratitudes in life has been the ability to travel to many destinations in the spirit of service and learning about the world. An even bigger gratitude has been being able to do so with my family. My family and I have volunteered and visited many countries and cultures around the world including traveling with our one-year-old daughter to South Africa to volunteer at the Isaac Booi school. I have also had very special opportunities to bring my daughter to Nepal twice, when she was age five and age seven. Although, if you ask her, she will tell you she has been there three times, the first time being when she was in my belly. She and I journeyed to Nepal in 2018 when I was about 20 weeks' pregnant. That is a story for another book.

We have grown as a family because of these experiences, and we integrate gained cultural learning into our everyday lives, including mealtimes, playtime, relationships, education, and inspiration for more service-learning and global travel. It is common in our house for my daughter and her two younger sisters, who will eventually join us in service-learning, to play "vacation" including packing a small suitcase with random toys, get on an airplane (their bunkbed), and go to Nepal. I love hearing their conversations like, "Today we are going on a hike to Champa Devi, and later we are playing Holi." It is also common for us to play "welcome dinner" during mealtimes, complete with joyful attempts to sing Nepalese songs and dance with fake fire.

Due to our experiences with service-learning and our immersive exposure to how other cultures in the world exist, we have made many changes to how our family operates and how my husband and I parent. Our family values deepen with each service-learning opportunity to have an open heart and connection with others in the world. Our family ideals and beliefs are rooted in diversity, equality, and multicultural competence as well as treating all humans with kindness and compassion.

My husband and I hope to continue to provide service-learning opportunities to our three daughters to instill global and relational values in them. Outside of service-learning we find ways to embrace cultural differences in our lives, specifically with their education. They are enrolled in a school that offers a K-12 International Baccalaureate curriculum that integrates cultural caring and awareness into each lesson.

Other values we have grown to adopt are rooted in letting go of fear and control, leading with gratitude, and finding joy in small moments. Letting go of fear and control has been a big lesson that has led to a hands-off parenting approach. To the average American, the following scenarios may seem risky or even dangerous and they would probably recoil at the thought of letting their children engage in some of these activities, but to our friends in other countries, these things make up their everyday lives. Letting go of fear and control is something that is learned in relationships, by modeling, conversations about varying beliefs and religious tenets, shared experiences, and sometimes by making a go-with-the-flow decision.

Some less risky things I have embraced while on service-learning trips have been letting my daughter ride in the car without a car seat or seatbelt, standing in the front of an open-air jeep driving on bumpy and sometimes treacherous terrain, driving in a bus on the side of the mountain that is only wide enough for one car yet somehow fits two, and adopting the ideas of co-sleeping. Slightly more risky moments have been allowing my friend Raj to carry my five-year-old daughter on his back down the mountain of Champa Devi, or allowing another friend, Bikram, to take my daughter on a motor bike without a helmet, or eat food served from dirty hands and unclean dishes, take a one-year-old sand surfing, or be among and feed a group of elephants. Riskier, and here is where it gets dangerous, activities include riding in a canoe-shaped, hollowed-out log down a mugger and gharial crocodile-inhabited river.

This last one was probably the riskiest, and admittedly scariest, situation yet. My husband and I, along with a member of our host family, were interrogated by openly armed members of the Zimbabwean National Guard because of our white skin. We were pulled over while driving down the main road just past the airport. Thankfully, we paid a small cash bribe and were able to carry on to our destination. At that time due to the political and economic climate, the Zimbabwean government utilized excessive force of their police and military to maintain internal security, for often nominal offences such as having a radio in your car. I think of that moment from time to time and scare myself thinking about the "what-ifs." Needless to say, these experiences among many others have contributed to, and heavily influenced, my way of living and parenting with less fear and control.

Leading with gratitude is a core principle in our home. As parents, we try to foster grateful attitudes and hearts within our kids. This principle is largely influenced by our experiences of seeing the lack of resources and often poor conditions in other parts of the world. Further, this value is influenced by the opportunities I have had to learn about my own privilege in the context of other cultures (Bennett, 2004). We model gratitude and remind our girls to lead with gratitude in various ways such as food, belongings, our home, our pets, our friends, and our family. The current focus has been on finding gratitude for food, specifically on waste and consumption. Not in a "there are starving kids in Africa" kind of way, but more in a practical appreciation for food. For example, shopping from the farmers' market, learning about how food is grown and harvested, and teaching our children about cooking and preserving food.

Another lasting impact on my family that has been fostered from global relationships has been finding joy in small moments. Leaning into joy has created strong family bonds among us and has further strengthened each of our relationships. From a parenting perspective, my husband and I try to be present with our kids including saying yes to connection opportunities. For example, in the middle of blueberry picking at one of our favorite local farms, it started to rain and then pour. My three daughters, each with half-full buckets of blueberries, began to cheer and celebrate the rain. My husband and I, not so cheerful about our now soaking wet clothes and thinking about the very wet car ride home, decided to embrace the moment and continued to pick blueberries with our daughters, in the rain. This moment led to lots of laughter and lasting joy in the form of "Can we go pick blueberries in the rain again?"

The true essence of service-learning is in its reciprocal nature. I have just shared so many blessings that have been gleaned from our service-learning adventures, it is hard to not feel gifted 100-fold because of the relationships formed with the served, but also how this has dramatically impacted and strengthened relationships with my own family and changed the very nature of my parenting style.

Colorful Moments

Integrating arts-based expressive therapy into service-learning was discussed in depth earlier in this book; however, using expressive therapy has undoubtedly been a catalyst for relationship building throughout service-learning. Expressive therapies, such as art making, music, dance, and play, are at the source of connection. Further, expressive therapies have been used to strengthen and build relationships during volunteer experiences as well as maintain relationships between visits, such as bracelet making and gifting of drawings and artwork.

During my time in Zimbabwe, I learned about the hardships the village members had obtaining resources like food and water, let alone access to art materials. In the spirit of connection and creativity I worked with a group of children to make art materials out of natural materials found in their environment. We gathered small sticks and tied them together with yarn to create makeshift drawing tools. We used our tools to draw basic pictures in the dirt like hearts and stick figure people. What I remember most about this experience was trying to write and pronounce each other's names. My attempts to practice using a clicking dialect to pronounce their names led to many laughs. This experience of creating materials together then using our materials to create symbols and names in the dirt fostered connection.

Another meaningful way to connect with others is through movement, often in the form of play and dance. When language is a barrier to communication or words are not an option, movement can be a way to connect and form relationships. I have had several experiences in service-learning where I have been invited to move my body in unison with others. These opportunities have deepened my understanding of the various cultures I have visited such as moving in a parade-like cadence to the sound of a drum with members of the Lakota Sioux or moving in a similar circular direction to the cadence of instruments with the Tharu people of Chitwan. Movement, dance, and play are abundant and practiced by both adults and children for a variety of reasons like dancing for fun to more serious versions of movement based on religion and tradition.

Some of the ways my family has been able to participate in building and forming connections in a non-visual arts way has been through movement. My husband has used his body to connect with others in various settings while volunteering. One story he shares is about a young boy in Peru who was nonverbal and lived with physical limitations. Ryan noticed the boy wanted to join his peers and the volunteers and play in the courtyard. He assisted the boy on the ground and then joined him on the ground to crawl and move around with the others. Ryan has also bravely used his body to participate in traditional dancing with native members of the villages of Gqeberha, which is always a cause for laughter and joy.

There is something so innocent and simple about being a kid. Regardless of race, language, status, or other difference, kids have an unspoken bond and understanding of one another through play. Through service-learning I have been able to witness my daughter build connections and relationships with others in this way. Her favorite form of play is the celebration of Holi where individuals honor each other and celebrate the festival of colors with powdered chalk and water. Those celebrating Holi will splash one another with handfuls of chalk and squirt guns full of water. This often includes running, chasing, playful screaming, and laughing. Holi is a way for both children and adults to move their bodies together and connect through the celebration.

These immersive experiences with dance, movement and playing Holi as well as so many more help connect the invisible and lasting strings of relationships with others, but also within my family. What started as a curiosity about service-learning back in 2013 when I was a graduate student, has totally transformed my worldview and the cultural context and awareness of others, has informed my actions, behaviors, and the way I approach the world. I have learned that creating and making room for relationships to form creates a ripple effect, which touches every aspect of a person's life. I am filled with gratitude, knowing that I am the lucky one to be able to do this work and look forward to serve as often as I can.

REFERENCES

Bennett, M. (1998). *Basic concepts of intercultural communication*. Boston: Intercultural Press.

Butler, L.L. (2022). *Red thread of fate*. Berkeley, CA: Penguin Random House.

Coll, C.G., Cook-Nobles, R., & Surrey, J. (1997). Building connection through diversity. In J.V. Jordan (ed.), *Women's growth through diversity: More writings from the Stone Center* (pp. 176–198). New York: Guilford Press.

Karst, P. (2018). *Invisible strings*. Boston, MA: Little Brown Books for Young Readers.

Cady, S., Ronan, M., & Taussig, H. (1986). *Sophia: The future of feminist spirituality*. San Francisco, CA: Harper.

Jordan, J. (1991a). Empathy and the mother–daughter relationship. In J.V. Jordan, A.G. Kaplan, J.B. Miller, I.P. Stiver, & J.L. Surrey (eds.), *Women's growth in connection: Writings from the Stone Center* (pp. 28–34). New York: The Guilford Press.

Jordan, J. (1991b). The meaning of mutuality. In J.V. Jordan, A.G. Kaplan, J.B. Miller, I.P. Stiver, & J.L. Surrey (eds.), *Women's growth in connection: Writings from the Stone Center* (pp. 81–96). New York: The Guilford Press.

Jordan, J. (1997a). A relational perspective for understanding women's development. In J.V. Jordan (ed.), *Women's growth in diversity: More writings from the Stone Center* (pp. 9–24). New York: The Guilford Press.

Jordan, J. (1997b). Do you believe that the concepts of self and autonomy are useful in understanding women? In J.V. Jordan (ed.), *Women's growth in diversity: More writings from the Stone Center* (pp. 29–32). New York: The Guilford Press.

Jordan, J. (2004). Toward competence and connection. In J. V. Jordan, M. Walker, & L. Hartling (eds.), *The complexity of connection: Writings from the Stone Center's Jean Baker Miller training institute* (pp. 11–27). New York: The Guilford Press.

Miller, J. (1976). *Toward a new psychology of women*. Boston, MA: Beacon Press.

Miller, J., & Stiver, I. (1997) *The healing connection: How women form relationships in therapy and in life*. Boston, MA: Beacon Press.

Roland, A. (1989). *In search of self in India and Japan toward a cross cultural psychology*. Princeton, NJ: Princeton University Press.

Surrey, J. (1991). The self-in-relation: A theory of women's development. In J.V. Jordan, A.G. Kaplan, J.B. Miller, I.P. Stiver, & J.L. Surrey (eds.), *Women's growth in connection: Writings from the Stone Center* (pp. 51–66). New York: The Guilford Press.

CHAPTER 6

Transformational Learning

By Megan Seaman

Transformation is characterized by change. It is fast and slow all at once; it is welcomed and avoided at all costs; and it is the one thing that all can depend on; it is inevitable. For those of us who choose the path of counseling and therapy, it is frequently the focus of many of our clients' treatment plans, and it is essential to foster the development of empathic, unconditionally accepting, genuine, ethical, professional, and culturally humble approaches to helping. Undoubtedly, change is "a-coming" regardless of whether we intentionally create it or passively allow it to happen.

Counseling and art therapy trainees transform through their program curricula both academically and personally. Therapists "knowing thy self" opens trainees' understandings of their ways of knowing, privileges, biases, prejudices, limitations, and strengths so that they can approach counseling with open-heartedness and compassion. Thus, counseling and art therapy trainees transform from "helpful" friends and family members when starting their master's programs into ethical, supportive, and culturally humble professionals who help their communities in the best ways possible.

Service-learning opportunities for graduate students in counseling and art therapy programs accentuate and accelerate the transformation process. I have seen students from various backgrounds and experiences volunteering, providing service, and acting as leaders with idiosyncratic reactions to the service-learning experiences; I have witnessed them deconstruct and reconstruct their worldviews; I have observed them engage in relationship-building and storytelling with new community members; I have viewed changes in their awareness of personal and collective comfort and discomfort, and empowerment and oppression. Through service-learning they internalize their transformations and externalize their perspective changes through critical reflection, dialogue, and activism. The change takes place and there is no going back to what they were.

Creating spaces and supporting opportunities for counseling and art therapy trainees to transform is an intentional process that is based on foundational theories and empirical research collected on transformation in adult education, as well as best practices of service-learning. In this chapter I present a discussion of transformative learning theory, and particularly how it relates to service-learning. I will illuminate Kiely's (2005) Transformative Service-Learning Process Model through examples of learning that I have encountered with my students. Following that, I will present a critique of traditional methods of understanding transformative learning. Finally, I will present an integrative approach to using traditional transformative learning methods with nontraditional affective and intuitive approaches that have fostered deeper change and dynamic activism in service-learning for me and my students.

TRANSFORMATION

To transform is to change in form, composition, or character (Merriam-Webster, 2025). For human beings, there are several expected transformations that take place as they progress in development from infancy through older adulthood, including evolving in physical, cognitive, and emotional maturity. For individuals who choose careers in counseling and art therapy, there are also expected transformations that are made in professional development, including increased familiarity with theories of practice, assessments and evaluations, and strategies and techniques to help clients address their concerns.

However, in adult learning there are potential changes that stand to undo former ways of knowing self and others, identities, values, beliefs, behaviors, cultural rules of engagement, and the meanings that are applied to ways of knowing. The meanings that adult learners assign to aspects of their lives become forever altered. Jack Mezirow (2000) defines transformation as "a movement through time of reformulating reified structures of meaning by reconstructing dominant narratives" (p. 19). In other words, transformation is not about adding new information or taking it away from one's point of view, but rather altogether creating a shift to new frames of reference in which to understand and assign meaning to self, others, and the world.

In the training process of counselors and art therapists, students learn to think differently. In a typical course, they read texts, reflect on the meaning of the information, integrate new information, reject old ways of knowing, and synthesize new understandings of themselves as helpers and the people they help. Yet, reading and reflecting alone cannot prepare students for the reality of being professional clinicians. It is through practicum and internship experiences that students move from learners to counselors and art therapists. They put their knowledge and skills to the test in empathizing and joining with clients to negotiate paths to goal attainment and healing. In their clinical practice experiences the real meaning-making and perspective changing happens. The actual application of counseling and art therapy with people from a variety of contexts and cultural backgrounds, and with different concerns and strengths, transforms what was theoretical into living and breathing reality. What meaning was applied to concepts of clinical practice prior to clinical experience takes on new purpose and quality in the active counseling and therapy processes. Thus, meaning-making is key to transformation, and transformation changes students into professionals.

Jack Mezirow (1997, 2000), the founder of transformative learning theory, describes that meaning-making is made up of two aspects: meaning perspectives and meaning schemes. Meaning perspectives refer to the sociolinguistic, psychological, moral-ethical, philosophical, aesthetic, and epistemic or ways of learning that are predisposed in how individuals understand information. Meaning schemes are conglomerations of beliefs, values, experiences, associations, feelings, and judgments that shape people's perspectives.

When individuals are presented with new information that does not fit their perspectives or schemas, there is a drive to reject it. However, at the same time there is a persistent need to make sense of the new information (Mezirow, 1997). In graduate counseling and art therapy training programs, students regularly are exposed to new information regarding counseling clients in consideration of their diverse backgrounds, social justice concerns, experience of power dynamics and oppression, which are meant to push trainees out of their comfort zones and into experiences of cognitive dissonance. Mezirow (1997, 2000) refers to dissonant experiences as *disorienting dilemmas*, or triggers for reflection. Triggers develop from experiencing major life-changing events or from the accumulation of related meanings that work to transform meaning schemas. The experience of disorienting dilemmas for counseling and art therapy trainees is an intentionally facilitated process that presents new perspectives and disrupts habitual perceptions of students so they cannot help but seek new ways to understand. In courses like cultural and socials issues of clients, students may find themselves initially rejecting new information in favor of maintaining the status quo of their meaning perspectives. Yet, to move forward in their learning, they must find ways to change their meaning schemas to organize new understandings of clients and their concerns.

Transformation then is a bigger force of change in adult learning. In the experience of counseling and art therapy trainees, transformation may include expected changes in professionalism as they matriculate through their plans of study. More importantly, transformation stands to change their views of self, the people they relate to, and those for which they are only just beginning to understand.

TRANSFORMATIVE LEARNING THEORY

Transformations in individuals occur because of development and time. Yet, there are intentional and structured approaches that can be facilitated with adult learners to move them to more expansive ways of learning. Primarily, transformational learning theory provides a model by which individuals change hegemonic perspectives to mindsets that are more inclusive and sensitive to alternative ways of experiencing reality. Mezirow (2000) describes transformative learning as

> the process by which we transform our taken-for-granted frames of reference (meaning perspectives, habits of mind, mind-sets) to make them more inclusive, discriminating, open, emotionally capable of change, and reflective so that they may generate beliefs and opinions that will prove more true or justified to guide action. [It] involves participation in constructive discourse to use the experience of others to assess reasons justifying these assumptions, and making an action decision based on the resulting insight.
>
> (p. 8)

Transformative learning becomes a deliberate process implemented to foster deep changes in meaning-making. Individuals' internal reflections and information processing shift the learning of how to think, feel, and behave in the face of novel experiences.

As mentioned previously, counseling and art therapy students' courses consist of topics designed to teach specific skills aimed at building trusting, compassionate, and culturally humble relationships. Additionally, students learn other instrumental elements of counseling including technical clinical skills related to assessment, strategies, ethics, and legal issues. Yet, learning can be both instrumental and communicative (Mezirow, 2000). In instrumental learning, transformation occurs through learning mechanisms of control and manipulation of the environment as a scientist may do to reduce a phenomenon to its essential elements. In this way, counseling and art therapy trainees learn and demonstrate specific tasks aimed at helping clients meet specific goals and objectives. In communicative learning, the process requires a more sophisticated pursuit of assessing the meanings of communications between the lines. It involves evaluating the truth or appropriateness of applying knowledge to new situations, peoples, and experiences, and it relies on observing the genuineness of individuals expressions of thought, feelings, and meanings (Mezirow, 2000). In communicative learning, there is a reliance on reflection, critical examination, contextual empathy and caring for others, and reformulation of knowledge and understanding to transform one's automatic belief systems. Internships and practicums serve as environments where communicative learning can occur, especially when it comes to demonstrating contextual empathy and caring. In supervision, trainees reflect and critically examine their conceptualization and therapeutic approaches and work on reformulating meanings. The purpose is to interrogate biases, prejudices, and foster cultural humility. One of the limitations of trying to support transformative learning in clinical experiences is that trainees may be working in environments that present different perspectives, or they may be working in spaces that foster their long-held mindsets, which limit transformative learning. Dependent on the clinical site, counseling and art therapy students may learn very instrumentally, but may not have the exposure necessary for communicative learning.

Transformative learning is about testing new theories with an open-minded positionality. In this way, adult learners question traditional, authoritarian, and status quo paradigms of understanding. Additionally, they reflect on the contextual influences of historical, political, and economic forces that oppress and subjugate or reward and support. Moreover, adult learners transform their understanding and change through reflective communication. Still, there are three concepts that differentiate transformative learning from other adult learning paradigms: transformative discourse, relationships and caring, and privilege and power.

TRANSFORMATIVE DISCOURSE

Discourse is a kind of discussion of organized thought. Other ways of defining it include an "exchange of ideas," an "action of running in different directions," or literally meaning a conversation (Merriam-Webster, 2025). In transformative learning, discourse is about creating reflective dialogue aimed at critically evaluating knowledge, clarifying meanings of differing cultural perspectives, and negotiating a collective interpretation of experience (Mezirow, 2000). Thus, discourse is a relational process with an exchange of ideas, coming from differing points of view, to be heard, understood, negotiated, transformed, and reconstructed. Transformative discourse is the vehicle to engage in the exchange of ideas and open-minded empathic understanding of viewpoints, resulting in new perceptions and behaviors.

Counseling and art therapy trainees are trained communicators. Learning how to convey empathic, genuine, unconditional regard to clients forms the foundation of their microskills training (Drcar, MacCluskie, & King-White, 2024). Nevertheless, trainees learn another important principle of practice: the counseling relationship is a one-sided relationship. The purpose of one-sidedness is to clarify and support that clients are the focus of attention in therapeutic relationships. Therefore, unless there are therapeutic benefits for therapist self-disclosure (i.e., in psychoanalytic countertransference is a necessary process), then most information shared is by clients and/or for the benefit of clients (Drcar et al., 2024). In this way, clinical experiences alone cannot foster the type of discourse that facilitates transformative learning. For transformation to occur, there must be a collective exchange of ideas and renegotiation of ways of knowing in relationships.

Discourse often takes the form of expressed words and their meanings held by the individuals involved. Individuals create dialogue about knowledge and meaning-making by construing words, phrases, and sentences together to convey various aspects of perception. In transformative discourse it is important to decipher cultural understandings, rules of decoding meaning, active listening, and empathy and caring for what information is presented in conversation or discussion. For counseling and art therapy trainees, learning how to foster dialogue about various perspectives of clients can be easily done. Students learn skills such as reflection of content, feelings, and meaning, asking open-ended questions, summarizing, and using prompts to create verbal communication (Drcar et al., 2024). Still, conversations between clients and therapists are not balanced exchanges of personal problems and strengths; rather, expression by the therapist is meant to facilitate exploration of presenting concerns and goal-attainment for the client.

Transformative discourse can take the form of alternative expressions in creative and cultural forms of visual arts, music, poetry, dance, and drama (Mezirow, 2000). Being able to imagine something different and create new ideas or concepts in context to new information demonstrates one of the most basic aspects of transformative learning. Thus, in transformative discourse,

> imagination is central to understanding the unknown; it is the way we examine alternative interpretations of our experience by "trying on" another's point of view. The more reflective and open we are to the perspectives of others, the richer our imagination of alternative contexts for understanding will be.
>
> (p. 20)

Discourse becomes an "extrarational way of knowing" in which meaning-making occurs through identifying symbols, images, and emotional and embodied forms of expression to create knowledge (Lawrence, 2012: 472). It draws on imagination and intuition.

It is not surprising that counseling and art therapy trainees often experience transformations from encountering their own creative expressions of knowing and witnessing expressions of their clients. In counseling and art therapy programs, students learn creative arts healing strategies to facilitate therapeutic processes in addition to traditional theoretical and evidenced-based approaches. They learn that using art as a form of discourse offers an alternative language for which to understand self and others. Art offers an alternative process of encounter, reflection, and transformation because it invites engagement in emotional and embodied expression and dialogue.

In teaching graduate students, we differentiate *art therapy* from *art as therapy* and creative arts healing approaches. What is implied in art therapy is that a particular therapeutic art technique will assess clients' presenting concerns or facilitate a specified therapeutic experience. However, in art as therapy and creative arts healing approaches, the act of engaging in art creation is communicative, relational, and healing, alone. Art creation is the transformative discourse.

RELATIONSHIPS AND CARING

As can be seen, discourse is a relational process. The premise of relationships is that individuals connect through mutual give and take, collaboration, sharing, and co-construction. Additionally, there is a mutual caring or concern for each other, even if it is transactional and instrumental. Relationships between individuals involve dialogue so that caring can happen. At least two individuals share information and perspectives, which allows them to experience mutual understanding and caring about what the other thinks, feels, and experiences. Perhaps caring on some level must happen in order for relationships to happen. Nevertheless, transformative learning cannot happen without considering the context of the caring and relationships that are encountered.

In transformative learning, Mezirow (2000) refers to relationship building and caring as *consensus*. In consensus, individuals engage in a collective and ongoing process to actively evaluate and judge knowledge tentatively. The process allows adult learners to "seek out and encourage viewpoints that challenge prevailing norms of the dominant culture in matters of class, race, gender, technology, and environmental protection" (p. 12).

However, interrogation of dominant paradigms can only be authentically implemented through mutual empathy, trust, connectedness, and security in relationships between people. Counseling and art therapy trainees' courses of study are based on the foundation of relationships and caring. Indeed, courses such as counseling theories, helping relationship microskills, and creativity and visual thinking teach the necessary skills of learning to relate to and understand clients in both verbal and creatively expressive ways. Communication, whether through reflective listening, empathic responses, and art can create environments of safety and connection (Lawrence, 2012). The sense of security and shared understanding is essential to experience caring and that one feels understood and heard or seen. Learning person-centered theoretical assumptions and strategies to effectively attend to clients, build trust in the therapeutic relationship, and unconditionally accept and understand clients serve as the cornerstones of relationship formation and transformation (Mezirow, 1997, 2000; Taylor & Snyder, 2012; Wedding & Corsini, 2019). When individuals feel genuinely seen and understood they are empowered to feel more compassion for themselves, and thus act in caring and compassionate ways to others and the environment.

Counseling and art therapy trainees learn to care for their clients. They learn to understand the positions of their clients based on clients' contextual backgrounds, interrogate their own points of view that stand to block therapeutic processes, and provide intervention plans to help clients reach their goals. In a way, trainees are tasked with transforming even before they get to the therapeutic table. As stated before, their curriculum is developed to support critical evaluation of bias and prejudice and ethical practice as they move into their clinical experiences. Nevertheless, transformational relationships and caring processes rely on a consensus that is demonstrated with mutual sharing of viewpoints that challenge norms of the dominant culture. In therapeutic relationships counselors and art therapists provide opportunities for insight and change, but mutual challenging of hegemonic perspectives is not a required experience in counseling, unless it relates to client goals.

PRIVILEGE AND POWER

One of the most important lessons for counseling and art therapy students to learn is that no matter how well-meaning a therapeutic decision may be, if they do not critically reflect on their privilege and power that color their decisions and actions, they may inadvertently (or intentionally) misinterpret their clients' presenting concerns, force their points of view, make microaggressions, and discriminate against their clients. Whether mistakes are purposeful or unintentional, they result in blocks to transformational discourse, breakdowns in trust between clients and therapists, damage to therapeutic relationships, and possible retraumatizing and oppressing clients. Counseling and art therapy trainees' responsibilities to know their privilege and use of power are imperative.

Historically, the presentation of privilege and power relations as part of transformative learning was not directly observed (Johnson-Bailey, 2012). Surely, facilitating disorienting dilemmas as catalysts for individuals to reflect on and change their thinking was emphasized (Mezirow, 1997, 2000). Transformative learning focused on critical reflection, support of discourse to speak about experiences, and creation of new schemas and incorporation into daily life. Nonetheless, privilege and power perspectives of adult learners going through transformative processes also depended on their personal awareness of privileged positionalities and power dynamics. As it was first proposed, transformative learning theory did not consider the social locations of adult learners that affected their learning and meaning-making (Johnson-Bailey, 2012).

New understandings of transformative learning illuminate Paulo Freire's work on conscientization (Johnson-Bailey, 2012). Freire was a Brazilian philosopher and educator who emphasized that traditional adult education paradigms were oppressive and controlling because they favored individuals in dominant positions of power (Harris & Roter, 2024). From his perspective, traditional education was designed to keep people situated in hierarchy of class. Conscientization is a way of encouraging knowing and learning through seeing and being different. Additionally, it is a dialogic process in that educators and students engage in reciprocal relationships asking questions about building a better world (Johnson-Bailey, 2012). Dialogue in reciprocal relationships is important in creating change and empowerment and supporting conscientization.

As mentioned before, counseling and art therapy students have numerous opportunities to reflect on their positionalities related to gender, class, ethnicity, racialization, age, sexuality, and other ways of identifying self. Engaging in questioning what is seen as universal or normal from the classroom environment in forum with other students and educators from varying backgrounds is a very useful process in interrogating the status quo. Indeed counseling and art therapy graduate program curriculum is organized to foster a type of conscientization that invites open reflection on other ways of being.

In the master's program that I teach, my colleagues and I have found that the addition of service-learning opportunities to curriculum adds the missing element that seems to make a profound difference in counseling and art therapy trainees' development. Students who engage in immersive service-learning have an opportunity to dialogue with people from other cultural experiences. Together, they see and are seen. They engage in dialogue that exposes positionalities in ways that are dynamic and different for everyone. They come to consensus at times and are still left with questions at other times. Whatever the experience, students report that they are transformed by the process.

In the following section, I discuss Kiely's Transformative Service-Learning Model as it serves as a structure to showcase dialogue and transformations that my counseling and art therapy trainees have reported. Though it is based on Mezirow's transformative learning, it engages dialogue that asks collective questions about ways of seeing and being that allow for questions about how individuals can make a better world, together.

TRANSFORMATIVE SERVICE-LEARNING

Service-learning has become an important addition to higher education curricula. It is a type of experience designed to combine institutional goals with community dynamics (Taylor et al., 2018). It brings together community service with academic learning and emphasizes intentional reflection based on certain learning objectives. Taylor et al. (2018) note that quality service-learning both supports intentional reflection but also includes critical examination of assumptions that "reinforce stereotypes, oversimplify complex issues, and lead to inaccurate conclusions" (p. 238). Moreover, service-learning aims to increase individuals' awareness of world issues and enhance intercultural communication.

My colleagues, students, and I have had the opportunity to travel within the US and internationally to engage in transformative service-learning, including yearly to the Cheyenne River Lakota reservation in South Dakota, and alternating years to Kathmandu, Nepal and Gqeberha, South Africa. Our goal is to foster partnerships that help our students build community through critical reflection of their positionalities in context to service-learning. Over the years, we have learned very much through intentional planning and organizing, as well as trial and error, that service-learning is best when relationships with communities are established with reciprocity and continuity. Because of that, we have been able to build relationships and continued dialogues with our community partners that have been maintained over the past ten years. Our relationships with partners from Cheyenne River, Nepal, and South Africa continue because of reciprocal awareness of world issues that is facilitated, and the strengthening of communication and dialogue with our world partners.

The purpose of our service-learning work is to facilitate communication and dialogue between our students, fellow colleagues, and community partners that fosters transformative learning within a counseling and art therapy framework. Community partners collaborate with us to create opportunities that build unique skills and expertise of our counseling and art therapy trainees and meet the needs of the community. For example, in Cheyenne River we work with the Cheyenne River Youth Project Center to host an art festival that promotes Lakota people's culture, language, and vocational opportunities. In Nepal, we work with a couple different programs that support social and emotional support of children who have been the victims of sexual abuse and who have been orphaned because their parents have been incarcerated. In South Africa, we join with community educators in the township schools to accentuate their academic curriculum with art and movement activities (see Figure 6.1). All our service-learning experiences focus on joining with community members, seeing and being seen, and supporting communication that transforms.

A good model to understand the service-learning engagement that my colleagues and students of the counseling and art therapy service-learning program experience is Richard Kiely's Transformative Service-Learning Process Model (2005). Kiely created five domains of transformative

Figure 6.1 Dr. Seaman and counseling students make art with children from Isaac Booi Primary School in New Brighton Township

service-learning based on Mezirow's (1997, 2000) ten processes of transformative learning. However, he made note of problems in traditional understandings of transformative learning, which included the absence of dialogue on positionality, social justice issues, and other expressions of knowledge, like spirituality and creativity. Kiely's five domains of transformative service-learning include: 1) contextual border crossing, 2) dissonance, 3) personalizing, 4) processing, and 5) connecting. In the paragraphs ahead, I will present to you my observations of transformative service-learning based on the work of my colleagues and counseling and art therapy students.

CONTEXTUAL BORDER CROSSING

In service-learning, there are personal, structural, historical, and programmatic factors that intersect to influence and form perspectives in which students interpret and understand the process of transformation in context of service-learning experiences (Kiely, 2005). Personal factors include individuals' personalities, learning styles, travel experiences, expectations, biographical qualities, and self-concepts. They are the unique interpretations of individuals' idiosyncratic experiences. Structural factors include elements of identity that individuals may categorize themselves or be categorized by society. For example, racialization, gender, age, socioeconomic status, and sexual orientation are aspects of identity both self-selected and assigned by society. Historical factors are related to happenings in the socioeconomic and political spheres of society. They can be based on past treatment and current experiences of macrosystem level influences. Programmatic factors include requirements of service-learning like intercultural immersion, direct service work, reflection and dialogue with diverse communities, and assignments that promote reflection on social justice issues. The aforementioned factors represent a picture of positionality that helps to understand the context in which individuals transform.

Kiely (2005) called the combination of contextual factors "biographical baggage" that influenced how adult learners processed their service experiences (p. 9). He found that service-learning work caused some students to "unpack" their biographical baggage and begin to question their positionalities that influenced their frames of reference. Additionally, he saw that with the inclusion of community collaboration, service-learning was designed with collective reliance on community partners to guide course planning and implementation of service work, as well as the creation of connective and reflective dialogue opportunities with community members from different political, economic, cultural, health, and spiritual beliefs.

My colleagues and I have seen a similar processing of biographical baggage in our service-learning experiences. For example, one student discussed her reflection on her ethnic identity as an African American woman in the context of the things she was learning on our service-learning trip in Gqeberha, South Africa. She disclosed:

> I knew about the racialized terms and designations of "white," 'colored," and "black" in the township schools, but when I was actually was [in the township] and saw the physical difference of being in a colored school versus a black school it made me reflect on the history of racism in America and my own ethnic heritage and oppressions.

This student came face to face with the intersection of structural and historical factors that caused her to think about her own ways of knowing and reflect on oppressions that influenced her perceptions.

DISSONANCE

Dissonance in transformative service-learning can be defined as the incongruence between individuals' frames of reference and the context of what they experience in their service-learning communities (Kiely, 2005). It can consist of low-intensity experiences that trigger learning confined to place, time, and content, and high-intensity experiences that create such a shift in perspective that ongoing learning is set in motion. Dissonance can be ignited based on incongruence in sensory, historical, environmental, social, physical, economic, political, cultural, spiritual, communicative, or technological experiences (Kiely, 2005).

Kiely presented examples of dissonance that included students' coming to terms with the physical nature of service-learning environments. He found that students reported feelings of discomfort with the sight and smell of trash on the streets, or the witnessing of stray dogs, cats, and homeless people. My colleagues, students, and I had similar experiences of dissonance. For instance, in Nepal, there were masses of people and very little traffic laws, lights, or stop signs (see Figure 6.2). Traveling in a vehicle often provoked a lot of discomfort because of the fast-paced driving combined with hundreds of vehicles and pedestrians on the street all trying to go the same way, without any traffic signals. They reported feeling "scared that we were going to crash" or "unnerved at how fast we were going." Dissonance in traffic represents low-intensity dissonance because students learned quickly the new normal of traveling through Nepal.

Figure 6.2 Walking down a city street in Kathmandu, Nepal

Yet, the kind of dissonance that seems to facilitate ongoing transformation is high-intensity dissonance. Kiely (2005) found that adult learners experienced high-intensity dissonance when witnessing the complexities of poverty, hunger, and sickness. Seeing individuals seemingly stuck in dreadful situations for which there was no immediate solution created long-lasting incongruence that channeled an ongoing desire to come to terms with the pain and suffering that was seen.

We saw high-intensity dissonance in our students' experiences too. Working at the Kathmandu shelter for girls who were sexually abused presented a mixture of emotions and resulting dissonance. Students met girls as young as four years old who had been removed from their homes and communities because they were sexually abused. Learning through dialogue with counselors at the shelter about the backgrounds of children and creating relationships with the children created high-intensity dissonant experiences. One student reported: "Learning [her] story and how she was abused and for so long was devastating. But then creating an All About Me Book with her was so different—she had so much creativity and joy in her book." This student felt profound incongruence that a little girl could endure such atrocities and still be so creative and happy. It created a long-lasting mark on her understanding of trauma and resilience, but more importantly left an emotionally felt realization that her dissonance was going to be an ongoing process of coming to terms with what she witnessed.

PERSONALIZING

Everybody's experience of service-learning is personal. Even students, faculty, and community partners who have created a long-standing relationship of partnership experience service-learning from their own unique frames of reference. Kiely (2005) presents another domain of transformative service-learning is personalizing. It involves personal emotional responses to dissonance, which may include anger, sadness, helplessness, fear, anxiety, confusion, joy, happiness, and cynicism. Emotional experiences signal individuals to get curious about what has happened and about their unique ways of responding to it. Students evaluate their strengths and weaknesses in processing dissonance.

Where social justice concepts of racism, sexism, poverty, and other forms of discrimination were just concepts, students gain a new understanding because of their embedded sense of despair, pain, or other deeply felt emotion connected to dissonant experiences. Kiely (2005) found that students could not dissociate from what they had been exposed—what had been a concept or a theory was now visceral and reality.

Our students experienced various examples of personalizing based on the contextual service work they were doing, but also included biographical baggage that influenced their unique points of view. One of our trips to Cheyenne River presented a contrast in personalization between two students. One student, I will call Charlotte, was new to service-learning, but had shown great professionalism and cultural empathy in preparation for our trip. Another student, I will call her Trudy, had been to Cheyenne River for three consecutive summers and so had a good understanding of contextual and professional aspects of the project. Charlotte quickly was moved by the poverty and homelessness she saw on the reservation. She felt anger at the US government and its history of oppression of Lakota people. She felt empathy for the community members that she befriended. She found herself experiencing a sense of empowerment that the work she was doing on the reservation was building community in a reciprocal and beneficial way. Yet, she was also dealing with some mental health issues that came to light on the trip. She had stopped taking her mediation that managed a mood disorder while she was in Cheyenne River. As a result, she experienced symptoms commensurate with mania, which dysregulated her emotional and behavioral management. Because of her unique contextual border crossings she misperceived experiences in the community and made decisions that were problematic.

On the other hand, Trudy had her own personalization of service-learning at Cheyenne River. She was on her third trip to Cheyenne River, and had insight about general things to expect related to the people and the work she would be doing. Though Trudy also experienced various emotions of anger, despair, and empowerment, she responded differently based on her contextual border crossings. For example, at seeing Charlotte's emotional reaction, Trudy felt compelled to join with her and normalize Charlotte's experience by telling Charlotte the story of her first trip to Cheyenne River. She reported:

> I was so inspired on that first trip. Don't get me wrong—I felt angry and sad and powerless that I could not do anything to repair a legacy of US oppression. But it made me want to learn more, and made me want to continue coming back to the people of this community.

Both students shared personal emotions about their service-learning experiences, but each had her own personalization of the work they did.

PROCESSING AND CONNECTING

In transformative service-learning, processing is more than an individual reflection on what was witnessed and learned. It is also a social and communicative phenomenon. It is an individualistic and collaborative experience that asks questions, searches for connections and causes, looks for problems and solutions, and fosters relational and reciprocal dialogue to get to the heart of the issues (Kiely, 2005). Therefore, it involves quiet contemplation as much as it relies on collective communication and forms of expression to co-create new meanings.

Connecting is interrelated to processing. Where processing can be seen as the tactical processes that individuals use to communicate, connecting refers to emotional and relational dimensions of transformative service-learning (Kiely, 2005). Processing and connecting are interdependent because they "explain how students experience transformation as both an abstract intellectual shift in their understanding of poverty, service-learning, and their citizenship role, as well as a profound change in their sense of moral affiliation and obligation" (p. 13). Processing and connecting can take on various forms of expression including sensing, sharing, feeling, caring, participating, relating, listening, and comforting, in activities such as personal journaling, group reflections, community dialogues, and sharing time by cooking together, playing games, going to religious services, doing chores, sharing stories, creating art, singing, dancing, and performing together.

Processing and connecting seemed to create some of the most valuable experiences. I recall one summer working in Cheyenne River. Some of my students, my colleague, Dr. Katherine Jackson, other volunteers, and staff at Cheyenne River Youth Project center were in the kitchen preparing community dinner. We were all circled around a large island area created by two stainless steel tables, and peeling potatoes for the buffalo stew that was being prepared. As we peeled, we shared about various topics, from grade school memories to past RedCan festivals to sociopolitical issues impacting Lakota culture. One of the staff members, Danielle, shared that a thing people outside the reservation got so mixed up was terminology to label or refer to Lakota people. Danielle expressed:

> This whole thing about referring to Lakota people as "Native Americans" is kind of offensive to me. The word "American" was a name given to this land by the Spanish. Just like the word "Indian," another word given to people of this land in error because Europeans thought they landed in India.

She went on to say: "It all depends on the person. Some Lakota people wanted to be referred to as Lakota, but some don't mind calling themselves being called 'Indian.' Some don't mind being called Native American." This dialogue with Danielle and the group opened my mind to the ways that different people of the Lakota tribe and Cheyenne River Reservation interpreted their identities and historical oppressions. Formerly, I was used to educating myself and my students on terms that were disrespectful and marginalizing. After that dialogue, I learned that the way individuals identified was not based on a politically correct terms handed down in a textbook, but rather based on dialogue and understanding relationships of the community members. There was no standard rule of relating. Dialogue and identity were fluid.

Another example of processing and connecting that has been experienced in context of our counseling and art therapy service-learning trips is the transformative learning that happens through alternative forms of communication, specifically art creation. The common denominator among all our counseling and art therapy service-learning trips is seeing and being seen and sharing space through art. Thus, a big part of the dialogic process is collaboratively creating with community members.

In preparation for our service work prior to trips, faculty, students, and community partners collaborate on creative activities including art experientials and dance and movement to foster connection with the community. For example, our group works with the arts program director at Cheyenne River Youth Project center to determine a list of organized activities to prepare for their annual RedCan Graffiti Jam art festival. The director usually has specific requests that match the needs and expectations of the Lakota community. Some include visual arts, like rock painting and the three-marker challenge. But others involve more tactile experientials including making moon sand and friendship bracelets. Relying on the guidance of community members we have collaboratively designed plans that meet their needs.

Another way we connect with community in Cheyenne River is to rely on and support local businesses. We have made it part of our process to use art materials that the community has available. In this way we give back revenue to the community, but also use materials that are accessible in a continuous way. One regular activity one would see Dr. Jackson and I engage in is making runs to the local dollar store, hardware store, and grocery store for various supplies to use in our art experientials. On our visits to local shops, we talk with community members and get to know them. They in turn get to know us. Connections are being made and processing is happening.

The real connection and processing comes from the dialogue that is facilitated during creative experientials. During RedCan Graffiti Jam at Cheyenne River Youth Project center one of our responsibilities is offering various art stations for children, parents, other community members, and even volunteers and staff to participate. We set up tables in the community and at the center where people can engage in art making. Usually, we have a table of hotdogs and a cooler of cold drinks to add to the community togetherness. Children and adults sit at a table with construction paper, scissors, glue, and old magazines. Students may guide them to create a collage or a keepsake box (see Figure 6.3). Soon all are cutting and pasting, folding and forming, and engaging in conversations about family members, favorite pop stars, what art means to them, and other aspects of life.

A particular memory stands out from our past trip to Cheyenne River. One student shared her experience working at a table where the 3-Marker Challenge was happening (see Figure 6.4). She told about a little boy and his mom who came to create. She expressed:

> He was just so determined about what he wanted to do. He chose his coloring page and his markers and started creating. I was caught up in his creativity. I got lost in the work. It was easy; effortless.

She went on to explain:

> I had worked with kids at summer camps when I was in college. When I came to grad school my goal was to work with older adults. But now I am starting to rethink that. I felt connected in a different way to the kids [at Cheyenne River Youth Project center].

In the experience of dialogue through art expression with the little boy she started to see herself differently. She started to transform her frame of reference about her role as therapist.

Figure 6.3 Counseling students facilitate a family arts festival at the RedCan Graffiti Jam, Cheyenne River Youth Project Center, Eagle Butte, South Dakota

As has been demonstrated, transformative service-learning is an adult education experience that creates a forum for dialogue and collective questions about frames of reference, ways of knowing, co-creating meaning, and change in context of individuals personal identities, experiences, and hegemonic beliefs. In addition, there are various domains of experience that provide a broad picture of how individuals perceive their realities, including understanding contextual border crossings, dissonance, personalizing, and processing and connecting. Counseling and art therapy trainees' experiences in service-learning fit the model of transformative service-learning in their encounters with their own identities, the interpretations and lived experiences of community members, and through dialogue that promoted communication about new ways of knowing.

Figure 6.4 Counseling student volunteer works with a child at the RedCan Graffiti Jam, Cheyenne River Youth Project, Eagle Butte, South Dakota

However, the transformative service-learning model is based on Mezirow's (1997, 2000) original process of transformative learning. Though both approaches have furthered understanding of adult learning, there are some important problems or cautions to consider in the use of transformative learning theory.

CRITIQUE

One important problem with the model of transformative learning is that it does not address other forms of discourse or dialogue (i.e., spirituality and forms of creative expression). In a critical review of the research on transformative learning theory, Taylor and Snyder (2012) found that across studies, researchers turned to alternative theories and models such as Africentrism, critical theory, critical social theory, and others because of the deficits in traditional transformative learning and its overlooking important forms of expression like spirituality and its importance in understanding social locations of individuals. Additionally, researchers found that concepts such as multidimensional learning and multiple ways of knowing in traditional transformative learning have been used interchangeably and do not clarify the different forms of discourse of dialogue facilitated to create transformative learning (Taylor & Snyder, 2012). For example, Yorks and Kasl (2006) discuss expressive ways of knowing, such as art, music, poetry, guided imagery, and storytelling, as related to fostering whole person knowing and transformation, which is a divergent understanding of transformative learning. Moreover, Lawrence (2012) found that engaging in the process of art making allowed one to create an expression of experience that was not represented adequately through words only. Art allowed individuals to make sense of their experiences, work through their traumas, create spiritual renewal and purpose. From a traditional perspective of transformative learning, other forms of expression and their importance in creating dissonance and dialogue have not been considered.

Another important problem is that transformative learning does not consider social justice issues and positionality. First, critics argue that transformative learning relies on a Westernized and individualistic approach of traditional education that operates to subjugate bodies and serve individuals in dominant positions of power (Johnson-Bailey, 2012). Paulo Freire viewed transformative learning as dialogic and an education of equals in its foundation (Harris & Roter, 2024). In Mezirow's (1997) model, emphasis is placed on the educator to create ideal transformative experiences for students. In this way, transformative learning is hierarchal.

One last critique is that transformative learning cannot be forced. Johnson-Bailey (2012) points out as educators we may not be aware that in pursuit of dissonance and transformative learning experiences for our students, we may be inadvertently traumatizing them. She presents that it is important to weigh the options: "what matters most: the possible growth through transformation or the potential harm or painful cognitive dissonance that may be experienced?" (p. 261). A further question might be: are we educators prepared for the consequences of transformative learning?

Moreover, researchers point to the difficulty in measuring transformative learning. For example, Johnson-Bailey (2012) found that it was complicated to understand the extent of transformation that individuals experienced because of differing positionalities, times and experiences, and personal ways of caring to know and understand others. As discussed in the section on transformative service-learning, there are multiple domains impacting learning and transformation. Anyone of those domains can help individuals to shift their mindsets, or they can act to create more concrete and hegemonic perspectives.

INTEGRATING TRANSFORMATIVE LEARNING, DIALOGUE, AND CREATIVE EXPRESSION

As previously presented, transformative learning theory offers a start to facilitating and understanding adult learning. There were limitations of traditional implementations of transformative learning theory as it related to the absence of alternative forms of discourse and expression. Additionally, it heavily relied on traditional individualistic principles of facilitating transformation that worked to support dominance and subjugation.

In Kiely's model of transformative service-learning the importance of considering the dialogic process of contextual border crossings that influence individuals mindsets, fostering high-intensity dissonance, supporting individuals personalizing and embedding of difference, and creating spaces for processing and connecting in communities was discussed. His model emphasized importance placed on individuals creating dialogues in regard to transformative service-learning domains.

However, another addition to this model is the transformative importance of creative expression. The work that my students, colleagues, and I have done using counseling and art therapy expressions as ways to see and be seen transformed that way students saw themselves in the communities that they served. Additionally, creative expression facilitated dialogue between students and community members that were organic and brought individuals closer together in relationships. Seeing and being occurred through individuals' drawings and collages, through their conversations while making food for a community dinner, and facilitated through nurturing visits to communities where relationships were continually being built through regular and consistent interconnections. To that end, the ongoing dialogues of transformative learning experiences seemed to foster another kind of continual communication, reflection, and transformation.

CONCLUSION

In conclusion, transformative learning in adult education is based on change. The kind of change that is possible is reflected in transformative discourse and empowering dialogue. It depends on individuals' consensus in relationships and acts of caring to change, and it must be understood from individuals' positions of privilege and power. For counseling and art therapy trainees, didactic courses and clinical experiences aimed at teaching transformative discourse, relationship and caring skills, as well as fostering interrogation of privilege and power is part of a standard curriculum. However, the dynamic and mutual questioning that is evident in a dialogic process of transformation cannot be fully realized by working in clinical settings alone.

Service-learning is an opportunity to engage in transformative learning. It is an active experience that facilitates changes to how individuals relate to their lives in unexpected ways. Moreover, using a transformative service-learning model in combination with approaches that foster artistic and creative expressions enhances individuals' understandings of themselves, others, and the world.

REFERENCES

Drcar, S.S.J., MacCluskie, K.C., & King-White, D. (2024). *Helping skills for counselors and health professionals: Building culturally competent relationships*. New York, NY: Routledge.

Harris, D.B., & Roter, D.L. (2024). Profound love and dialogue: Paulo Freire and liberation education. *Health Literacy Research and Practice*, 8 (3): e118–e120.

Johnson-Bailey, J. (2012). Positionality and transformative learning: A tale of inclusion and exclusion. In E.W. Taylor, P. Cranton and Associates (eds.), *The handbook of transformative learning: Theory, research, and practice* (pp. 260–273). San Francisco, CA: Jossey-Bass.

Kiely, R. (2005, Fall). A transformative learning model for service-learning: A longitudinal case study. *Michigan Journal of Community Service*, 12 (1), 5–22.

Lawrence, R.L. (2012). Transformative learning through artistic expression. In E.W. Taylor, P. Cranton and Associates (eds.), *The handbook of transformative learning: Theory, research, and practice* (pp. 471–485). San Francisco, CA: Jossey-Bass.

Merriam-Webster (2025). *Merriam-Webster dictionary*. Accessed September 13, 2025 at webpage: https://www.merriam-webster.com/

Mezirow, J. (2000). Learning to think like an adult. In J. Mezirow & Associates, *Learning as transformation: Critical perspectives on a theory in progress* (pp. 3–33). San Francisco, CA: Jossey-Bass.

Mezirow, J. (1997). Understanding transformation theory. *Adult Education Quarterly*, 44 (4): 222–232.

Taylor, K.B., Jone, S., Massey, R., Mickey, J., & Reynolds, D. J. (2018). 'It just had to settle': A longitudinal investigation of students' developmental readiness to navigate dissonance and experience transformation through international service learning. *The Journal of Higher Education*, 89 (2), 236–260.

Taylor, E.W., & Snyder, M.J. (2012). A critical review of research on transformative learning theory, 2006–2010. In E.W. Taylor, P. Cranton and Associates (eds.), *The handbook of transformative learning: Theory, research, and practice* (pp. 37–55). San Francisco, CA:. Jossey-Bass.

Wedding, D., & Corsini, R.J. (2019). *Current psychotherapies, eleventh edition*. Belmont, CA: Brooks/Cole.

Yorks, L., & Kasl, E. (2006). I know more than I can say. *Journal of Transformative Education*, 4 (1): 43–64.

CHAPTER 7

Cultural Competence

What is cultural competence? This question is a hot topic query in today's world and has many clinicians asking themselves if their skills measure up to be culturally competent. Counseling and art therapy have their roots in an ethnocentric monoculture of European values and mores (Sue & Sue, 2022). This stilted view of therapeutic practice is beginning to unravel and deconstruct, as to best practices in working with non-European-descended people. I have found that to be culturally competent one must understand one's own personal framework or worldview, including background, ancestral practices and relationships, immigration patterns, affiliated ethnic groups, and early teachings by parents, teachers, and caregivers about multiculturalism. Once the clinician can identify their own implicit biases, and the context from which they have grown out of, it is possible to work with others from other cultures. It is best to attend to cultural competency by practicing cultural humility, a term coined by Tervalon and Murray-Garcia (1998) which implies that clinicians need to have self-awareness of their own culture and belief system and recognize cultural imbalances that occur when working with cultural difference, and those who are marginalized or underserved. As expressive arts therapists, it is important to study cultural art practices, be it art making, music, dance, or drama, to get a feel for what materials and methods work in specific populations.

LOST BOYS OF SUDAN

From 2001 to 2006, I had the pleasure of working at Catholic Charities Migration and Refugee Services with the Sudanese "lost boys," a group of young adult men from the Dinka and Nuer tribes, who had been the victims of the second Sudanese civil war, a conflict between Muslim groups in the north and Catholic groups in the south. The "boys" who were actually young men, ages 18–22, had been resettled in Cleveland, Ohio as part of a large global resettlement effort, housing small groups of about 40 refugee youth in various cities around the United States. Art therapy had been a viable method of helping the Sudanese boys cope while they were at refugee camps in Kenya awaiting their resettlement. Catholic Charities was keen on hiring an art therapist a few hours a week, and thus my part-time art therapy consultant job was created to help the young men acclimate to their new home once they arrived in Cleveland. I learned a valuable lesson in cultural competence in my art as therapy practice with them. On the first day of my consulting art therapy job, as there were about eight young men in my group, I set out paper, pencils and markers as just a quick and easy, "get to know you" activity. The young men did not understand how to use the markers and pencils, and even the paper was foreign to them. I was confused as to how these simple materials were a mystery to these young men. After some back-and-forth attempts at communication and the aid of an interpreter, I soon discovered that the Sudanese had never been exposed to traditional art-making materials such as paper and pencil. These young men had been shepherds in the fields and helped with farming, etc. They had not attended formal education and if they did they used a small chalk board and chalk to do simple tasks in the classroom. However, after some exploring, I discovered that the young men were adept at working with earthen clay, which is abundant in Sudan. The young men had had a good amount of access to earthen clay as they tended their animals out in the fields. They were expert clay builders and could make any animal, tree, or plant out of clay.

    I purchased a large block of earthen clay and presented it to the young men at our next group. The young men became animated and quickly went to work building various animals and imagery from their experiences in Sudan. One young man, Nico (pseudonym) created a bull out of the clay. He was able to share that he had many cows and bulls that he tended on his farm in Sudan. He was also able to share, through an interpreter, that he had run from the terrorist group that had burned down his village and killed his family. He had left all his livestock and everything he had to find safety. Nico had later met up with other lost boys as they all fled the scene of the war and pillaging. Making the bull (Figure 7.1) was empowering to Nico, in that he felt a sense of being rooted/grounded and connection to his homeland. Nico was also able to process his traumatic experience, through the depiction of his clay bull figurine, and this started a lasting relationship between myself and Nico. Nico and some of the other young men, a few years

CULTURAL COMPETENCE 103

Figure 7.1 Nico's white bull

after living in Cleveland, presented their clay figurines at a gallery exhibit to educate the public about the plight of Sudan and its people. The gallery exhibit helped Clevelanders become more culturally aware of events in Sudan, Africa. Most of the gallery goers were unaware of the horrific trauma and genocide that had rampaged through Sudan, and to this day continues.

This experience for me was a real eye opener to understanding the complexity of "right" art materials. Since working with Nico and his fellow lost boys, I have taken a proactive stance on making sure I am aware of art practices in whatever community I am serving or helping in. Once I understand traditional art making of said culture, it is easier to find "goodness of fit" between the art material and the maker.

WORKING AMONGST THE LAKOTA SIOUX

As mentioned earlier, we have been going to Cheyenne River Reservation each summer for years. So much discrimination and oppression have been projected and placed on Native American people by well-meaning but ignorant majority-culture Americans. There are no words to describe the suffering that the Lakota and other tribes have experienced. It is a miracle that the Lakota tribe members are still in existence, and not totally killed through genocide, disease, and terrible conditions placed upon them by early settlers, the United States government, and others greedy to take land away from Native persons.

Many of my students and volunteers are unaware of the history of hardship for Native people, who have been living within the Americas for over 10,000 years. Over 500 tribes roamed different parts of what we now know as the United States. These tribes had diverse and unique ways of being in the world, speaking different languages and different cultural practices. The Lakota Sioux tribe have specific cultural ways of living life. As students and volunteers, we need to be allies of the Lakota tribe; to watch, listen, and learn from the elders about appropriate ways to engage with members. Part of being culturally competent is to use cultural humility, coming to any encounter with an open and free mind, allowing for new information to be acquired and assimilated as needed.

Being a part of the drum circle, the tipi raising, cleaning bathrooms, picking up trash, etc. are paramount to understanding the needs of the community. Assessing and understanding the needs are part of what Block (2003) calls servant leadership. When acting as a servant leader, there is no task to menial or lowly that merits attention. Once given the directive by the tribe members to clean up trash, wash floors, or organize the kitchen, it is the service-learning providers' job to pitch in and get the task accomplished. This in essence is servant leadership.

Community meals are a big part of the Lakota Sioux. At the Cheyenne River Reservation there is a two-acre garden, where organic vegetables are grown and tended to. Gardening, mostly by weeding and transplanting small seedlings, is a popular activity among my students and volunteers. The harvesting of the vegetables that are grown in the community garden is given freely to members of the community. There are also community meals that feed up to 350 folks at a time. Being asked to help prepare and serve this massive community dinner is an honor and one that we always agree to help with. Historically food has been scarce for Native tribes and the ability to join in and help with meal prep is humbling. There is no waste of any food item; all is saved and used again.

A few years ago, I had the opportunity to help prepare a buffalo heart, a delicacy in the Lakota tradition. Although I am a plant-based eater, I relished this special opportunity to be of service to the Cheyenne River Youth Project founder Julie Garreau, who was teaching myself and a few others how to prepare the buffalo heart in the traditional manner. It is important to put aside one's own cultural framework and embrace the new cultures frame of reference in order to learn. From this experience, I learned how important the buffalo was to the Lakota and how they have lived in harmony with buffalo for millennia. Historically the buffalo provided many needs that the Lakota had, including food, warmth, spiritual practices, and ritual. Every part of the buffalo was used after a mindful slaughter, in that the relationship between the Lakota and this majestic animal were in harmony, co-existing together.

Another interesting aspect of the Native American tribes, including the Lakota, is the concept of place. Historically there is no land ownership within the Lakota tribe, but rather a land custodianship. Native people traditionally moved around within a large geographical location, not wanting to overuse the land. The native people believe that the land/earth provides, but that it is a reciprocal process, one that honors give and take from both mother earth and the Lakota. In order to be culturally competent, these land ownership ideas need to be understood. When the United States government pushed native persons into reservations, the land on the reservations was dulled out in multi-acre parcels. This was a unique way of thinking and acclimating for the tribes. What I have noticed in staying at the reservation every year, is that there is a communal framework that exists, regardless of land ownership. The tribe members look out for one another, and make sure that no one is without a roof over their head or food to eat.

CULTURAL COMPETENCE IN NEPAL

Nepal is a very old country steeped in ancient traditions and ways of being. Nepal, although progressive in many ways, still possesses a patriarchal worldview. As a feminist, living in a patriarchal United States, I understand this basic structure and idea. However, each country has their own unique view of patriarchy. In Nepal, the concept of girls attending school is a relatively new concept, as well as the concept of women having rights and working outside the home. Child rearing is considered to be women's work, whereas providing for the family is considered men's work.

At Prisoner Assistance Nepal (PA Nepal), children are placed in a residential home because their mothers have been placed in jail. The reason many of these women are in jail is because of petty stealing to raise money for food and clothing for their children. There is very little legal representation for women who have no money to pay for a lawyer, thus these women remain incarcerated. From a United States view, it seems that if the mother is in jail, then the father will take care of the children. In Nepal's cultural view, however, the fathers are not the primary caretaker of children, and thus the children end up in a residential facility. If this residential facility did not exist, children under the age of five go to prison with their mothers. Cultural competence in this situation means trying to understand the traditions and norms of Nepalese culture, without trying to change them or becoming outraged or railing against the system. This is the way of Nepal, and as a service-learning provider, we work within the context and framework provided.

Likewise, high in the mountains and hill towns of Nepal, there are other problems for young girls and women. Hill tribes have existed in Nepal for thousands of years, and have survived by subsistence farming, trade, and animal livestock. Increasingly, there is less ability to farm and raise livestock due to the ever-changing landscape riddled by environmental changes, major earthquakes and increased population. These indigenous Nepalese are very poor and have little resources. Many times, girls are the victims of this difficult environment. Sex trafficking and child bride trafficking is on the rise within the hill tribes of Nepal. Families need money, so they "sell" their daughters to seemingly good people, thinking that the girls are going to help out another family with domestic service and/or childcare. Another issue that affects the girls in rural Nepal is the alcohol addiction of parents. There is a pure grain alcohol, made out of rice, called raksi. This drink is widely consumed in Nepal and has led to serious addiction issues, most notably in the remote areas. When parents are inebriated, girls (sometimes boys as well) can become the victims of sexual abuse, by their own parents, or neighbors. Antardristi, a safe house in Nepal, has made it their mission to rescue girls from these horrendous conditions.

As a woman living within the United States, it is hard to hear these stories. It is normal to want to write letters to authorities, create a protest, support with money, etc. The important part of being a culturally competent service-learning provider is to remember that we cannot change the system. Folks working on the inside of the system are much more likely to change the system, thus people of Nepal are the best choice for change here. It may seem like a "cop-out" to not help in changing systemic oppression of women, but it is simply not the job of the providers to do this. The service-learning providers should be compassionate; help empower the children and teens by teaching coping skills and increasing self-esteem. There are tragedies that occur all over the world, and as a compassionate observer it is hard not to try and help. In over-helping, we take the role of colonizer, suggesting that we can save this country and its people by knowing better or doing better. If a country specifically asks for help from outside their country, then it is up to the helpers to decide if they can help, but without an invitation there is no room for trying to make systemic changes. One of the codes of being a mental health service-learning provider is to be able to wait for the invitation. The country that has requested our help knows what is needed and what might help. We as non-natives to the country or culture simply cannot begin to understand the multiple layers of cultural norms and mores.

MULTICULTURAL COUNSELING INVENTORY

As part of my work as the service-learning director at Ursuline College, I wanted to use a measurement that could assess our students' growth in the form of multicultural competency. From 2017 to 2019, I assessed 49 students, using the Multicultural Counseling Inventory (MCI) by Roysircar-Sodowsky (1993). This research, which was approved by Ursuline College internal review board (IRB), utilized a pretest and posttest to students attending service-learning trips from 2017 to 2019. The results yielded an interesting outcome.

The MCI measures four competency areas; multicultural competency in skills, awareness, relationship, and knowledge. Examples of questions used are "I perceive my race may make clients distrust me" and "I examine my cultural biases" (Roysircar-Sodowsky, 1993, p. 2). The MCI was administered a few months before the service trip and then re-administered right after the service trip.

Formal inferential statistical analysis completed to test the hypothesis showed that the mean post-trip scores were higher than the mean pre-trip scores showed statistically significant results for three categories: total Multicultural Counseling Inventory scores, Multicultural Counseling Skills Subscale scores, and Multicultural Awareness Subscale scores.

The test of total inventory scores yielded a p-value of 0.0093 meaning that the likelihood of seeing the increase in post-trip scores due to chance is only 0.0093%. There is a very strong likelihood that the service-learning trip experience led to these results. The result of the test for Multicultural Counseling Skills scores was a p-value of 0.0069, signifying that the likelihood of the post-trip mean score being higher than the pre-trip mean score due to only chance is 99.31%, again strong evidence of the positive impact of the trip. Finally, the output of the test comparing the mean post-trip Multicultural Awareness score to the mean pre-trip score was a p-value of 0.0051 indicating that the likelihood of results showing that the mean post-trip score is higher than the mean pre-trip score occurring by chance is 0.0051%.

What does this all mean? It appears that time spent volunteering while immersed within a different culture has clearly increased the participants' level of multicultural awareness and multicultural skill. Student volunteers self-reported that they did feel more culturally competent and learned greatly from this immersive experience.

I followed up after the students had taken the MCI by asking some additional questions, to get a qualitative view of learning acquired by student volunteers. I asked the following questions to 49 volunteers:

1. What did you learn about yourself from attending a service-learning trip?
2. What did you learn about others from attending a service-learning trip?
3. Do you believe that your view of others (religions, cultures, and ethnicity) has changed because of the service-learning trips?
4. Do you think service-learning opportunities help counselor/art therapists/others grow and evolve as humans?

In response to question 1, "What did you learn about yourself from attending a service-learning trip?" I received many responses, but Shaun and Kristy's (pseudonyms) responses seems representational of many, Shaun expressed:

> I learned from experience that significant cultural differences and considerations can exist between populations of people. These disparities cannot be categorized as "right or wrong" or "better or worse." They just are—that is, they exist and characterization should be avoided. Helping someone means to help them from their own perspectives and needs, and not those of the practitioner or clinician. Previous to this trip, these realizations were academic, and to some extent recognized through experience. But considering the vast differences between American and other cultures, these issues became rather crystalized for me.

Kristy, a seasoned service-learning alumnus, wrote:

> I found that going out of my comfort zone was worth every smile I received from the children we spent time with. I developed a deeper appreciation for what I have in life, particularly relationships. I have become more aware of and impacted by world events.

In response to question 2, "What did you learn about others from attending a service-learning trip?" Mary (pseudonym) expressed the following:

> I learned that while there are indeed differences between people, even those in a seemingly homogeneous groups, certain universal principles also exist. It seemed to me that people are rather hard-wired for joy, connection, and collaboration. We all, in general, desire to be together and improve our conditions. That may be by sharing a meal or comforting a person in need.

Another volunteer, Ray (pseudonym), expressed:

> Some of my most connected human moments were in Zimbabwe when we stayed at the Peniel Center. There were late night talks with some of the boys, playing pool on a table that saw its better days 30 years ago, eating lunch squatted against the side of a building, but all the while laughing and being connected in the moment. I learned we are all different, but also similar. Everyone wants to connect and belong with others.

In response to question 3, "Do you believe that your view of others (religions, cultures, and ethnicity) has changed because of the service-learning trips?" Rachel (pseudonym) wrote the following:

> I have a stronger appreciation for cultural differences. Learning and experiencing these differences when given the opportunity can open doors to a richer experience in life. It has also helped me to put into perspective the problems that are faced across cultures and the resolve and adaptability people have in dealing with such.

Melody (pseudonym) expressed her views after visiting the Cheyenne River Reservation:

> I read the recommended materials and knew even before finishing the books about the systemic oppression and devastation of the Native Americans brought on by settlers. But I think that going to South Dakota and getting to know the children and community members reiterated my personal value of connecting with other people. As different as people think that different cultures are, I think that there are commonalities and that most people want to form meaningful connections with others. I was reminded that I can relate to many different people with different beliefs and be okay with that.

The fourth question, "Do you think service-learning opportunities help counselor/art therapists/others grow and evolve as humans?" was answered by Lee (pseudonym) in an insightful and life-changing way:

> I know it has helped me during stressful situations in my everyday life. It has allowed me to have an understanding of a greater community. The stressful things I encounter aren't life and death nor are they

> really that big of a deal. Once I was able to see with my own eyes what poverty and struggle *really* are, most of my issues and the issues around me became trivial. Once that became a truth in my life, I began to see what really matters and began to focus my efforts on those areas.

Stephanie (pseudonym) thoughtfully answered with the following response:

> Yes. How could it not? As long as the counselor/art therapist/other participates in the experience from a place that is in the moment and present-centered, there are no reasons why these opportunities would not lead to at least some sort of growth and evolution, even if minor. Those that engage more fully can probably expect more significant growth. This might even have some sort of direct relationship.

In pouring through the responses of many volunteers (students, alumni, and community members), I was struck with the theme of interconnectedness of all humanity. To be reminded that human beings are more similar than dissimilar is important, but also to take into account cultural differences and learn from these unique differences feels central to the lessons learned from my participants. Human beings look at the world based on their unique cultural experiences. Thus, when raised in a high-rise apartment building sharing space with many other families, one's worldview shifts to becoming more tolerant of other human beings inhabiting space. Whereas someone raised in a remote region with few human interactions may experience a unique comfort with aloneness or crave solitude. These seemingly insignificant ideas can change one's perception of the world and the people that reside here. As mentioned earlier, language can change the perception and worldview as well. Likewise, certain cultural customs, rituals, and traditions can also have an impact on how one perceives reality.

The United States and other Western countries are experiencing a feeling of lack of connection. There are movements and trends, such as meet up groups, to help people find like-minded people to engage with. The history of the United States, began by early settlers searching for new destinations that were less crowded, less community oriented. Many English and European pioneers longed for religious freedom and the ability to live their lives as they saw fit. Ideas such as manifest destiny, the belief that white colonizers were divinely ordained to settle and take over the Americas, killing Indigenous persons who were in their way, was and is a popular concept. What we call the United States was a large region of the Americas that had Indigenous people living there already. In fact, history estimates that there were about 8 million Native people living in North America in the late 1400s, but by 1900 only about 250,000 remained, due to manifest destiny practices (Wilson, 2000).

To be part of the United States and a citizen of this country holds us complicit in the degradation of Native persons, but also consciously or unconsciously contributes to our worldview of the United States as a majority white-skinned nation, where independence, civil liberties, and justice for all prevail. Just opening the newspaper or web page suggests that the early ideals of the United States are not so easily seen or manifest in today's world. My point here is not to degrade the United States, or any other culture or nation, but to show how worldview and cultural concepts of justice or independence changes one's reality and perception of the world. It is extremely difficult to extricate oneself from one's genetic and learned culture, to not be influenced by intergenerational beliefs and teachings. The person can be taken out of their culture, but one cannot take the culture out of the person. Learning to be culturally competent is a lifelong avocation, and one that needs continual tending due to deeply held beliefs and/or worldview of one's home culture. Staying aware and mindful of biases and judgments that inhabit one's mind is crucial. In student's/volunteer's responses, this idea is echoed in many students suggesting that their awareness of poverty and their own appreciation of their abundance are at odds. The responses are full of learning and deeper understanding of worldview and cultural awareness. Yet, the majority of responses distilled learning down to experiences involving compassion, love, relationship, and common humanity. Thus, there is a paradoxical view here: we are all so different based on early cultural teaching but also so similar, because human beings all want to be safe, to be loved, and to make connections with others. I am reminded of my son Max and a little boy named John (pseudonym) in Zimbabwe as they played and wrestled with unconditional love and joy. These moments show the very best in human beings and break down barriers. It is love and connection that join us together, but also sorrows and suffering, which are part of being human.

REFERENCES

Block, P. (2003). *The answer to how is yes*. Oakland, CA: Berret-Koehler Publishing.

Roysircar-Sodowsky, G. (1993). *Multicultural counseling inventory*. Keene, NH: Antioch University Press.

Sue, D.W., Sue, D., Neville, H., & Smith, L. (2022). *Counseling the culturally diverse* (9th ed.). New York: Wiley.

Tervalon, M., & Murray-Garcia, J. (1998). "Cultural humility versus cultural competence: A critical distinction in defining physician training outcomes in multicultural education." *Journal of Health Care for the Poor and Underserved*, 9 (2): 117–125.

Wilson, J. (2000). *The earth shall weep*. New York: Groove Press.

CHAPTER 8

Social Justice and Service-Learning

There is much talk in today's culture about social justice and advocacy, especially in the fields of art/expressive therapy and counseling. In the American Counseling Association and the American Art Therapy Association's code of ethics, social justice and advocacy have been redefined and highlighted as a role that mental health therapists can play in educating and at times liberating others from oppressive practices or understanding systemic racism. Einfeld and Collins (2008) suggest that social justice and civic engagement grow out of service-learning experiences. Likewise, Stoecker (2016) explains that knowledge is power, and that the persons that are oppressed and need serving can begin to be a part of knowledge production by understanding oppressive systems that are in place. Stoecker (2016) further explores the concept that outside interventions of social justice, created by well-meaning service-learning providers, can "just as easily weaken a community as strengthen it" (p. 105). It seems that every outsider or service-learning provider that wants to help needs to understand the ripple effect that can be created by helping in a way that is not congruent with a specific culture or group of people (Warren, 1998). I am reminded here about my colleague Carrie (pseudonym) who helped groups of girls in India. Her goal was to help girls in the "untouchable" caste system rise up and create better opportunities for themselves. From a United States perspective this sounds fabulous; however, India is steeped in the Hindu ideals of a caste system, and everything in this culture revolves around one's place in that caste system. In teaching the lowest caste girls, she was creating waves that rippled out ten-fold. Carrie was asked to leave India and not return for what was deemed subversive activities. With this background and story of India, I begin this section on how to integrate social justice into a service-learning approach.

DOI: 10.4324/9781003643432-8

People and their lives are all interconnected; like the game of dominoes, when one goes down, they all go down or at least are affected. Events that happen and systems in place all work to affect each other. Stoecker (2016) adds to this idea by saying, "there is no such thing as treating the individual because that individual has relationships with others in the local community and changing the individual will impact their relationships" (p. 105). Of course, often changing the community oppression is the end goal, but this is not always possible due to stakeholders' or community leaders' unwillingness to unbalance or change the status quo. Service-learning volunteers can be a part of the process of change, but only if agreed upon and supervised by people in the community that is being served. Hence, volunteers must understand and work within the community and for the community in order for change to occur (Boyle-Baise & Landford, 2004). It is also important to note that it is not the volunteer's job to solve or fix the problem, but merely to help those in the served community to achieve goals or changes in line with social justice or advocacy that is desired or needed.

CHEYENNE RIVER YOUTH PROJECT

Recently, the National Endowment for the Arts (NEA) grants, supplied by the federal government to help support the arts in nonprofit help-oriented sites, was suspended, leaving nonprofits on unsteady footing, with no funding for creative and life-affirming programming. I discovered this grim reality helping at the Cheyenne River Reservation in the summer of 2025. The RedCan Graffiti Jam, which I have mentioned previously, was destined to be canceled and put on pause indefinitely due to these funding cuts. Luckily, the Cheyenne River Youth Project, run by Julie Garreau, was able to secure private funding to host the 11th annual RedCan Graffiti Jam, an arts and culture festival and celebration of Lakota heritage and community. However, the lack of funding has put this organization in a crisis.

This past summer, my colleague Dr. Megan Seaman and I were tasked with interviewing the artists, volunteers, community members, and leaders/elders of the Cheyenne River Reservation to provide evidence to support the arts, for Julie Garreau as she traveled to Washington, D.C. to give testimony on the de-funding implications for her program. The interviews that were conducted were chock full of reasons for arts continuation and also provided fodder for continued social justice and advocacy of Native American tribes. Interviewing many team members and players was in itself an act of social change and advocacy, in which Megan and I grew in awareness and insight. The fact that we were able to provide a 14-page single-spaced document to Julie Garreau to take to Washington,

D.C. was a good way for us as allies to show our support and rally behind the Cheyenne River Youth Project.

Biafra, a Minneapolis-based graffiti artist who attends the RedCan Graffiti Jam every year, had some interesting things to say regarding the importance of the arts. First, he shared a quote said by his father after Biafra's high school arts programming got cut. He said, "the point of art and music making is not to be a professional, rather the point is to expose oneself to shaping our brains to think outside of the box" (personal communication, 7/10/25). Biafra went on to say:

> The worst thing you can do is put yourself in a box. You need to follow your passion. RedCan and CRYP help kids to think outside the box and offers opportunities that expose them to things beyond. When the CRYP kids came to Minnesota we took them to the Minneapolis Institute of Art art museum. Kids were exposed to life in the city, and they had so many questions—questions I didn't even consider. It gave them an opportunity to see something outside of the box. Especially kids at CRYP this year seem way more engaged and engaging than past years. Wakiyan, art director at CRYP, guides them, gives them that confidence. He bonds with them, engages with them, and exposes them to things outside the box so that they can see things differently. As a result, youth artists are way more confident.
> *(Personal communication, 7/10/25)*

Biafra is talking about how the arts have boosted confidence and sense of purpose with the youth at the Cheyenne River Youth Project (CRYP). Empowering kids by teaching and admiring art is a form of social justice. The kids from the reservation can utilize "out of the box" thinking to create a new or different narrative for themselves that can incorporate Lakota ways of being as well as new ways of being in the world as a Native American person.

Jorge Camacho, known as "J.Duh," is a graffiti and mural artist from San Jose, California. He sees art as social justice on a daily basis, but was surprised at how powerful his experience at the RedCan Graffiti Jam was. Jorge said:

> Creative arts, especially in the form of large public murals and graffiti, communicate emotions and things that are hard to verbalize. The RedCan event is interesting because I was able to teach, inspire, and help the development of a local youth artist in the creation of their art.
>
> Art has impacted me in that I am able to have a job; I am able to give and be service based; helping people and exchanging ideas and achievement of goals. I can foster a space for youth to create and adapt to changes and circumstances.
>
> I can't see my life without art. I started when I was 3 years old, because I stumbled on a nonprofit that supported community mural making. I was feeling lost, and I had no other goals or skill sets that were clear. Art is so accessible to everyone.

> I never thought I would be in South Dakota, but because of art I am here. The power of art is to help us reach beyond borders, travel and connect across the country and world.
>
> Here in Eagle Butte, it is beautiful to see the Lakota tradition being carried on. As a kid, I felt separate as a Nicaraguan American, like I didn't belong, and I was different. But kids at CYRP are supported to follow art traditions and encouraged to honor their heritage. They fit in and belong. I was paired up with a youth artist, Eric (pseudonym). I found out he was more punk rock than me and had a sense of him not fitting in. But he's making art happen. I hope he continues his development as an artist. He created the Weiner Dog mural—he told me that it's his new hangout place, which tells me that he feels proud of his creation and the skill he put into his work. Just a couple of cans of paint is the start of many more marks that he will leave on the world.
>
> I see that in Eagle Butte, the locals, the city, people support the arts. I see locals checking out their neighborhoods being transformed not just art for artists, but art for the community. I am a friend of Wakinyan (art director at CRYP), and I knew him when we were making art in a graffiti art collaborative in California. Seeing my friend now, I see how he has transformed. He is so happy to guide youth in their own creating of art. He is taking leadership to guide the kids of Eagle Butte. I notice CRYP is so community-based. Everyone shares. I see people accept the arts without hesitation. Times when things are most stressful are when art shines; it saves people. It brings people together.
>
> (Personal communication, 7/9/25)

For Jorge, art making is the change, it is his life, and he believes art making saves people. In this way, it creates social change, and social statements to others who view the art murals and graffiti. Jorge was especially excited about his work with the youth Eric, who he was able to mentor and reach in a way that was needed. The fact that Eric was able to create a large-scale mural with Jorge's assistance will be a lifelong memory and transformational moment in time. The Lakota people, and primarily the youth, can become empowered in art making as a creative expression of their artistic voice, thoughts and ideas.

Creating murals and graffiti that represent social justice and advocacy messaging may seem like a drop in the bucket as far as making change, but I can assure you that the community of Eagle Butte, South Dakota is held up and promoted in the light of these beautifully crafted statements honoring the Lakota. At a trip to the local hardware store in Eagle Butte, an employee told me that she loves seeing the Lakota words stenciled onto the wall murals around town. She said it helps her remember her heritage and reminds her to feel proud of her culture. After years of oppression and suppression of Native American Indian rights, this is social justice in action. The murals are lifting up the people, helping them reclaim a part of themselves that was lost in the hundreds of years of poor treatment and genocide that has plagued Native Tribes.

NEPAL: ANTARDRISTI AND PA NEPAL

As previously mentioned, Antardristi and PA Nepal are in many ways subject to mores and cultural oppression when it comes to creating change within the patriarchal views of Nepal. Although certainly changing, there is still much stigma around women caught in unfortunate circumstances. At Antardristi, many times the girls who have been sexually abused are victim blamed and shamed. Likewise at PA Nepal the mothers of the kids in residence who are incarcerated are seen as "bad" people, even if their petty crimes were made due to family economic hardships. Providing advocacy from a social justice or social change perspective is important to these groups. As volunteers it is our job to help and assist within the framework of these organizations, if we can.

At Antardristi, we have been supportive of a yoga marathon day where every March an open-air yoga class featuring 108 sun salutations is held to promote awareness of the work in rescuing sexually abused girls in a community wellness activity. In yoga, the number 108 is considered a sacred number with deep symbolic meaning, representing spiritual completion and interconnectedness. It's believed to be a bridge between material and spiritual realms, connecting yoga practices to a greater cosmic good. In doing this practice 108 times, the young women hope to find peace and spread the word of healing and wellness to others who participate in this yoga session. This quiet yet effective activity is a form of social change and advocacy. By showing up and doing this yoga practice, it spreads the word to help keep young girls and women safe from sexual abuse.

At Prisoner Assistance Nepal (PA Nepal), Indira, the founder of this nonprofit, began adopting all the children whose mothers were not likely to get out of jail and whose fathers were absent. The children that were adopted by her had no birth certificates because they were born in rural mountain areas, and thus no ability to ever qualify for documentation to be able to own material items, work a traditional job, or leave the country for a trip. She made it her business to formally adopt about 50 children, so that they could have the proper documentation to live better and fuller lives with more opportunities. This small service was an act of love and social change and advocacy. Those children are far better off now, because Indira cared enough to ensure their future. We have aided in helping this organization with donations of books, art materials, and money. These donations have paved the way for the kids to gain knowledge and pursue hopes/dreams. All the children at PA Nepal go to school for free, their school fees paid for by Indira and the contributions and donations that are obtained.

ECUADOR

I have said little about our trip to Ecuador, where we worked with street children and also those in primary school. Quito, the capital of Ecuador, is a gorgeous mountainous city full of rolling hills and old Spanish colonial buildings. We had seen an article about the excess of street or homeless children in Ecuador and wondered if we could help in some way. Thus, our journey to Ecuador was launched. Upon our arrival, we did notice an excess of children living on the streets in an effort to make money for their families that lived in the mountains outside of Quito. For some children, parents must leave them at home alone during the day because of income deficiencies that prevent suitable daycare. It is common for families to lock their children under five years old in a bedroom, to keep them safe until they return from work. Such extreme childcare problems are hard to imagine in the United States. While we were in Quito, we met a woman named Rosa. Rosa was a woman who had dedicated her life to taking in other people's children during the day so parents could work. She had cleared out a partial basement of a rather run-down and dilapidated house to have a safe space for the kids. There were mattresses on the floor, and a toilet and sink with no walls for privacy. Rosa needed help to secure a better space for these kids; therefore with the help of the local "on the ground" liaison for United Planet, we began raising money for Rosa to fix up her space. We were able to raise the 1,200 USD that was needed to add walls to the bathroom and finish the basement space, so it was not open to the elements. In this situation, we attempted to create social change in a small way. If Rosa had not asked for help, we would not have provided it. It is important to work within the scope of our service. In helping fund a safer and more feasible space for Rosa and her daycare children, we hopefully facilitated a slightly better outcome for the kids. The ripple effect of doing this type of "repair" work is hard to measure, and we have rarely resorted to helping in this way, always discerning if we should or should not help. In this particular case, it felt like the right course of action to take. Our intentions always are to do no harm, and to provide what is needed in the community. It is a tricky balance to understand the true needs of those we serve, not ours. In this way, I think we can stay true to social justice and social change ideology.

SOCIAL JUSTICE AND SERVICE-LEARNING THROUGH EXPRESSIVE THERAPIES

Lastly, I wanted to share how we have used art making and other expressive therapy practices to facilitate or engage in social justice. At Cheyenne River Youth Project, we have utilized graffiti and wall murals to create social justice statements and positive affirmations that can bring communities together. Through the RedCan Graffiti Jam, we have helped artists create important Lakota words that help remind the Lakota of their ancestral ways. Recently, graffiti artist Biafra and Wundr created a graffiti mural that simply said "Many Thanks," or "Wopila Tanka" in Lakota. It is on a building in the small downtown area of Eagle Butte. It is a thank you for everyone's contributions to the greater good, a thank you for showing up, a thank you for remembering the ancestors. Our role is strictly supportive while trying our hand at graffiti painting. It is important to empower those who are Indigenous, to create the artwork for these building walls and other billboards in their hometown.

During the Hindu springtime celebration of Holi, we have made it a point to purchase all the colored pigment for the kids at PA Nepal and Antardristi, so that they could participate in this colorful celebration of spring. Providing the colored pigment is empowering to the youth and allows them to be participants in their own cultural Holi holiday. This is a statement of social justice, making available what is usually not available. The kids feel included in this celebration, not sidelined due to lack of resources.

On our visit to El Salvador, our first service trip, the nuns who ran St. Dominics school asked us to help the children create murals that would embody virtues from the bible. Regardless of our faith and belief system, when asked, our answer is always yes. We set about creating murals on the outside school building walls. The murals represented peace, love, charity, and hope. There was an extra small mural honoring mother Mary that one of our student volunteers offered to paint by herself. These murals are still present at St. Dominics school, 12 years later, a testament to the social change and affirmation the murals offered to others as they viewed these art pieces day after day.

HUNGARY: WORKING WITH THE ROMA

I want to take this opportunity to relate our trip to Ozd, Hungary. We had decided to go to Hungary to work with the burgeoning population of Roma (also known as Romani people) children. We became interested in this because one of our alumni, an art therapist named Zsuzsa Csepanyi, had grown up in Hungary and had volunteered with the Roma previously, therefore she had connections and was a fierce advocate of the Roma.

There is a sizable population of Roma people in Hungary, which makes this group the largest minority in the country. The Roma originally come from northwestern India, and have been "travelers" around Europe since the 14th century. They were nomadic people that traveled from city to city, country to country, finding work in whatever location they arrived at. In more modern times, it has not been possible to be nomadic, so many Roma have settled in large cities or towns and have assimilated into local culture. However, the Roma in Hungary face discrimination and are considered social outcasts, making the plight and history of these people tragic.

In Ozd, a small northern city on the border with Slovakia, there is a large population of Roma who experience many hardships. The Roma children attend school with other Roma children, and are mostly segregated from Hungarian children. In Ozd, many of the Roma kids lacked resources, and the ability to have special programming let alone special visitors. We decided to work with the kids in the Roma schools to provide art as therapy and other expressive therapies, such as song, dance, and bibliotherapy.

We saw working with the Roma to be a form of social justice advocacy in that we were providing special care for the Roma kids who were not provided what other Hungarian children received. In our work with the kids, we provided empowering art as therapy type activities, like making paper plate crowns, using loving kindness, played, and created relationships. One of my favorite activities was to read books and then draw or create using the story as a prompt.

The use of animation and gesture became especially important, in that Hungarian people rarely speak or know English, and the Roma have their own unique language, thus translations were challenging. Therefore, we resorted to pantomime and nonverbal communication.

Social justice and social change help people feel empowered. Working within frameworks that are culturally true and accepted is important. It is not for us as volunteers and service providers to determine what we like or do not like, it is our job to be of service and to help where needed. Reiterating here once more, we take our lead from those we are helping, always wanting to uphold the served group in high regard, with dignity and respect.

REFERENCES

Boyle-Baise, M., & Langford, J., (2004). There are children here: Service-learning for social Justice. *Equity and Excellence in Education*, 22 (2): 187–202.

Einfeld, A., & Collins, D. (2008). The relationship between service-learning, social justice multicultural competence, and civic engagement. *Journal of College Student Development*, 49 (2): 95–109.

Stoecker, R. (2016). *Liberating service learning and the rest of higher education civic Engagement*. Philadelphia, PA: Temple University Press.

Warren, K. (1998). Educating students for social justice in service-learning. *Journal of Experiential Education*, 21 (3): 134–139.

CHAPTER 9

Indigenous Art-Making Practices as Connection

What makes an art practice indigenous to a specific culture? This is a hard question, due to the intermingling of cultures throughout the world over a long period of time. There are some art practices that do seem to be original to certain cultures. In the United States, Indigenous art-making practices are those native to this country before colonization.

In ancient cultures within countries in Africa, Asia, and Native American culture, there do seem to be some original practices that can be traced over millennia. Many of these practices were designed for utilitarian or ceremonial reasons and utilized natural elements that were easy to obtain from the natural environment. For example, in Africa, clay works, beading, and wood carving are found in prehistoric grave goods and archaeological digs. In Asia, there are sophisticated pottery practices, calligraphy, and watercolor paintings. Within the Native American culture, we see evidence of beading, wood carvings, basket weaving, various tattoo and scarification practices. Many of these art crafts are seen in each of the cultures mentioned, but the creativity of difference utilizing the same materials can be seen and easily recognizable due to the artistic style used.

LAKOTA SIOUX ART PRACTICES

In today's culture, the idea of appropriation is a valid concern. Can non-Native people use traditional cultural art-making practices? Is traditional art-making practice to be used only by specific cultures? Of course, this is a gray area, and one that requires communication and permission if using a traditional art-making practice that belongs to another culture. In working with the Lakota Sioux tribe, we have discovered that

DOI: 10.4324/9781003643432-9

permission and invitation are needed to engage in traditional art-making practices. For example, on our first visit to the Cheyenne River Youth Project, we wanted to use the story of "White Buffalo Calf Woman" to create a puppet theater production with the Lakota youth. This story is about a supernatural sacred figure, the white buffalo calf woman, who is revealed to the Lakota to remind them to stay connected to the creator and their Lakota heritage. Because of the near annihilation of the Lakota tribe, we believed that sharing a story using puppetry would be honoring for the Lakota youth. However, before we put this plan into action, it was discussed with the Native elders and, with their permission, we were able to utilize the book and re-tell a story important to Lakota heritage.

"White Buffalo Calf Woman" is teaching the Lakota ways to the youth puppeteers. This drama-therapy enactment was meaningful to the youth and helped them re-remember this story and how it relates to their ancestors. These types of Indigenous themed arts can connect the Lakota youth to their history while at the same time creating a community of art creation.

Another example of utilizing culturally indigenous art making with the Lakota is in using rocks from the reservation for rock painting. With permission, the Lakota youth and our group gathered rocks that were strewn about in roadways or grassy areas. We cleaned the rocks and painted one side of the rocks to make it easier for the youth to paint small pictures, images, or words on the rocks. These small rocks served as reminders or talismans of something special that the Lakota youth could take with them and keep in a pocket or backpack. Traditionally painting, carving, or scratching on rocks has been a form of storytelling for the Lakota, thus this art project incorporated traditional practices in a more modern and portable way.

Graffiti arts are not traditionally Native American; however, within the Cheyenne River Reservation, graffiti art making and tagging have become synonymous with the Lakota in this part of South Dakota. The RedCan Graffiti Jam festival has been a fixture every summer on the reservations since 2015. This festival brings in other Indigenous graffiti and street artists to decorate the town buildings, as well as bringing social justice awareness. None of our volunteer groups have been graffiti artists, but we have all taken a turn at creating graffiti art with permission from elders and leaders of the arts festival. Children are allowed to learn graffiti-type art making as well, within a manufactured "art park" where large billboards have been erected to hold graffiti arts images.

Each year that we have attended the Graffiti Jam, we have made stencils that the kids can use for spray painting and creating their own graffiti. It is a joy to see the "pop-up" graffiti stencil station outside of the local dairy queen. Each year, we create a "pop-up" art station somewhere in the community, for example a grocery store parking lot, an abandoned building's front yard, a gas station, or other business grounds. With stencils, kids can learn the art of spray painting by using a stencil to guide the image making. As the kids grow up, they can perfect their graffiti skills free hand or by sketching on the wall with a pencil as a guide to follow to help create their image. The RedCan has become famous across the United States and embodies what the Cheyenne River Reservation and Youth Project are trying to create. This opportunity empowers youth and reminds adults and elders of the healing power of art making, to enjoy beauty, to seek justice, and/or to be a part of a creative growing and thriving community. One tribe member, TammiJo created a large graffiti piece entitled "Have you seen my sisters" to educate the community about the missing Indigenous women from reservations. There are more missing Native American women than any other group in the United States. Sex trafficking, abduction, and murder are common occurrences for Native Women. This graffiti image on a large brick wall, makes the image of native women missing, real. Some of the figures in the image are devoid of facial features, indicating the lack of regard and care for Native women. Making a statement about systemic oppression in the form of missing women is important for the community as well as visitors who may be volunteering at the Graffiti Jam. This kind of social justice gets attention and immediately makes the point, without words or needing to read anything, thus every member of the tribe and community can understand and be more watchful for their fellow women community members.

Clay making is also a part of Native American traditional art practices. Although due to the nature of the pop-up art-making stations, earthen clay is hard to transport and use, we have substituted model magic clay or play doh to create animals, bowls, symbols, and self-figures. The Lakota kids love to create with clay, and making butterflies, snakes, turtles, or small pinch pots are a hit. Figure 9.1 depicts the author and two young girls making snakes and other animal creatures with model magic. We like using model magic because it dries quickly and has many bright color varieties. There is lore and stories about different animal totems, and the children can usually tell me what "snake medicine" is. In this particular case, the little girl was educating me about the meaning of snakes; in her words, "snakes are about transforming, because they shed their skin, with a whole new skin underneath!" This knowledge seemed wise beyond her years, and I felt honored to be a student of this little one's teachings.

Figure 9.1 The author and two Lakota girls: snake medicine through clay making

NEPALESE ART-MAKING PRACTICES

Nepal has many lovely traditions of art making, calligraphy, watercolor flower and plant painting, hand-painted mandalas, as well as pottery and clay crafts. As I have been to Nepal many times, I have enjoyed learning about these crafts. What has impressed me greatly is the patience, delayed gratification, and discipline it takes to become proficient at Nepalese arts. There are not many abstract or free expressionist modes of making art and thus learning the various art crafts is a process of much practice.

Mandala a Sanskrit word for wholeness or interconnectedness is a common art product of Nepal. There are mandala painting schools that teach this art form to apprentices from an early age. To be a master mandala painter takes upwards of 15–20 years of experience, at which time master artists are allowed to sign their names to their pieces. Traditional mandala paintings use earth pigments that are harvested from the surrounding mountainsides. There are usually four quadrants to a mandala painting signaling doorways or openings to the soul and life. Women are becoming master mandala painters, a craft that was closed to women

Figure 9.2 Woman master painting a mandala

until recent history (Figure 9.2). In the past decade or so, more non-traditional mandala styles have emerged engaging in more cosmic or abstract-oriented images. The image below shows a woman mandala painter adding color to a traditional mandala scene; notice the four gateways in the center of the mandala.

Understanding the culture's reverence for mandalas, not only as a meditation, but also as a spiritual or religious tradition, we asked permission to create a version of mandalas with the girls in the safe house. We decided to buy inexpensive coffee filters to serve as the circle for our mandala project and then used markers to color the mandala. Once the colors were in place, we used a water bottle spritzer to soak the coffee filters and allow the colors from the markers to run and merge, creating an abstract-looking piece. The girls really enjoyed this process and patiently waited for the filters to dry. We laid them out on the patio deck to dry in the sun, then later we hung them up from the rafters of the porch overhang, reminiscent of stained glass. Lakshmi (pseudonym) patiently waited for her coffee filter mandala to dry so she could hang it up with the others (Figure 9.3). Without the distraction of social

Figure 9.3 Lakshmi waiting for her coffee filter mandala to dry

media and other Western technology, quietly waiting and admiring one's artwork can be a worthwhile pursuit.

Traditional Nepalese women have enjoyed using, jewelry, hair accessories, and brightly colored fabrics to adorn themselves. One of the things we noticed in working with the girls from Antardristi safe house is that they loved having long hair, and either braiding it or tying it back with ribbons, and gold or silver clips. Furthering this tradition in art making, we decided to use inexpensive tissue paper, bought at a local store, to create tissue paper flowers and butterflies that we then affixed to rubber hair bands that the girls could wear in their hair. The girls were delighted with this beautification art practice and soon got to work on folding, fluffing, and manipulating the tissue paper in a way that showcased their gorgeous long thick dark hair. The girls at Antardristi have very few belongings and what they do have is treasured. Thus, making space for the girls to create hair fashion indulged their girlishness and also satisfied their sense of accomplishment.

Human beings have a desire to decorate and create beauty within their environment. When young women and girls have been through a life-changing trauma, such as sexual abuse, like the girls at Antardristi, even simple beauty can be life affirming. Nita (pseudonym) was a young nine-year-old girl from the hills of Nepal. She had been rescued from sexual abuse by her family, and had been brought to Antardristi, to seek refuge, counseling, and reside in a safe space. Nita had little resources and wore no jewelry. Some of the girls wear earrings or bangles, which signifies their family's wealth, but when a girl has nothing, the living conditions are usually pretty grim. Therefore, when Nita made her tissue paper hair ornament, she glowed with excitement. She displayed her efforts proudly as she tied her hair into a ponytail using her new hair accessory (Figure 9.4). Using resourcefulness and observational skills regarding the arts practices of a culture can have far-reaching effects in the ability to work within the cultural framework of artistic expression.

Figure 9.4 Nita with Tissue Paper Hair Ornament

GQEBERHA, SOUTH AFRICA: ORIGAMI BOXES

In Gqeberha, we noticed that the kids were quite adept at utilizing three-dimensional art-making activities. South Africa is home to jewelry crafts, ceramic productions, wood sculptures, and other carvings out of native material. Wood, jewelry, and ceramics were out of our reach to acquire for the kids, so we made a decision to teach the kids origami box making using construction paper which was readily available at the local "crazy store" in Gqeberha. It seemed like origami would be an easily acquired skill due to the 3-D nature of the kids' aptitude. Sure enough origami boxes were a popular artistic experience.

We had the kids in the schools of Gqeberha create origami keepsake boxes, utilizing markers and stickers to decorate the boxes. On the inside of the boxes, the children were directed to write a secret or important message to themselves that they could view whenever they chose. The idea of writing an affirmation, or encouraging words, was based on providing an opportunity of empowerment for the kids, who are already in a "less than" status within the local South African caste system. Two girls enjoyed making boxes together, which they adorned with words, stickers, and special messages inside (Figure 9.5). Inside their boxes, as they giggled, they each wrote "I love myself" which was a suggestion from one of the student volunteers and seemed like a novel idea to these young girls. The idea of personal affirmations was a new addition to the girl's repertoire of

Figure 9.5 Two girls making origami boxes

self-care knowledge. I wondered: is the new knowledge or idea that one can say they love themselves a hindrance or some help to girls struggling with daily necessities of life? Is the addition of a new idea a colonizer mentality or just simply an idea that may assist? I find myself reflective and thoughtful quite often when making these types of executive decisions. It is important to use ideas and concepts that are part of the culture and are mainstream to South Africa. In the end, I decided to let this addition of new self-care ideas stand and hoped that it would not in any way negatively impact the girls. When kids are struggling to just get buy, it is hard to judge what may or may not be helpful. These words could be seen as superfluous to anxious parents eking out a living. Whatever the case, this cross-pollination seemed to have a positive impact on these two girls engrossed in their box creation.

Along with Origami boxes, the kids also decorated 3-D name cards to help us identify them, but also as a way to express their creativity and leave their mark in some way. We have found that the children enjoy the name placards; it makes them feel seen and heard. There is a lot of effort put into the writing and drawing various symbols and fun images that denote their interest. We work with a group of girls and boys using hearts and flowers to decorate their name tags. Volunteers also make name tags so the kids can easily identify us. We try and simplify our names as needed so the kids can more easily pronounce them. Although the kids can speak some English, many times the pronunciation is tricky. It can also be challenging for volunteers who are unaccustomed to African names. We try and say names out loud many times to ensure the accuracy of our pronunciation and to plant it inside our memory. Using construction paper to make 3-D arts and crafts projects seems to work well in South Africa. The kids have access to construction paper and are used to making things using this medium.

A final 3-D arts project utilizes construction paper interlocking rings. In South Africa, the leaders of the schools are keen for the kids to hope and dream about their future. As many therapists and teachers know, having hope is crucial for kids to achieve. Using strips of construction paper, we have the kids write down one to three wishes for themselves; it can be a career, family, or personal wish that they deem important and want to write down on their paper strip. Once they write down their wish, dream or hope, the kids speak their wishes out loud to the other kids. Everyone claps and gets excited about the wishes and dreams. The kids help us close off the rings by using tape and then link them all together to form a paper chain. These very long paper chains are then hung from the ceiling or blackboard of the classroom. Having your wishes and dreams honored and known by others is a form of setting intentions and being accountable to oneself and others to try and achieve this dream. Many of the wishes and dreams highlighted education and health for family. All of the kids in South Africa seem so eager to get educated, whether it is to become a doctor, lawyer, beautician, teacher, etc. Kids in the lower socioeconomic and colorists caste systems know that it will take furthering their education to be able to break out of their current situation. I asked the principal and other leaders in the Gqeberha community how often kids get to attend college or vocational training and was told that it only happens about 20% of the time. So, even though kids are expressing their hopes and dreams, the harsh reality is that few will make it past high school. This reality gives me pause to contemplate how very difficult it is to be oppressed by a system that judges kids on their family wealth, skin color, and ability to speak Afrikaans or English.

CHAPTER 10

More Creative and Expressive Arts Practices

As mentioned earlier, dancing, playing, singing and other creative arts practices can be beneficial when working with people from other cultures. I do believe that there is a universality to creative arts, not in the specific songs or dances, but by the fact that all cultures dance and sing. It is a bridge that can foster growth and communication and further knowledge along the way about specific cultural practices.

SOUTH AFRICA DANCE AS STORY TELLING

Story telling is a common experience and way to convey historical knowledge in South Africa. Each year that we go to South Africa, we learn more and more about the dances and the stories behind them, specifically Zulu and Xhosa cultures, which are native to Gqeberha. The dance stories tell of animals, families, relationships, the great spirit, and more. Each dance has ritualized movements that are recognizable to the Zulu or Xhosa viewer. In this way, spoken words are not important; it is the dance steps, the rhythm, and the accompanying drumbeats that weave the tale. At each of our visits to Gqeberha, we participate in a bush camp experience where food is cooked over an open fire, and dancers tell the history of these distinct tribes of people. Once the food is eaten, the dancing starts, with a narrator helping us understand. The dancing is rhythmic, thumping, and undulating in its pulse. It stirs the heart. Once the dancing is well underway, our group begins to join in the dances. We are taught certain moves and try to keep up as best we can. The lead woman dancer, Suki (pseudonym), encouraged me to do a shimmy movement reminiscent of a bird's mating dance which caused a cacophony of laughter from my students. There is such joy in joining in and performing the dance. These moments capture a union of sorts, people

DOI: 10.4324/9781003643432-10

coming together and sharing, without a distinction that belies us or them, but a fun joyous reunion of our African kin.

During many years of apartheid and ill treatment of native Africans since colonization by the Dutch and later the English, the South African people created various dances and music to communicate with each other. One of these dances is called gum boot dancing. There were many African people working in the mines, whether it was mineral, gem, coal, or salt mines. These dark and dangerous underground places to work required careful attention and many times voices could not be heard due to the underground rock cavities. The miners had to wear gum boots (similar to rubber rain boots) due to the wet conditions underground. They created a way to tap and stomp the boots in order to communicate with each other underground. This is similar to other African traditions of using drumbeats as a way of communicating. Miners came up with elaborate and intricate ways to communicate based on the sounds of the jumps, stomps, scoots, and taps of hands and/or boots on the ground. We have experienced lots of fun and embarrassing moments attempting to learn gum boot dancing. Together as a large group we are taught the steps and meanings of the steps, little by little, until we have an entire nonverbal script of sorts. This dance is intricate and fast paced, requiring a lot of attention to detail. It also has many slaps, claps, and stomps that create a cacophony of sound! As volunteers it is important to learn about the culture and about the resiliency and "work arounds" that were accomplished by Indigenous Africans during their hardships. This experience sets the stage for more awareness and insight into the people of South Africa.

YOGA IN NEPAL AND SOUTH AFRICA

In today's world the Hindu practice of Yoga has become synonymous with exercise. However, the ancient art has four limbs: restraint, observances, postures of yoga, and breath. Although in the West only the postures of yoga and breath are typically taught, it is important to be mindful of yoga's multi-layered meaning and purpose. Originally yoga was practiced by priests and holy men but gained much popularity in the United States in the late 19th century, due to the philosophers Emerson and Thoreau's writings about the philosophy of yoga. By the mid-20th century, yoga had transitioned to a method of exercises/postures and less of the philosophy of yoga was relayed.

When we are in Nepal, yoga is an accepted practice that most individuals understand as encompassing all four limbs of yoga, therefore including yoga in our work with the children and young adults is not surprising.

Most of the youth that we work with have a keen understanding of the various asanas/postures which create a fun atmosphere for those of us that are yoga practitioners. My co-facilitator, Dr. Megan Seaman, and I are both registered and trained yoga teachers, and we utilize our skills to implement "kid-centered" yoga practice as part of our creative expression. Having the youth create a large circle while participating in a sun salutation routine can be quite fun and energizing for the kids. We are not only teaching yoga but reminding them of their Hindu culture (80% of Nepal is Hindu). Re-teaching the kids about Ahimsa, which is a part of yoga that reminds us to "do no harm," is important in our work. What does it mean to do no harm to others? Does this include all people and animals, or just people in Nepal? These are wonderful questions to ask the kids to get a thoughtful response. In addition, many of the youth we work with have been harmed, so it is important to begin to determine how they may feel about not harming others, even if others harmed them.

We also teach breath control or breathing practices. These are again part of yoga but can also stand in for a way to cope with hard times. We teach the youth how to breathe slowly in and out to deal with hard times. There is mindfulness that comes with controlling the breath, which can be helpful for the youth, especially the youth that have been severely traumatized. In this way, we are merely the facilitators of what is already a large part of the culture.

In other countries, such as South Africa, there is less familiarity with yoga, but a general willingness to learn an interesting practice. In South Africa, we have held yoga sessions in the dirt, grass, classrooms and broken concrete parking lots. There is very little space within the schools we work within in South Africa; therefore, any spot of unclaimed territory works for yoga. The South African kids love the kid-oriented yoga that we teach, making sure to incorporate poses with names like "lion" and "lizard" and "downward facing dog." There is usually much laughter and joy within this practice. Along with the joy, we also teach the same principles as we do in Nepal, making sure to teach deep breathing, ahimsa (do no harm), and other disciplines that may be helpful such as "use right communication or be truthful with your words." Using yoga as a teaching and relationship-building experience has been quite fruitful in our work, and we almost always incorporate this ancient art with kids we serve.

PLAY AS THERAPY FOR KIDS

Human beings, especially kids, respond well to just simple old-fashioned play. We have experienced this over and over again. The field of play therapy is the intentional pairing of a developmentally matched medium with a therapeutic relationship through which children play out their experience and express their thoughts and emotions (Malchiodi, 2023). Although we are not play therapists, we do use play in a way that can be therapeutic for the kids we work with. Some of the play opportunities have been shared in previous chapters but let's take a closer look at the profound connection that can happen when adults and kids play and interact together in a "non-task"-oriented way.

Piggyback rides, swinging through the air, chasing, and hide and seek are a few of the many ways we engaged the kids in Gqeberha. We used play as kids were milling around, between classes, or just waiting for a group to form to do art as therapy. Kids in South Africa have proven to be a boisterous group, and play discharges energy, relieves tension, and helps kids be more peaceful and calmer once creating art with us.

One such child, Mohammed (pseudonym), was a hyperactive and mischievous little boy, probably around eight years old. He would pull the girls' hair, tap someone on the shoulder and run away, take and or hide pencils or markers, and generally misbehave. One of my students, Joanne (pseudonym), started a chasing game with Mohammed, which created lots of laughter and smiles. Once she caught him, she would hold onto him and swing him in the air around and around in circles. Mohammed loved this activity, and it kept him focused on Joanne, not on mischievous behavior. Mohammed became Joanne's shadow and soon we realized that he was just starved for attention and would go to great lengths to get attention, even if negative. Once we had figured out what helped Mohammed stay focused, we continued engaging him in playful activities, and he became a great helper to Joanne and even exhibited some leadership skills within our art-making group.

Other forms of play include playing with art materials, playing games such as checkers or jump rope, as well as group games such as "Simon says." There is a version of "Simon says" in every culture, even if the name is not Simon. This repeating movements and listening game helps kids listen carefully and move their physical bodies, and helps us bond with the kids with no expectations—everyone can play. Movement by running and jumping is also a playful pastime. While in Nepal we held piggyback races with kids atop our student volunteers (Figure 10.1). The joy on the children's faces was priceless, and they cheered to do it again and again. In this race, there were no real winners, just exhilarated kids and volunteers racing around the courtyard of the school, high fiving one another if they successfully made it to the other side of the concrete play yard.

The holiday of Holi is another play celebration opportunity in Nepal. The Hindu holiday called Holi celebrates the coming of spring. It is said that Lord Shiva, who is represented by blue skin, wanted to celebrate all the colors of spring, not just his own blue color. Every March, Holi is celebrated by throwing powdered pigments on people and their clothing.

Figure 10.1 Piggyback races with volunteers and Nepalese kids

The powdered pigments are a water-based powdered tempura paint that adheres quite well to hair, skin, and clothing. The children of Nepal like to add water by using plastic spray guns to soak individuals to enhance the colors adhesive coating. Our volunteer group always goes the second week of March, and thus we always celebrate Holi. We wear white t-shirts to enhance the color staining of the pigments, and also have a nice souvenir of our time to remember once we are back in the United States.

As we walk around the streets and play with the kids, everyone in the entire city of Kathmandu is shouting "Happy Holi" and throwing powder with glee. For hardcore aficionados powder can be smeared on the face and teeth, and can find its way up the nose as well! By the end of the day, people are running from each other so as not to continue to get powder everywhere. Amidst the colored powder throwing chaos, there are moments of genuine affection and care. Savannah, a volunteer, had a heartfelt moment in the form of a hug from a little girl, while the Holi festival raged on all around them. I remember stealing a glance at their embrace within the chaos of flying pigment and running children.

I have found delight in allowing powder to be thrown and smeared at will all over me. There is a "letting go" of inhibitions, and a carefree attitude that is needed in stressful times. The kids we work with in Nepal have very little to look forward to and seem to grow up too quickly, thus encouraging them to "act like kids" is needed and appreciated by all.

Playing and singing music is universal in totality. In South Africa, drumming, yodeling, and singing is center stage. In Nepal drumming, playing the sitar, and other string instruments as well as gestural singing and dancing are important. On the Cheyenne River Reservation, it is singing Lakota folk songs and learning jingle dress dances (the dresses literally sing with each movement, by chiming and clinking).

In South Africa, tunes encompassing acoustic harmony were made popular by groups such as Ladysmith Black Mambazo, and artists such as Paul Simon who utilized African beats in his music. African music, but more specifically South African music, uses a deep almost vibratory beat that is meant to be felt in the heart and soul. The music traditionally has been folk songs that highlighted everyday life of the community. There are songs for working, funerals, playing, and worshiping to name a few. Each folk song is meant to help carry the person through whatever endeavor is needed at that time.

In Nepal, much of the music utilizes hand gestures (similar to the hula in Hawaii) telling a story with hands and body. Similarly to South Africa, there are songs for storytelling, incorporating Hindu religious stories as well. In Nepal, a call and response music type called Kirtan is quite common. The lead singer will sing a line, often from a Hindu Vedic text, and the audience or others present will repeat this verse. The verse is repeated over and over until the entire community is singing. This type of call and response offers people a way to meditate and be mindful within the mantra of repeated words.

On the Cheyene River Reservation, traditional Lakota songs are sung during the morning and evening prayer circles, including drumming. The singing/chanting and drumming call the ancestors and kin to come together in sacred community and union. Singing honors the earth, the animals, all the Lakota, and others who have come before. It is an offering of sorts to connect and ground people within the Lakota ways.

In all three cultures, using books as teaching or therapeutically slanted moments has been successful. Sitting in a circle with kids, avidly watching a story come to life through a book or by way of a traditional orally told story from memory is a sight to behold. The volunteers and I always bring books that highlight simple life lessons or feeling expression. The kids listen to the story, with a translator nearby if needed, and then create artwork, a drama re-enactment, or other play based on the themes of the story. We try to bring books about African, Asian or Native American children, to help the kids see versions of themselves represented in the literature. This is important because so many of the books that the children have to read are based on

European white characters that are hard to relate to. Famous author Adichie (2015), growing up in Nigeria, confesses that all her childhood books were based on white characters, snow scenes, and lush green countryside, none of which were in Nigeria. She had a disconnect of sorts in not seeing herself or her country reflected in popular literature. Adichie now writes books based on African characters and landscapes. With Adichie's experience in mind, we incorporate multicultural children's books.

Within the cultures and traditions mentioned thus far, we as service-learning providers and volunteers are guests who have been invited to share and witness these special moments. We have been invited to dance, share stories, play, and sing in all three cultures and have been welcomed with much enthusiasm. I can't help but wonder if the general population of the United States set the stage for such welcoming of others, what would our country feel and be like?

In a both joyous and grim testament, on our first trip to Nepal, the Nepalese children were teaching us some songs with hand gestures; it was a cultural sharing. The kids excitably taught us and laughed as we tried to mimic and learn the Sanskrit language words to the sacred Hindu songs. After much giggling, one of the little girls asked us what songs we had to share with them that are from the United States. We were at a loss for what to say. What songs could we possibly sing? We decided to try the national anthem of the United States, but most of us did not know all the words and found the verse too difficult to sing. Another student decided that we should teach the "chicken dance" song, which is a popular song played and acted out at weddings and other parties. What is comical about this song is that it is actually a German song, not an American song. Amidst some guffaws by our volunteer group, our worry turned to the Nepalese kids who now believed that the chicken dance song is somehow one of our treasured songs. Laughter, whether based on just good fun or honest misunderstandings of cultural practices, is good for the soul and unites all of us together through joy.

REFERENCES

Adichie, C. (2015). *We should all be feminists*. New York: Vintage Books.
Malchiodi, C. (2023). *The handbook of expressive arts therapy*. New York: The Guilford Press.

CHAPTER 11

Planting the Seeds in Helping Professions

Service-Learning in Undergraduate Education

By Heather Denning

My introduction to cultural exchange and service-learning occurred when I was 18 years old, the same age as of some of my undergraduate students I am teaching today. What I remember about this time in my life was a desire for connection to others, adventure, and a spirit of unwavering optimism. A trip to the Soviet Union in 1988 during a period marked in history by Mikhail Gorbachev's policy reforms of perestroika (restructuring) and glasnost (openness) created opportunities for more cultural exchange and travel. I traveled to the Soviet Union to attend and participate in a Youth Summit through the program Youth Ambassadors of America. The mission of the program was to promote relationships between youth from different countries, develop mutual understanding between youth, and encourage community service. One way I sought to connect to youth from the Soviet Union was through art. In advance of the trip, I painted a banner with the message "Love Heals the World" to present to a school we were visiting in Saint Petersburg. Russian teens smiled as I unrolled the banner and requested a group photo before the time of selfies and smartphones (Figure 11.1). Their positive response was affirming on many levels allowing me to feel a connection despite significant cultural differences.

One of the most memorable experiences was visiting a teen named Evelyn and her family in their home, an apartment flat in Moscow (Figure 11.2). The outside surroundings were stark. The buildings appeared uniform and

Figure 11.1 Interacting with Russian youth

nondescript; however, this contrasted with the inside of the apartment where a welcoming Russian family resided. The family shared their culture through preparing a dish in their small kitchen. They included us, several American teens, donned in denim and big hair (as this was the eighties) in their cooking. I do not recall what the meal was, but I remember the warmth the family showed us despite language barriers, different political backgrounds, and a large geographical divide. Being exposed to people from an entirely different culture allowed me to recognize common human threads that bind us together. No doubt this first service-learning opportunity influenced my decision to pursue art therapy as an undergraduate student and ignited a desire that still resides today as an educator—to learn from and connect to others through art.

Now as an undergraduate educator, I hope to impart valuable information to my students; however, I recognize it is these service-learning experiences that seem to deepen knowledge in a more meaningful way. I have been fortunate to participate in service-learning with my students, colleagues, and friends; some of these inspiring journeys are described within this book. I have been privileged as an educator to have the resources to travel and participate alongside my students in these opportunities. I have taken the stance as a "fellow learner" walking alongside my students in service much like Schroder's stance of "walking beside"

Figure 11.2 Cooking with a Russian teen Evelyn

clients, but know I am also being served through these human connections (Schroder, 2005, p. 37).

Interacting with those from other cultures reinforces our similarities and highlights differences to be respected and celebrated. The success of these learning experiences is ultimately formed by reciprocal relationships, foundational to helping professions. Thus, service-learning can spark the beginnings of developing cultural competence and more importantly cultural humility during undergraduate studies. Service-learning is defined in Chapter 1. Additional sources similarly present service-learning as an engaged model of scholarship that is under the category of community-based experiential education and occurs outside the traditional classroom in the community (Welch & Plaxton-Moore, 2019). Key components to community based experiential education include being respectful and responsive to communities, addressing critical societal issues and contributing to the public good (Committee on Institutional Cooperation, 2005; Kellogg Commission, 2001). While cultural competence is important, cultural humility deepens relationships and self-awareness both important to student development. Cultural competence is addressed in more detail in Chapter 7. Cultural humility is a lifelong pursuit recognizing that others are experts in their own cultural identity (Jackson, 2020; Tervalon & Murray-Garíca, 1998). Exploring cultural humility prompts us to be more aware of our own cultural identity, biases, and beliefs and can include the use of art for self-reflection (Jackson, 2020).

This chapter describes an undergraduate service-learning experience in Italy which involves use of the arts; therefore, an additional term, art-based service-learning, is provided. "Art-based service learning brings together the power of the arts with the essential components of service-learning in a mutually empowering way" (Krensky & Steffen, 2008, p. 15). Art-based service-learning places the arts in the community to meet a community need, make connections, develop empathy, build a sense of community, and provide a teaching method in art-based education (Feen-Calligan & Matthews, 2016; Krensky & Steffen, 2008). As the arts engage our senses and provoke emotions, art-based service-learning prompts affective learning which is "concerned with how learners feel while they are learning, and the ways those learning experiences war internalized to help shape ... attitudes, opinions, and identity (Jacobs, 2023, p. 6). Jacob's study on the experiences of education students found arts-based service-learning to elevate mood for both the students and participants and resulted in greater optimism and positivity. I have also witnessed and felt joy in engaging in the arts with others during service-learning on our service trip to Italy, learning regional dances, being with small group of women to create a collaborative drawing, and making a friendship bracelet with a small child in a Roma community. All these interactions filled me with happiness and, although only a short period of time, reinforced human connection in a profound way.

In this chapter, I hope to share my experiences as an educator with service-learning with undergraduate students. This chapter will focus primarily on service-learning experiences abroad in Italy although I have also overseen and joined in service-learning with my students in the local community and within the United States. Student narratives will be presented to highlight their experiences, growth, and learning. Additionally, I have participated in service-learning with undergraduate and graduate students together allowing me to observe some similarities and differences between these educational levels. These experiences provided me insight to the needs of undergraduate students informed by personal observation and developmental theory. Information is offered for educators regarding a connected course implemented to support service-learning and consideration of the educator's role. The chapter emphasizes student learning; however, in practice, the service was conducted in a collaborative manner with the communities we worked in.

SIMILARITIES AND DIFFERENCES: UNDERGRADUATE AND GRADUATE STUDENT EXPERIENCES

Research specifically comparing undergraduate and graduate student service-learning appeared limited. Lack of research on this topic was also found in the expressive therapies fields. One study from arts education compared service-learning between undergraduate music education and graduate art therapy students at the same university (Feen-Calligan & Matthews, 2016). Service-learning occurred on campus for music education students teaching beginning musical instrument classes to homeschool students ages 9–13 while the art therapy students were placed in agencies off campus. Both student groups were given reflective assignments, essential to service-learning; however, they varied. Both student groups provided written responses. Art therapy students created visual reflections in addition. In analyzing these assignments, the authors found the students had similar experiences and identified three common themes: expectations, professional transformation, and personal transformation. Student expectations of the service-learning experience elicited anxiety in relation to encountering a new group of people and their own abilities to perform at their sites. Professional growth developed as students learned how to prepare for interactions with others and recognized people as individuals. Personal growth occurred as students gained more personal awareness and reflected in more depth (Feen-Calligan & Matthews, 2016). The themes outlined in this research aligned with my observations regarding the similarities between undergraduate and graduate students in service-learning.

Similarities were also identified in another study comparing the impact of community-based research paired with service-learning projects for undergraduate education students and graduate physical therapy students (George et al., 2017). "Community-based research (CBR) generally acknowledged as an iteration of service learning ..." is a collaborative research method providing reciprocal learning and mutual benefit to community members (George et al., 2017, p. 15). While the sample size was small and examined the impact of CBR specifically, helpful information can be gleaned as the CBR was highly connected to the service-learning projects. Unlike the previous study cited, both student groups completed the same service projects: implementing and facilitating an aquatic program and an exercise program designed for youth. Accompanying student research projects evaluated the impact of these programs on the children. The survey instrument, the Student Learning Outcomes Survey of Community Based Research, addressed "professional skills, educational experience, academic skills, personal growth, and civic engagement" (George et al., 2017, p. 18). Similar results were reported for undergraduate and graduate students: deepened understanding of individuals from different backgrounds and improved perceptions of competencies working with children and their families. Areas of greater difference were the rates of perceived improvement in the ability to listen to others (86% undergraduates, 40% graduates) and increased interest in college (86% undergraduates, 50% graduates). The authors concluded that both student groups improved the understanding of local and social issues and gained confidence in their roles related to their fields of study.

Outside of the fields of the arts, a study comparing service-learning from business education for undergraduate and graduate students found that student perceptions of service-learning were similar (Moorer, 2009). Additionally, in Moorer's implications of the research, he presented the idea of providing service-learning projects simultaneously with undergraduate and graduate students where graduate students serve as mentors. George et al. (2017) also supported cross collaboration between student groups in different departments. I have observed graduate students giving support and advice to my students when I had opportunities to co-travel in service-learning projects. Although this mentorship occurred spontaneously, these dynamics warrant developing a more formal process of mentorship with students spanning education levels.

The studies, although limited, and my observations support the idea for general student populations, there are more similarities than differences between undergraduate and graduate students and service-learning. Mainly, both groups can serve a population or community members in a mutually beneficial way and gain meaningful life experiences. All three studies discussed reinforce that service-learning increases student confidence and skills. However, competencies and learning objectives between undergraduate and graduate students specific to expressive therapies fields will differ as graduate students are striving for a higher level of competency as "therapists." The most significant differences noted between undergraduate and graduate students and service-learning related to developmental stages experienced from adolescence to adulthood.

Developmental Factors: Undergraduate Students

Developmental factors should be considered by educators in service-learning experiences. While psychological theories provide a framework for understanding students' emotional development, educators should also respond to students as individuals with various familial, cultural, generational, and socioeconomic backgrounds which impact the enormous milestone of transitioning into adulthood. My experience with undergraduate students and service-learning has been primarily with students ages 18–22 who fall within the developmental stages of late adolescence or early adulthood which is marked by growing independence and developing a sense of autonomy and identity (Erikson, 1993; Gilmore & Meersand, 2023).

Undergraduate students are typically younger than graduate students; therefore, they have less life experience compared to students studying at the master's level whose developmental stages span more widely. However, educators are recognizing age demographics shifting in the classroom. Educators may now interface with "nontraditional students" well beyond their 20s and teens entering undergraduate and conversely graduate students who are as in their early 20s. Students have more opportunities to earn college credits while attending high school through dual enrollment and advanced placement (AP) classes. The rate of dual enrollment has increased over the last two decades (Fink 2024; Velasco et al., 2024). In the 2022–2023 academic year, almost 2.5 million high school students registered for a least one course in higher education (Fink, 2024). Although these rates have increased, it is important to note, these opportunities have not been equitable to students from lower socioeconomic levels and identified in the study as Black or Hispanic (Velasco et al., 2024). According to the College Board, 35.7% of U.S. public high school graduates in the class of 2024 completed at least one AP exam compared to 32.8% by the class of 2014 (College Board, 2025). These opportunities accelerate the timeline to earn degrees in higher education and may impact the age range of students presenting in classrooms.

Emerging Adulthood

The concept of emerging adulthood was initially defined by Jeffrey Jensen Arnett in 2000 and refers to a period of development from ages 18–29. Emerging adulthood describes the transitional, exploratory nature of the early adult stage of development (Arnett, 2000). Arnett (2000) noted the presence of common themes in emerging adulthood "a focus on identity and self-discovery, a sense of possibilities and change, a value placed on self-reliance and independence" (Gilmore & Meersand, 2023, p. 54).

The emergence of this developmental model was shaped by changes in society including advances in technology and more careers requiring a college education. In 1959, around 2 million teens attended a university (Gilmore & Meersand, 2023). While recent rates of undergraduate attendance have fluctuated, between 2021 and 2031 total undergraduate enrollment is projected to increase to 16.8 million students (National Center for Education Statistics, 2023). With expanded time spent in higher education, many young adults are delaying marriage, the start of families, and obtaining stable work to later in life compared to earlier generations. As a result, financial independence has been postponed (Arnett, 2000).

Most of my students were financially dependent on their families; therefore, even making the decision to travel abroad to an unfamiliar community for service-learning often hinged on a parental decision. Parental influence also intersects with technology and communication. Technology has changed the ways college students interact with their parents. Students are easily in contact with their parents allowing them to extend their parenting practices long after they have left home (Arnett, 2023). I observed frequent and daily communication home to parents especially in the beginning of the experience then lessened as students immersed themselves in the projects and gained confidence.

As the volunteers were legally adults but also students taking a connected course to service-learning at a university, educators must pay attention when communicating with parents and being aware of federal laws related to confidentiality in higher education. Often, I needed to educate families in addition to the student in advance of the experience to allay misconceptions and fears about the projects and travel. Sometimes parents inquired about information that was protected under the Family Educational and Privacy Act (FERPA) which required written consent for a response (U.S. Department of Education, n.d.). Most families were excited for their student as they embarked on their journeys. Parents of undergraduate students were more often at the airports at departure and arrival, some with tears in their eyes as their student embarked on these journeys. While young adults may benefit with parental support, this may also delay adult responsibilities such as making independent decisions (Arnett, 2023). One student asserted her independence traveled to Italy for service-learning despite her families concerns related to her health history. Ultimately, this assertion proved to be a big step towards independence and increased confidence.

Early Emerging Adulthood

Building on Arnett's theories, Gilmore and Meersand (2023) focused on the first segment of the decade of emerging adulthood and defined *early emerging adulthood* as the period between ages 18 and 23 as its own phase where individuals both expand social opportunities and face challenges as they break away from the structure of high school and family life. This phase is highlighted by an increased capacity for independence and the ability to adjust to novel environments and experiences which are encountered in college and by interacting with others from diverse backgrounds. Early emerging adults are influenced by youth culture; frequently moved by social issues, interact with social entities, and lead efforts of social change (Gilmore & Meersand, 2023). Service-learning projects typically present as novel environments giving students the opportunity to tap into internal resources, explore, and develop their identity and in turn confidence (Gilmore & Meersand, 2023). These factors position service-learning and undergraduate students with this developmental phase.

Undergraduate Service-Learning Settings and Populations

Other distinct differences are considering the projects, location, and populations served and what is most suitable for undergraduate students versus graduate students in clinical training. Since the undergraduate student is not being prepared as a therapist, careful consideration should be made to the selection of the service projects that align with the appropriate level of education and learning objectives. Community settings enhancing wellness and cultural exchange, versus treatment centers, or agencies addressing illness are typically more appropriate for undergraduate students. One example to illustrate this point was a service-learning trip to Nepal where both levels of education were represented. While we shared many cultural outings, the undergraduate students volunteered teaching art at a school while the graduate students provided art therapy services at a safe house for youth who had experienced human trafficking and sexual abuse. Each project supported the knowledge and skills needed for their educational level. Additional consideration was given to initially introducing familiar experiences for service-learning. Subsequent projects challenged students to expand beyond their comfort zones to promote personal growth and learning.

Nonna Roma

One example was volunteering at Nonna Roma in Rome, Italy. This organization focused on bettering their local communities through addressing societal issues such as lack of access to healthy and nutritious food (Nonna Roma, n.d.). This site was our first project during our service-learning trip to Italy and allowed students to work "behind the scenes" packing food boxes and restocking shelves than more directly interact with others during the food distribution (Figure 11.3). Many undergraduate students were familiar or had volunteered in the past at "soup kitchens or pantries" in high school, college, or faith-based organizations; therefore, service in this manner was more familiar and comfortable as a beginning project. I observed students who were more tentative to interact directly with the recipients still being able to serve through

Figure 11.3 Students preparing food for distribution

organizing and packing food items while those who felt more confident to interact with the public distributed food directly and practiced greetings in Italian. Students had the opportunity to volunteer in both capacities. Some choose initially to remain behind the scenes and cited the language barrier as one reason to initially avoid direct interactions which for some students elicited anxiety.

Gillian, an undergraduate art therapy student, shared this experience from volunteering at Nonna Roma. She stated that during our first service experience she was "nervous" but also sensed a "familiarity" since she had worked in food pantries and soup kitchens before. She also noted how the staff, some who were former recipients, and current recipients at Nonna Roma were teaching us about how their organization operated, the tasks at hand, and Italian words and greetings. This highlights the reciprocal nature of service-learning. Gillian reported feeling a sense connection by the end of the visit even completed tasks which might seem simple like restocking shelves. She also shared an interaction with an older man who was receiving food telling her "stay away from the boys" in Italian. She experienced this as a universal interaction where a grandfather figure may tease a young woman. Shane, another undergraduate student, studying graphic design, experienced the language barrier at this site as a challenge, but noted at the conclusion of the project the recipients and staff's appreciation helped him to understand that even a seemingly little service made a big difference.

Afghan Community Center

The students visited other service-learning locations after our initial experience at Nonna Roma. An additional community center was visited that provided support to individuals from Afghanistan in Rome, Italy. The community center offered a range of support services and community-building activities to help the Afghan community adjust to life in Italy. The community center, located in a former home, nestled in a neighborhood hosted us for cultural exchange activities. The community center director was from Afghanistan himself and sought to offer a community center for those who fled the Taliban regime during or after the war. Several activities with young adults were planned: time for art making, an Afghan community dinner, and dancing. This experience required more direct interaction with others compared to our beginning point of packing food. Part of this direct interaction included art facilitation where our students lead planned art activities. Art facilitation is within the scope of undergraduate education and involves guiding a group to successfully complete an art task by imparting knowledge, such as providing the directions and steps to create art, within a supportive environment (Denning, 2022; Schwartz et al., 2022). It can involve role modeling or demonstrating use of materials which can be important especially when there is a language barrier. Art facilitation requires leadership and interpersonal skills to develop and maintain the group's activities and relationships. Graduate students can also serve as art facilitators; however, graduate-level education prepares students to be group therapists and expands their role to learning how to provide treatment to group members presenting with mental health symptoms, developmental challenges, medical conditions, and other presenting problems (CAAHEP, 2024; Denning, 2022).

Abby, a junior psychology major and art therapy minor, provided leadership for several art activities in small groups in the art facilitator role. These art activities included a planned art task creating artist trading cards then a spontaneous activity of making origami cranes. While drawing, a woman shared her sadness about leaving her family in Afghanistan. Abby reported:

> One woman in the group told us about the cards that she made. She told us about her family, specifically her father and her dog, who were back in Afghanistan. Her image reflected how we are all united under the same sky, and that our families are always close in our hearts.

What initially started as an art activity led by our students became a time for sharing about the love of family. In the art facilitator role, students created the environment for the art activity and listened, but unlike a therapist did not delve into deeper emotions related to grief and loss.

While we were waiting for dinner, Abby initiated a second art activity spontaneously showing flexibility and adapting our "planned" activities. This narrative also demonstrated how the nature of service-learning is reciprocal as Abby shared what she gained from this interaction:

> Our small group transitioned from leisurely drawing, to creating paper cranes. Together, we slowly showed everyone, fold by fold, how to create a paper crane. I noticed as people were joining in, those who had been following along began to teach the new members and tried to catch them up. My most favorite part about the entire night was when everyone's faces lit up after their final fold was completed. It was a beautiful moment simply being able to bring joy through a tiny little piece of paper. In some Asian cultures, cranes are referred to as 'birds of happiness', and this experience strengthened this meaning for me on this trip. I was able to connect with people by showing them how to make paper cranes and now every time I make a paper crane, I think of how much happiness they can bring.

Table 11.1 Distinctions and intersection between undergraduate and graduate students

Undergraduate Students	Intersections	Graduate Students
Developmental Phases:		
Early Emerging Adulthood (Ages 18–22)	Emerging Adulthood (Ages 18–29)	Wider of Range of Developmental Phases
Approaches:		
	Art Facilitation Art-Based Service Learning Art-Based Activities Community Arts	Expressive Art-Based Therapy Group Art Therapy Art as Therapy Community-Based Art Therapy
Curriculum Content Areas from Pre-Art Therapy & Art Therapy Education		
Community Art Facilitation: Students will demonstrate group leadership skills necessary to effectively facilitate creative art experiences for a wide range of participants and purposes in a range of community settings, while establishing and maintaining effective … community participant relationships (AATA, 2025, p. 21).	*Graduate art therapy students also perform community art facilitation	Group Work: Students will have the "opportunity to integrate theory, processes, and dynamics of group work to form and facilitate ethically and culturally responsive art therapy groups that have been designed with a clear purpose and goals for the population served" (CAAHEP, 2024, p. 19).

Table 11.1 presents topics related to service-learning that are distinct and intersect each level of education. Many approaches overlap as both undergraduate and graduate students can facilitate art experiences. However, approaches requiring additional competencies and advanced education are listed in the column for graduate students. Applicable educational content areas connected to service-learning are cited from the art therapy field as my experience is primarily as an art therapy educator (American Art Therapy Association [AATA], 2025; Commission [CAAHEP], 2024; Schwartz et al., 2022). While students' experiences of service-learning generally encompass wider content areas and specialties, "community art facilitation" is featured as an example for undergraduate art therapy students working in groups.

PRACTICAL CONSIDERATIONS

Course Connection

Much of the work of the undergraduate educator begins well in advance of the service-learning. For service-learning involving travel abroad, it is recommended to partner with a non-profit organization that specializes in service-learning who is familiar with community members needs and form sustainable partnerships. These organizations will have valuable resources for educators, students, and communities being serviced. We partnered with United Planet, an organization described earlier in this book. This partnership has provided many innumerable benefits and ongoing support.

For our service trip in Italy, many of the practical considerations and much more were addressed in a connected course offered in advance of travel and service-learning. As the service trip to Italy was designed for undergraduate students meeting the university's criteria in the study abroad office, and not specific to the undergraduate art therapy program, consideration was given to broaden course descriptions, objectives, and student learning outcomes. This model volunteering with undergraduate students with a wide range of majors compared to my experiences with graduate students studying art therapy and counseling was an additional difference in comparing my experiences. While graduate art therapy and counseling students are intentionally entering a therapy field, undergraduates with a range of majors brought more diversity in the student group. Students who registered tended to be from human service-related majors as the service-learning component offered was unique compared to the other study abroad opportunities at the university. Students' majors ranged from art therapy, psychology, music therapy, social work, graphic design, and intelligence studies.

Combining service-learning with a credit bearing course was ideal as more preparation and reflection could occur before and after the project within the structure of a course. At times, the course was a deciding factor for families whether to support financially as the experience "counted" for an academic requirement and offered credits. Students were provided a framework in which to prepare and share thoughts and feelings about the project in advance and after the service-learning projects were completed. Connecting a credit-bearing course to service-learning can assist faculty, especially if the course is considered part of their contracted teaching load. While service-learning and travel are wonderful opportunities for faculty, they also incur additional responsibilities and roles.

The course description included supporting students in interfacing with individuals and communities from different cultures and building cultural humility. Additional goals included planning and developing art directives and other activities to build cross-cultural connection. A planning guide was presented to assist students in these assignments and building leadership skills (Figure 11.4). Although we learned to be flexible and adapt activities as needed, the planning guide provided students an opportunity to conceptualize an art directive or activity in advance. This was especially helpful in considering the cost, sustainability, and quality of materials as well as practical aspects such as obtaining supplies in country, or prior and transporting.

Course activities included: language and history lessons (with collaboration with faculty in other departments), creating an art journal to accompany service-learning for reflection, creating an art tote to transport supplies (which would be left with remaining supplies to sites after asking and if welcomed), mapping out a walking tour from our accommodations, brainstorming ideas for art directives and activities, then presenting later in class once ideas were more solidified. Course lectures, discussion, reading assignment, and reflections included many topics addressed and defined earlier: cultural competency, cultural humility, multiculturalism, and interculturalism.

The Educator's Role

Upon travel, I found my role as an educator expanding from the traditional classroom setting to providing emotional support, tending to physical illness, and addressing culture shock. Boundaries in the student–educator relationship can change or encompass more roles including mentor, role model, and a "pseudo" parental figure. This expanded role prompted me to consider the "teacher–student" relationship in a more flexible and fluid manner, but at the same time follow ethics related to this relationship (AATA, 2013; Art Therapy Credentials Board [ATBC], n.d.; International Expressive Arts Therapies Association [IEATA], n.d.). In art therapy, one of the expressive therapies fields, codes of ethics dictate that educators should be aware of their influence on students and not engage in a therapeutic relationship (AATA, 2013; ATBC, n.d.). While both educators and therapists can provide mentorship, educators should focus this support on learning and service versus ameliorating mental health symptoms.

Other educators who have engaged in educational experiences abroad with students have noted similar dynamics and experienced expanding educator roles. Kim (2022) described boundaries with students during study abroad as becoming more "permeable and overlapping" as depicted in Markus and Kitayama's model of the interdependent view of self. This model of identity describes a person seeing themselves a connected to others rather than independent which is linked to more individualistic cultures

Template: Service-Learning Art Directive/Activities Planning Guide	
Student Name:	Date:
Name of Art Directive/Activity:	Theme:
Timeframe: (preparation, completing activity, clean-up)	
Goals: State two clearly stated goals for your idea (how does this support a multicultural exchange or benefit to the participants?) Goal #1: Goal #2:	
Participant/s:	
Cultural Considerations:	
Art or Activity Materials: Be specific. Provide a list of materials with amounts of materials needed. Considerations (Preparing, transporting, getting through customs, safety, cost, accessible to population?):	
What are the benefits of this activity?:	
Directions: Provide a statement describing the directions for the art directive or activity. Include clearly stated steps. Consider selected participants, age, and appropriate level of simplicity or complexity of directions.	
Variations (at least two): Offer ideas on possible variations in materials. (Simplified version? Related game, activity, song that doesn't require materials.)	
Other Information if Needed	

Figure 11.4 Template planning guide

as within the U.S. (Markus & Kitayama, 1991). Pasquarelli described "faculty hidden roles" (the first aider, mentor, problem solver, and guardian) in her experiences leading multiple short-term faculty lead trips to Italy with her students (Pasquarelli, 2022, p. 41). I found myself relating to these roles and accompanying examples provided such as navigating medical care for students and providing support for homesickness. Having an additional faculty member or co-leader is ideal to cover the expanded roles required of service-learning abroad described above.

Related to the mentor role, Gilmore and Meergand noted the importance of other adults serving as "nonparental mentors and positive role models" which include college instructors and advisors during the developmental phase of early emerging adulthood (2023, pp. 62–63). For all the students traveling, I was their instructor and for many also their primary academic advisor. Adult mentors, not associated with a students' childhood, can offer support, advise, and teach skills without associating them to childhood and foster for students a sense of being capable and more independent (Gilmore & Meergand, 2023).

CONCLUSION

Having the opportunity to interact with people from other cultures beginning in my own early adulthood to more current service-learning experiences as an educator in mid-adulthood has shaped my own identity, values, and career path as an art therapist and educator. I still carry that spirit of optimism from my youth as service-learning has reinforced my belief in the power of human connection through the arts. These experiences have offered me knowledge shared in this chapter which I hope in turn inspires and helps other students, professionals, and educators in the expressive therapies and human services fields engage in service-learning with undergraduate students. These experiences for undergraduate students can be formative personally, educationally, and professionally and shape one's path to more meaningful connection with others. Returning to the metaphor of "planting seeding in undergraduate education," I have seen my students grow during service-learning in many ways—gaining independence and leadership skills, building empathy, expanding outside their comfort zones, and being more flexible. I have also reflected on my own growth in realizing my own privileges and shifting stance of "volunteer" to approaching as a reciprocal experience. For me, the knowledge gained in service-learning is a continual process that is still unfolding and growing, as I process its impact on my own life, my students, and the people in the communities we engage with.

While the chapter highlights some related literature and my narrative experience in mainly one experience abroad, it cannot encompass all perspectives of undergraduate service-learning for students and the community members interacted with. My students and I have engaged in service-learning projects in the local community which were not described here. It is important to note service-learning can occur in a wide range of locations and communities and maybe most importantly in one's own community as these partnerships may be more sustainable. Additionally, while information for educators was present to prepare for service-learning having a balance between preparedness and inviting the spirit of spontaneity is paramount. Being in the moment with others is at the forefront for service-learning experiences.

There are many individuals who have enriched the experiences of service-learning for me personally and as an educator. These include many students, colleagues, family, and friends who are innumerous to name; however, deep gratitude is extended to Dr. Katherine Jackson who initially invited me to a service-learning trip to Nepal in 2016. Additionally, I am grateful to Jodi Staniunas-Hopper and the students who accompanied me to the service-learning trip in Italy described in this chapter and my parents who encouraged and did not limit my idea to travel to the Soviet Union as a teen.

REFERENCES

American Art Therapy Association. (2013). *Ethical principles for art therapists.* https://arttherapy.org/wp-content/uploads/2017/06/Ethical-Principles-for-Art-Therapists.pdf

American Art Therapy Association. (August 2025). The American Art Therapy Association's undergraduate pre-art therapy education guidelines. American Art Therapy Association.

Arnett, J.J. (2000). Emerging adulthood: A theory of development from the late teens through the twenties. *American Psychologist,* 55(5), 469–480.

Arnett, J.J. (2023). *Emerging adulthood: The winding road from the late teens through the twenties* (3rd ed.). Oxford: Oxford University Press.

Art Therapy Credentials Board. *Code governing standards of practice, eligibility for and regulation of credentials, and disciplinary procedures.* https://atcb.org/ethics-appeals-lp/code-of-ethics-conduct-and-disciplinary-procedures/

College Board. (2025). AP program results: Class of 2024. Retrieved from https://reports.collegeboard.org/ap-program-results/class-of-2024

Commission on Accreditation of Allied Health Education Programs (2024). *Standards and guidelines for the accreditation of educational programs in art therapy.*

https://cdn.prod.website-files.com/5f466098572bf97f28d59df/67409c1d5deb73d057fa43aa_ArtTherapyStandardsApproved11-15-24.pdf

Committee on Institutional Cooperation. (2005). *Engaged scholarship*.

Denning, H. (2022). Beginning concepts of group work (pp. 451–491). In M. Rastogi, R. P. Feldwisch, M., Pate, & J. Scarce (eds.), *Foundations of art therapy: Theory and applications* (pp. 451–491). London: Elsevier.

Erikson, E.H. (1993). *Childhood and society* (2nd ed.). New York: W.W. Norton & Company.

Feen-Calligan, H., & Matthews, W. (2016). Pre-professional arts based service-learning in music education and art therapy. *International Journal of Education and the Arts*, 17 (17): 1–9.

Fink, J. (2024, August 26). How many students are taking dual enrollment courses in high school? New national, state, and college-level data. *The CCRC Mixed Methods Blog*. https://ccrc.tc.columbia.edu/easyblog/how-many-students-are-taking-dual-enrollment-coursesin-high-school-new-national-state-and-college-level-data.

Gilmore, K.J., & Meersand, P. (2023). *Emerging adulthood: A psychodynamic approach to the new developmental phase of the 21st century*. Washington, DC: American Psychological Association.

George, C.L., Wood-Kanupka, J., & Oriel, K.N. (2017). Impact of participation in community-based research among undergraduate and graduate students. *Journal of Allied Health*, 46(1): 15–24.

International Expressive Arts Therapy Association (IEATA). Code of ethics for registered expressive arts therapists. https://www.ieata.org/reat-code-of-ethics/

Jackson, L. (2020). *Cultural humility in art therapy: Applications for practice, research, social justice, self-care, and pedagogy*. London: Jessica Kingsley Publishers.

Jacobs, R. (2023). Affective and emotional experiences in art-based service-learning environments. *International Journal of Emotional Education*, 15(1): 4–20.

Kellogg Commission. (2001). *Returning to our roots: Executive summaries of the reports of the Kellogg commission on the future of state and land-grant universities*. Washington, DC: National Association of State Universities and Land-Grant Colleges.

Kim, P.Y. (2022, August 15). Rethinking interpersonal boundaries with students: Lessons learned while leading a short-term study abroad program. *Christian Scholars Review*. https://christianscholars.com/rethinking-interpersonal-boundaries-with-students-lessons-learned-while-leading-a-short-term-study-abroad-program/

Krensky, B., & Steffen, S.L. (2008). Art-based service-learning: A state of the field. *Art Education*, 61 (4): 13–18.

Markus, H.R., & Kitayama, S. (1991). Culture and self: Implications for cognition, emotion, and motivation. *Psychological Review*, 98 (2), 224–253.

Moorer, C. (2009, May/June). Service learning and business education: Distinctions between undergraduate and graduate business students, *American Journal of Business Education*, 2 (3): 63–72. https://doi.org/10.19030/ajbe.v2i3.4050

National Center for Education Statistics. (2023). *Undergraduate enrollment*. https://nces.ed.gov/programs/coe/indicator/cha

Nonna Roma. https://nonnaroma.it

Pasquarelli, S. L. (2022). Faculty-led, short-term study abroad programs: Stories and dilemmas of practice. *Beyond: The ISI Florence & Umbra Institute Studies in International Education*, 5, 30–49. Washington, DC: Association of State Universities and Land-Grant Colleges. https://docs.rwu.edu/sed_fp/72

Schroder, D. (2005). *Little windows into art therapy*. London: Jessica Kingsley Publishers.

Schwartz, J.B., St. John, P.A., Lagstein, C.G., Pate, M.P., & Denning, H.J. (2022). Instructional content in undergraduate art therapy education. *Art Therapy*, 40(1): 31–39. https://doi.org/10.1080/07421656.2022.2131356

Tervalon, M., & Murray-García, J. (1998). Cultural humility versus cultural competence: A critical distinction in defining physician training outcomes in multicultural education. *Journal of Health Care for the Poor and Underserved*, 9 (2): 117–125. https://doi.org/10.1353/hpu.2010.0233

U.S. Department of Education, Student Privacy Policy Office. (n.d.). *Family Educational Rights and Privacy Act (FERPA)*. Protecting Student Privacy. https://studentprivacy.ed.gov/ferpa

Velasco, T., Fink, J., Bedoya, M., & Jenkins, D. (October 2024). The post-secondary outcomes of high school dual enrollment students. A national and state-by-state analysis. New York: Community College Research Center, Teachers College, Columbia University.

Welch, M., & Plaxton-Moore, S. (2019). *The craft of community-engaged teaching and learning: A guide for faculty development*. Boston, MA: Campus Compact.

CHAPTER 12

Best Practices, Logistics, and Wisdom Learned from Service-Learning

After 13 years of running a service-learning program through Ursuline College, there is much to share in terms of best practices, logistics, and wisdom garnered via these experiences. To date, we have explored El Salvador, Ecuador, Peru, Zimbabwe, Hungary, Cheyenne River Reservation, South Africa, and Nepal. About seven years ago, we started to get a sense of which service-learning destinations were best suited for our needs, and thus the focus of most of this book has been on Cheyenne River Reservation, Nepal, and South Africa, with a few exceptions and highlights from other places peppered throughout.

BEST PRACTICES

There is an old adage that goes something like this: "You don't know what you don't know until you know it." This phrase sums up much of the learning accumulated over time with service-learning. As mentioned in the preface and elsewhere in this book, I am the daughter of Presbyterian missionaries and spent my early childhood (until 2nd grade) in the Democratic Republic of Congo (DRC). This is important to understand, in that missionaries are providing help in the way that is needed by the people who need help, but also providing help in the form of the Christian religion. There is a contextualized meaning, sometimes left unsaid, that the missionary is the teacher and the culture being helped is the student. This (although unwittingly) smacks of colonization. Thus, the inference is that there are superior folks and poor Indigenous folks who don't know better and need to be educated. I am not intending to sound harsh and certainly much good has been done under the care of missionaries, my parents and grandparents being some of the best open-minded people I am proud to descend from. But likewise, there has been some less good "helping" in the form of white superiority brought in by worldviews of well-meaning people from the United States. The United States since World War I has been in the "big brother" protector role for many parts of the world. This ideology worked for a long time but in my humble opinion is no longer a viable context to base action upon, and should be re-evaluated for efficacy.

I also had the experience of working with refugees and asylum seekers through Catholic Charities for about six years in the early 2000s. These two experiences (growing up in the DRC and working at Catholic Charities) informed me greatly on expectations and cultural considerations, and created a fearlessness and intrepid spirit to travel and help where help was needed. However, I quickly understood by my first trip to El Salvador and later to Cheyenne River Reservation that helping in "my own way or what I thought was needed" was usually not acceptable, and that I needed to help the way the people in need wanted or needed to be helped. As mentioned earlier, bringing gifts, hand-me-downs/used clothing, and other extraneous goods are not helpful if not asked for.

In this next part of this chapter, I have highlighted best practices for providing service-learning experiences for students, volunteers, helpers, and those who are receiving help. These best practices have not come easy, and were earned by trial and error and quite a lot of "foot in mouth" experiences, which later proved invaluable in my "baptism by fire" journey to understand and implement service to others.

BEST PRACTICE 1: WAIT FOR THE INVITATION

In our fast-paced world, full of emotional reactivity and task-oriented lenses, it is almost impossible to consider the idea of waiting, or just "being," and using patience. The biggest lesson learned and best practice in relation to service-learning is to wait for the invitation from the people who are needing help or requesting service of some kind. When considering the therapeutic arena of counseling, this is a mirror. In providing counseling/art therapy, the client first must find the therapist, make an appointment, attend an intake session, and finally tell the counselor/art therapist what they would like to work on. It is not the job of the therapist to determine the goals without the aid of the client. The helper and helped are involved in a collaborative relationship, where both become focused on the wants and needs of the client/recipient. Together clear, concise, and manageable goals are set, and together the work begins in service of the client.

Likewise, service-learning meanders down a similar path, maybe not quite as clear-cut as the therapeutic office, but just as important.

Our very first time in Nepal, working at Antardristi, we collectively had a "great" idea to bring sanitary pads, underwear, and bras to the girls at the safe house. We also brought some hair ties and other "girly" accessories that we thought would be appreciated. These gifts and items were received with gratitude; however, these items were not used, and we wondered why? The girls took the items we gave them and hoarded them, to give to extended family members that might visit or use them as trade for other items. They would rather live with what they had than use the new products we gave them. This was shocking to us as volunteers, but I understood. We had guessed what we thought they might need or want, and we had been incorrect. The house mother at Antardristi tried to explain with disapproval that the girls give away all new clothing or any items; they don't hold onto anything. She explained, "These girls are happy with what they have and do not want anything else." From our American worldview, this seemed unbelievable: how could this be, the girls had so little?

We had made a grave mistake in assuming that we understood the girls' needs based on what American girls might want. We had not taken into consideration differences in the accumulation of material wealth or abundance of needed items. These girls, despite their sexual abuse trauma, were seemingly happy and did not need material possessions to bring them joy or help them feel supported. They were content with what they had and the environmental circumstances they existed in.

For the service-learning providers to deem the girls' conditions or state of mind to be less than ideal contributes to the girl's oppression and contributes to a colonizer mentality. We have many material possessions and so much abundance in the United States. Even people that are below the poverty line in the United States most likely have more than the girls in Nepal. But happiness and life satisfaction are not measured by material possessions in Nepal; it is measured by family, friends, community connection, and love. Of course, this seems like a beautiful and rather refreshing ideal, but very hard for a typical American to comprehend due to the capitalistic structure imposed in our culture.

The girls need to be shown care and love, and to be empowered from within. We quickly learned that the invitation for us was to be in relationship with the girls, to mentor them as women, to form bonds with them, to support their dreams and aspirations. These were the real nontangible items that were needed. We did correct our thinking and behavior and quickly got in step with what was actually needed. As service-learning volunteers, we now know building and maintaining relationships is the goal, and that this right relationship has a ripple effect and changes many things.

BEST PRACTICE 2: UTILIZE RESOURCES AVAILABLE IN THE COUNTRY

I like to think that most Americans are generous beings, who like to give to others if asked. However, what happens when we over-give or give the wrong items, similar to the story of the Nepalese girls who were given sanitary pads. Like an invasive species of plant that destroys the native plants because there are no natural predators, so too can we get off track with doling out resources that are unneeded.

On our first service-learning trip to El Salvador, we brought a whole suitcase filled with pom-poms, stickers, foam paper, door hangers, scented markers, googly eyes, shiny sequins, and a host of other arts and crafts materials that cannot be found or purchased in El Salvador. In our excitement to "give kids cool stuff" we neglected to see the harm in not providing materials that can be found/purchased in El Salvador. The kids had fun using the novel materials, but once used could not be acquired again. The unspoken message here is, "Hey kids, we brought you all this cool art-making stuff, but you can only get it in the United States because the USA is better and has more stuff than you do." This type of thinking, even if unconscious, creates a "less than" mentality for the persons being served. We are "rubbing it in" that they don't have pom-poms and stickers, making them less than, and we do have pom-poms and stickers, making us greater than. I am embarrassed by my own naivete in allowing this to happen in the first place; however, it was a valuable lesson.

After our trip to El Salvador, we no longer bring art materials that cannot be found at location/country. We do bring along some extra art materials and supplies at times, but only supplies that we know can be acquired in the country we are visiting. We try our best to shop in local shops or gather natural materials (with permission) from the environment. In this way art making and creative endeavors can be sustainable, and can be created and practiced by the service-learning recipients long after we are gone.

BEST PRACTICE 3: JOIN IN WITH LOCALS AROUND DAILY PRACTICES

Do you remember a vacation where you are just one of the many tourists participating in tourist-curated activities? How was that? From my perspective, being only a tourist puts a person firmly on the outside of a culture looking in. This can be a lonely and awkward place to stand, and is the epitome of being the other, or the observer of others. Our motto in the service-learning program is to join in and lean into our discomfort in order to learn, grow, and evolve ourselves into a more full and robust citizen of the world and cultures.

We try to live and stay where local people are living. Eating traditional foods and trying exotic new foods is also important to understanding the worldview and context of people's lives. In Nepal we participated in a Newar celebration of food and prayer. The Newar are the original Indigenous people of Nepal, and many of their traditions are still practiced. We gathered together at a community space, sitting on the floor with other local Newar people. As guests, we were greeted and blessed with a tika on our foreheads and then led to a space to sit on the floor. We awaited drink and food. The food was served by "grandmas" out of big pots that they each carried around and gave us small servings from. Another grandma carried a large ornate pitcher of the homemade rice moonshine "raksi" that we were given in thimble sized cups. The food was very spicy with interesting dishes such as sheep intestines, animal marrow, various vegetables, and leafy greens, as well as an assortment of ultra-spicy rice. Once eating, my mouth was on fire; the heat of the spicy food was almost intolerable to my American palette. The locals quickly came around again with a large bottle of Coca-Cola filling our glasses with the American beverage. The Coke actually cooled my mouth down and was a nice accoutrement to this unbelievably spicy meal. We learned quite a bit about spicy food and why it is served. Nepal is quite warm most of the year, and the spicy food helps folks sweat, which ultimately cools you down. In addition, when winter does occur (in December and January), the spicy food helps people feel warmer. The food is in harmony with the environment and weather of Nepal.

Another experience of joining in happened on our trip to Zimbabwe, where we stayed in the Peniel Center orphanage. We stayed in huts and primitive lodgings just like the kids. In one of the huts, there were roosting birds that randomly defecated on us, the inhabitants dwelling below. We took showers in the same sawed-off pipe jutting out of a wall, with water warmed by sunlight, as the children. This particular trip was challenging and difficult because the accommodations were so different than our American way of living and caused much discomfort. For example, to get to a toilet (hole in the ground) or shower, it was at least a half-mile walk. Much of the day spent at the orphanage was about just taking care of daily hygiene and clean water needs. The watering hole used by others in the village was about a three-mile walk, with a large bucket on the head. The fact that we had a cistern water catchment system at the orphanage made us privileged. What must it be like to live this way every day? To take a shower, one must plan carefully and make sure there is enough time to do so. This gave us a unique perspective on life in Zimbabwe, but also on human beings' ability to survive even in difficult conditions.

In Gqeberha, we usually stay at a hostel that is mostly used by South African or African natives. In the hostel, there is a community kitchen, where folks come together to cook meals and share food with each other.

We have been fortunate to have a local woman help us prepare food and serve dinner at the hostel, but it has been stimulating to visit with the more local people while there. We learned that many of the guests at the hostel are traveling workers, who come to Gqeberha to get part-time work. Some of the people have been from Zimbabwe, where work is hard to find, and thus they travel south for opportunities. Hanging out with non-American people has been educational. There are many issues that we would not know about if we were staying in a fancy hotel somewhere. Likewise, we have visited Cape Town in South Africa a few times, more for tourism than service-learning, but the places we have stayed have also been backpacker hostels, where lots of different folks are present. A few years ago, there was live music at the Cape Town hostel, and present were a few people from different African countries, a German family, a few folks from Britain, an American, and all of us. This made for lively conversation and also connection with fellow travelers seeing and enjoying the same sites as we were.

As part of our travels, we also visited and did service work in Hungary, Peru, and Ecuador. What is similar to all of these countries is the sharing of food with local people. We worked in schools in each country and as part of the school program all children were provided with a warm lunch. As volunteers, we were included in the meals with the school kids and sat with and participated in this lunchtime practice. In the United States, volunteers and/or teachers rarely eat with kids; it is separate. Therefore, having this opportunity at first was jarring, worrying about proper boundaries etc., but we discovered that there is no better way to get to know the culture and people, especially kids, than by sharing food. We learned what foods are "good" and important to the children, and also the honoring that takes place in having food provided. The children, unlike many American children, ate all of their food. There were no choices, only what was served. There was a gratitude that was palpable in these meals. Immersing oneself in food is a way to celebrate differences, learn something new, and enjoy.

BEST PRACTICE 4: ACCEPT INVITATIONS WHERE SKILLS CAN BE UTILIZED

As noted earlier, it took some time to determine where we needed to provide service-learning. We were invited to many countries, and at first we accepted all the invitations, as a way of understanding the needs of a certain community. As we volunteered within many different countries and cultures, it became clear where our best fit was. On some of our first trips to El Salvador, Ecuador, and Peru, we learned the reality of "not the best fit." We had been tasked with working within the school system in each country. What we discovered is that it is hard to describe art or expressive arts practices to systems that do not have such folks working in their school. Certainly, there are art therapists in El Salvador, Ecuador, and Peru, but not in the areas where we were volunteering. The translation of art therapy was expressed like art teacher, and therefore we were expected to teach art. Of course, teaching art and art as therapy are maybe not too far off, but it does require a shift in mindset and some pivoting. My team handled this flawlessly, but we discovered that teaching art or just making art was not really our skill set. The first schools in El Salvador and Ecuador were full of typical kids, who enjoyed art making, but our skills were maybe better aligned with working with kids who suffered or had a difficult experience in life. Fast forward to Peru, where I attempted to let the leader know of our interest in working with more troubled children. This was translated as working with kids with severe intellectual and physical disabilities. I was not aware of the mistranslation, and no one was more surprised than I when we showed up to our volunteer work with multi-handicapped kids. We were 100% unprepared and lacked knowledge. After several team meetings and again pivoting, we were able to salvage this experience by narrowing our focus to kids with intellectual disabilities and those with hearing impairments, and managed to make some strides.

Of course, in each situation, we provided loving kindness and care, and did the very best we could to help or provide whatever the site needed. I write about these ill-fitting placements to make a broader statement of understanding that finding good fits between server and the served is a process and can be lost in translation very easily.

A juxtaposition of this is our work in Nepal, South Africa, and Cheyenne River Reservation. These particular sites understood the nature of creative arts therapies and these types of treatments were already in place; even if the site did not call it "art therapy" there was a natural kinship with the healing arts. I have found that once working with a "good fit" site placement, everything flows much easier. I think remembering goals is important, in that if the goal is to use art making and other creative tasks as healing opportunities, a site that needs and honors this is a must. If the goal is just to provide service in any capacity, the parameters of the service-learning trip can be much loser.

BEST PRACTICE 5: SEE AND BE SEEN

Providing service-learning using expressive arts/art therapy and counseling skills is not providing therapy. It would be unethical for us to provide any type of "real" therapy to those being served, in that we are only visiting for roughly two weeks. What we can provide is therapeutic friendship and holding space for art as therapy to work its magic. As noted earlier, the art as therapy ideas from Kramer's third hand intervention, in the service of the client or those being served, works perfectly within service-learning (Kramer, 1986). Although many of us are trained expressive or art therapists, and or students learning how to be art therapists, we can use our skills to simply be fully present and engage with the kids/adults we work with.

To be seen, really seen, is a gift, and one that I believe changes everything. When the people being served can be approached with cultural humility, an open-minded and open-hearted approach, there is a felt sense of being seen. Likewise, in this "seeing," the server is also being seen in the light created by clearly looking at the served. I cannot think of anything more gratifying to have the feeling that someone truly sees, understands, and wants to know more about a person's life. This is the true nature of service-learning to be reciprocal, an ebb and flow, give and take. For example, as a volunteer shows empathy, compassion, care, and kindness to the served, these feelings come back a hundred-fold. This is not why we provide genuine acts of kindness; it is just the inevitable natural consequence of showing love. This reciprocal process of seeing and being seen is a cultural exchange of sorts, and also the most therapeutic way of being that moves beyond served and server and takes into account each person's humanity.

LOGISTICS

Intrepid traveler, foolhardy risk taker, itinerary-bound planner, or shy wallflower? Which are you? I have been all these things in my work as the leader of a service-learning program. I would like to write that I have been totally put together and well versed in all aspects of service-learning. However, quite honestly, the learning that I now have has been slowly acquired through trial and error. Let me put emphasis on this last statement: trial and error, good times and hard times. One cannot begin to know everything about each trip, country, and culture. In fact, even the countries that we return to each year, like Nepal, are always slightly different, in that the leaders may change, the schedules might change, the kids we were supposed to work with have important tests they must take that hampers visitation, there might be a monsoon that unexpectedly changes plans, and so on. This has happened so much that the other co-leaders and I have joked that we need a t-shirt that reads, "I don't know, things may change," and thus just point to our shirts instead of continually using the phrase, "I don't know!"

On our first trip to Nepal, we worked in the Samata School and PA Nepal simultaneously. We happened to be in Nepal in June, which is the beginning of the monsoon season. From my perspective, I was thinking that monsoon meant heavy rain and downpours. Much to my amazement, the monsoons did come toward the end of our trip, while we were volunteering at the Samata School. Just to put into context, the Samata School is a bamboo-constructed school, made available to all children, for free. The buildings are constructed of bamboo which is a fast-growing sustainable wood that can be easily and quickly put together. The roof of the school building is made of tin, which is not watertight. While finishing up an art-based project, it started to rain, in fact it rained so much that the entire school floor and school yard became a river. The only safe exit out of the school was to walk along the window ledges high above the rapidly rising water. Imagine my shock at this scenario. We were rescued by our "land rover" vans that could drive through a few feet of water.

On that same trip to Nepal while at PA Nepal, we had been walking under some trees shielding ourselves from the heavy rain of the monsoons, when suddenly black lumps started falling from the trees. We thought at first that these dark semi-round objects were dead leaves or budding flowers of sorts, but soon realized that they were leeches that lived in the trees during monsoon season. With blood now running down our arms and legs with many leeches attached to our appendages, we had difficulty remaining calm. Imagine leeches falling from the trees! Luckily the local Nepalese were accustomed to such things and were able to expertly extricate the leeches from our legs and arms. After floods and leeches falling form the sky, we only go to Nepal in March now, before monsoon and leech season.

In yet another harrowing story, while in Zimbabwe, visiting the Peniel Center orphanage run by Youth with a Mission (YWAM), we encountered a perilous situation as well. We had gone to Zimbabwe with the help of alumnus Rebecca Chilcotte, and had put together the itinerary and planned the trip ourselves, as best we could. Once there, we came across a wide range of difficulties, as I have mentioned earlier in previous chapters. One of the biggest lessons I learned was in utilizing transportation services. The folks at YWAM had a few older cars that they used to transport the kids at the orphanage and any volunteers who happened to be helping. It was common practice for volunteers to drive vehicles to be of service to the leaders and staff. We had visited a remote area of Zimbabwe, called Chibi, a tiny village (more like ten homes tucked together) where kids were waiting for us to provide some art as therapy groups, and also some outside yoga for the community. On our way back from Chibi, my son Max who had joined our trip (age 19), volunteered to drive the two hours back to Bulawayo in one of the cars, a Toyota sedan. In Zimbabwe, the roads are rather rough with little financial infrastructure to make repairs, so potholes and loose gravel are a mainstay on the two-lane highways. Max had three student volunteers in his car when suddenly without warning his car hit loose gravel and flipped over traveling on its roof into a gulley, just feet away from a dangerous ravine.

This experience was one of the worst of my life: not only did I witness my son's car crash, but also three students were in peril. This was a "praise the Lord" moment in that all four of the travelers unstrapped themselves from seatbelts while hanging upside down. My son and the students were ultimately fine, but there were black eyes, bruised shoulders, cracked ribs, and general aches and pains that ensued. To be cautious we took everyone to the clinic, which only had Tylenol available and no doctor present. This was not sufficient, so we had to drive into Bulawayo city, call the doctor at 2 a.m. in the morning, offer a bribe for him to come to the hospital to take x-rays, and make sure the car crash victims were not badly injured. All in all, everyone survived with minor injury.

Lesson learned here: never let any volunteer drive, make sure drivers are professional licensed people. From this trip forward, we have only had professional drivers and most of the time we have used a volunteer organization, such as United Planet, to plan itineraries, hire licensed personnel, and deal with on-the-ground logistics. We also have insurance for all members of our volunteer team and have legally prepared consent forms for everyone to sign. Regretfully, many of these commonsense procedures were not in place in the early days of service-learning.

UNITED PLANET: A NONPROFIT VOLUNTEER GROUP

This terrifying experience led us to work with United Planet, a volunteer nonprofit, founded by Dave Santulli after 9/11 in 2001. Dave founded this organization out of his own experiences traveling and living abroad in a service capacity, and he hoped to help student groups and other volunteers to develop what he calls relational diplomacy, connection, and peacebuilding skills. He was concerned by the blatant bias and mistreatment of Muslims after 9/11 and also foreigners in general, and wanted to help spread good will to other countries, and also help volunteers understand that "we are all connected." One of the taglines of United Planet is borrowed from poet Ryunosuke Satoro: "Individually, we are one drop. Together, we are an ocean." This sums up the entire philosophy of United Planet and its founder.

United Planet works with over 40 countries, providing facilitation in the United States and then linking groups to "on the ground" local nonprofits in various countries that help plan and organize the volunteers' service experiences. For example, in Nepal, United Planet partners with Social Tours, a local grassroots nonprofit in Kathmandu providing meaningful opportunities for volunteering and eco-tourism. Social Tours was founded by Raj Gyawali, and he personally works with us each time we visit. There are many partnerships like this one, all curated relationships started by David Santulli. In this ingenious collaborative framework, the volunteers are working with locals at the volunteer sites, and United Planet is working behind the scenes in the United States to ensure that all necessary documentation, safety plans, state department registry, and insurance is in place before volunteers depart for their destination.

Meanwhile, the local nonprofit is securing hotels, volunteer site coordination, all transportation needs, language translators, touring and sacred site visits, as well as opportunities to be with locals from the area to facilitate a more immersive experience. Working with United Planet has made leading service trips a more manageable and definitely less dangerous experience.

BREAKING BONES AND SICKNESS

What if you went sandboarding or trekking up a small mountain and fell? What if you broke your wrist? What if while playing "duck, duck, goose" you slipped a disc? What if you ate some street food which caused extreme gastro-intestinal problems and needed intravenous fluids? What if you got Covid? What if you developed the flu or other virus with a fever? What if you got bitten by some horrible bug and your ankles swelled up to the size of grapefruits? What if you were in a foreign, less developed country when any of these things happened? What would you do? Let me repeat my earlier query: intrepid traveler or foolhardy risk taker? Service-learning especially in developing countries can be risky and sometimes dangerous as I have previously noted in relaying the details of the car accident in Zimbabwe and then asking many reflective questions in this paragraph. The reality is that all of these things have happened on our trips, not because we were not careful but because service-learning is a type of adventure traveling not for the faint of heart. We are quite literally immersing ourselves in local culture and participating in a more intimate way, like the locals. The difference is that we are not locals, and what locals may be accustomed to, we are not. Hence, it is easy to have a mishap, in the form of an accident or sickness.

In Nepal and South Africa, two of our adjunct faculty at Ursuline College broke their wrists. Diane, an experienced art therapist and adjunct professor, decided to dune board along with the rest of the group. Dune boarding requires a person to wax a sandboard, which looks almost identical to a snowboard. One must take the sandboard up to the top of a sand dune, put one's feet into the straps, and push off. The result is like snowboarding down a mountain, except on sand. This is great fun, but plenty dangerous. The sand, although looking soft, is not soft if you fall. The sandboarding experience was part of a cultural immersion, in understanding the beach culture in South Africa. It is a popular sport/activity among the locals. Diane, on her way down the sand dune, had a tumultuous fall and ended up breaking her wrist. At this time, we were quite far from a hospital or help, therefore we kept her wrist elevated and wrapped and proceeded to get to the emergency room as quickly as we could. As one might imagine, we had to get all the students dropped off at the hostel, then proceed to the local hospital emergency. Needless to say, Diane needed surgery and a caste, which a young doctor, looking very handsome (we both took note of this), cared for my colleague. Because we had global health insurance, the entire procedure cost about $250 USD.

Six months later, on our trip to Nepal, my other colleague Judy fell after our hike up Champa Devi. Judy is a seasoned art therapist and adjunct faculty as well. She had completed the hike, and was walking with us to get lunch, when she just fell on some gravel and broke her wrist in two places. This particular break was a little more severe and required surgery and pins to hold the bones in place. This was a calamitous situation, in that it was difficult to be in a foreign land without the creature comforts of the United States. In both cases of broken wrists, Diane and Judy showed their grit and determination to not let a broken bone deter their experience. Armed with ibuprofen, a sling, and lots of help from fellow volunteers, they persevered. It was a good lesson in teamwork and also gratitude that we were able to get medical attention when needed.

Currently, there are many systems in place to guard against broken bones and sickness. For example, as mentioned earlier, we have global health insurance and consent forms that are signed prior to a trip. I have also found that educating volunteers on the dangers and joys of service-learning creates a mindfulness and awareness that they must be careful, and to be thoughtful about an activity that they deem unsafe for their comfort or strength level. We now offer alternative excursions for those not wanting to sandboard or hike a mountain. Also, there are requirements for regular exercise at least six months before the trip. It seems clear that students and volunteers who have at least a moderate level of fitness do better in difficult environmental conditions. Many of our volunteers form walking groups or attend exercise classes together to get ready for the service-learning adventure.

EMOTIONAL BREAKDOWN OR SPIRITUAL AWAKENING

Author and speaker Brene Brown (2010) sites in her TED Talk "The Power of Vulnerability" that individuals who feel as if they are having an emotional breakdown should change the narrative and express that they are having a spiritual awakening instead. Brown comments on this with a sheepish grin and tongue-in-cheek humor. However, I do believe this to be true at least about service-learning experiences. There is nothing like providing service-learning to completely break someone open, create extreme discomfort, and push people to their very edges. The growth and transformation, as noted in an earlier chapter, cannot happen without much discomfort. No one ever grows when they are comfortable. Putting students and volunteers in situations where everything is different facilitates this un-ease, which ultimately leads to a growing experience.

Let's walk through a scenario that a student recently shared with me. Imagine a student volunteer who has never been out of the United States, and now is arriving in Nepal. The landing of the airplane into Kathmandu is frightening, in that Kathmandu is in a valley surrounded by the Himalayan range. Therefore, the airplane must land using drops, like walking downstairs, not a diagonal descent that is routinely expected when flights land. An airplane descent, creating stomach in throat or motion sickness, can be disarming for many. Next, the student is greeted by massive amounts of human beings at the airport, overcrowded luggage carousels, squatty potties in the women's bathroom that smell of strong urine. Once out of the airport, riding in traffic, where traffic signals do not exist and traffic rules are suggestions, not the norm, wondering if they will die before they get to the hotel. Next, marveling at the monkeys and cows ambling about, with traffic weaving around these animals. Once at the hotel, discovering that the bed is a board, the toilet minimally functioning and a shower that brown water is pouring out of. This 30-minute scenario is just the beginning of the "breakdown" that begins to emotionally crack open even the most experienced traveler. It takes a few days to fully acclimate and begin to see the beauty of Nepal and her people, because the discomfort and culture shock have been so intense.

In another such breakdown, my co-leader Dr. Megan Seaman was part of our trip to Zimbabwe. We had arrived at the Peniel Center Orphanage and were shown to our room As I have previously intimated earlier in this book, Megan and I were to share a very small room with about six students, sleeping in sleeping bags on the floor. Megan felt something wet strike her and noticed that she had been sullied by bird poop. Once we looked up, we saw that birds were inhabiting the rafters of the roof which were exposed to the elements. Taking a deep breath, she went to use the toilet, and discovered the toilet was not working, the water in the sink turned off and the bathtub also had no water. At this moment, my colleague, broke down and began yelling at our alumnus Rebecca, who had helped us plan this trip. Megan and I could both see that the living conditions were not safe with chances of getting sick from bird excrement rather high. In addition, other small creatures like rats could also get into this space. Megan is a lovely beautiful human being, who I care about immensely. She is wise and compassionate and would never yell at others; however, in this situation, it was just too much. After a long flight, many delays, being held at gunpoint at the airport on our arrival, because we were white foreigners and not trusted, and then making the long dusty journey to the Peniel Center to work with the AIDs orphans, it was just too much. We did ultimately find a way to remedy this situation in that Megan and I were able to move to a room less "exposed to the elements" and we figured out how to walk to the shower and toilet that was a short distance away. We are all human and ultimately vulnerable and fragile at times, prone to breakdowns when our discomfort level has risen to a dangerous point. This very difficult experience has made Megan and I more resilient and more compassionate, but we first had to be quite human and have a "fall apart" moment to be able to come back together and regroup. Our Zimbabwe trip was the roughest and most unsafe of all our trips, and yet it has taught us some of our greatest lessons and greatest joys. To this day, we both look back fondly at the Zimbabwe trip as a profound transformative experience.

WISDOM GARNERED

How does one even begin to write about the volumes of wisdom acquired and downloaded into the collective brains of myself and all the volunteers over the course of so many service-learning trips. Wisdom is something that comes from experience, age, living through difficulties, and awareness of oneself and others. Over the tenure of many years of service-learning, I am forever changed, transformed, and knowledgeable about many aspects of service-learning. I will admit, that although I do know many things, I don't know everything, even after so many experiences. There are always new challenges, new joys, new people to meet, and one cannot begin to be an expert, when there are so many moving and changing variables on each and every trip. In this next section, I will attempt to extol the essence of the wisdom learned, in hopes that these nuggets of knowledge may help instill the phenomenological nature of service-learning.

EXCEPTIONAL HUMAN EXPERIENCES

My professor when I was getting my PhD in Psychology, Dr. William Braud (2001), wrote a paper entitled "Experiencing Tears of Wonder Joy," examining a concept that he called exceptional human experiences (EHEs). These exceptional experiences in a person's life are magical, ineffable, profound, transformative, and can at times bring tears of joy. Many times EHEs occur during a flow state, or when an individual is fully present in the moment. Sometimes, EHEs happen when a person has a powerful dream, ancestor visitation, is looking at the beauty of the natural world, or during the process of great spiritual connection. Braud (2001) had an EHE while visiting a Russian Orthodox church on a vacation to Russia. He was moved to tears as he witnessed the lighting of candles and incense by the priests.

Likewise, many of us have had EHEs on the service-learning trips. During my first visit to Nepal we worked at the Samata School, educating children ages 5–18, who are underserved and economically disadvantaged. It was our last day at the school and the kids were putting on a dance performance, featuring traditional Nepalese dances. The volunteers and I were seated in a circle on the ground in the courtyard of the school. The kids were in the middle of our circle dancing, when suddenly they broke into a "flash mob" style dance party inviting us to join. We all started dancing to loud Nepali-style modern music, with a strong beat. We ended up jumping, twirling, swaying, and vibing to the beats. I had become close to a young man, named Roshan (pseudonym), and we had shared so many things about each other's cultures. He was the same age as my middle son, and he had "adopted me" as his alternate American mom. In the midst of the dancing, Roshan, found me and began twirling me around and dancing with me. As we danced, we looked at each other, with deep eye contact, an intimacy rarely allowed in American culture. He then put his hands together to form a "heart" shape and held the heart to his heart and thus shared his love and appreciation with a nonverbal gesture. I echoed his sentiment by my own hand heart gesture. At this moment, I began to cry tears of such joy and wild abandon. I was fully in the moment, body moving to the music, looking at this handsome young man, who had the world in front of him. There was such joy, love, and an ineffable feeling of profound gratitude in this EHE moment that, even as I write this, I can feel tears of joy prick my eyes. These EHEs are few and far between for most people, and to have this experience forever changed me. In that moment of dancing, I understood so many things: Roshan's culture, my own culture, his earnest longing for a better life for himself, my own humility, and shock at having experienced such closeness with this dear young man. It's as if the world made perfect sense in that moment, and our differences did not matter, we were just two people locked together in mutual affection and gratitude in the moment. It has been a decade since this experience with Roshan and he and I are still in touch via Messenger. He is doing well and has attended university, and now works as a hotel manager in Kathmandu. I have seen him several times since my first visit and we both share a mutual affection and care for each other. I have to wonder here, what if we allowed ourselves to connect, to really see others in this way more often? What a world we could live in if we took the risk to love and be vulnerable with others, especially those different from ourselves.

A PICTURE IS WORTH A THOUSAND WORDS

In working at Antardristi, the safe house for sexually abused girls, we have grown very fond of the girls and young women, and I feel a mother-like protection of them. We have spent years cultivating a relationship, not just with the girls, but also with the leader and founder, Binita, as well as the other helpers and mental health support persons onsite. One year, we brought a Polaroid camera with us, as a way to gift the girls pictures of all of us together. Photography and social media posts are limited and rare due to the vulnerable nature of these girls' sexual trauma, therefore having a memento of our time together felt right and a way to practice object permanence of sorts, letting them know we are here and will be back. The Covid crisis, delayed our return to Nepal, and thus it had been about three years since we had been able to visit. Many of the girls had been adopted by relatives, returned to their original homes, or graduated from the program, leaving just a few girls at the safe house that we remembered. I was sitting with one of these girls, Ananda (pseudonym), making a friendship bracelet, and she said, "Auntie, I have something to show you" (Auntie is the common term for an adult you are friendly with). Ananda left the room and when she returned she held up a frayed and faded Polaroid picture of she and I from many years ago. She explained that she had been holding onto it and looking at it, reminding herself that I would return to see her. This type of connection is priceless. The photo helped her have hope and trust that my volunteers and I would return. It got her through the loneliness of Covid and of not being with her family. The wisdom here is to never underestimate the impact that relationship has on others. Sharing loving kindness and compassion can change a person's life. It is hope that gets us through hard times, and the promise of being together again can keep the fires of love and care burning. The fact that Ananda kept this picture of us all these years is testament to connection and forming bonds that can fortify and create a sense of hope, even in the direst of conditions.

ABUNDANCE EVEN WHEN LACKING

What gives me pause is to recognize that human beings are innately generous and will try and help even when they have little. In our world today, it is hard to remember this, and many of my colleagues and friends believe that humanity has lost its soul and folks are not as generous or kind as they once were. This may be true in some cases, but ultimately I have seen generosity in spite of hardship so many times that I choose to believe in the good of human beings and that love and light prevail.

As I have mentioned previously, the students/volunteers and I arrived in Bulawayo, Zimbabwe in the midst of the dictator Robert Mugabe's regime, which meant machine guns and suspicions of travelers at the airport, and checkpoints on the roads, requiring bribes be given to the local police. Once cleared to proceed after hours of questioning at the airport, we made our way to the Peniel Center. The Peniel Center is a local compound, similar to a rustic camp, set up to house orphaned children whose parents have died of AIDs. There are several grass-roofed cottages, and a main building where a few guest bedrooms and kitchen are housed. In the best of times, there is a sustainable garden, but the last several years have been plagued by drought, so this was not tenable. As we toured the grounds, we saw that the garden crops were brown and not growing. There was no water for the plants and what little water there was needed to go to the livestock and human beings living on the compound. The food that was served was scarce and in very small portions. The ladies cooking for us in the kitchen managed to kill a scrawny chicken to serve on our first night, and managed to spread the remains of that chicken to all of us. They explained that they rarely kill the chickens because they need them for eggs, which can sustain folks further. For the most part, meals consisted of sadza, a cornmeal mush served with wild greens, which I have spoken of in Chapter 3. What is astonishing to me is the sharing of food stuff, even when there are limited resources available. The lady cooks used every inch of that chicken to create a feast for about 20 of us total, stretching the meager chicken flesh, as well as providing a watery tomato sauce served over the sadza with greens. The meal was consumed with no leftovers, food was respected, and gratitude for having food was prayed about.

Later, on our first night there, Gideon's (the pastor and leader of Peniel Center) wife Jennifer, asked me if I would like to take a bath. As I have shared a little about this already earlier in this book, and after our experience in the hut with birds and recognizing there was no water in the bathroom, I agreed wondering how this was going to be accomplished. Much to my embarrassment, I learned that they needed to get water in large tubs from the cistern (half a mile away), light the wood stove, and warm the water over a flame. Once the water was warm, they filled up the bathtub little by little. What ensued was a shallow somewhat warm bath. The effort that it took to create a bath for me, to help me feel more comfortable, was more than I could emotionally take. I felt incredibly guilty and ashamed of my privilege while at the same time feeling so much love for these kind people. They had suffered and toiled to make sure that I was taken care of in the best way they had. Wisdom gained here is that many times people in the worst circumstances continue generosity of spirit and helping others. Gideon and Jennifer were grateful for our assistance, and therefore wanted to show their support by offering whatever they had to give.

In Nepal similar experiences have happened to us. Working at PA Nepal, we recognized that the kids that are in residential care have very little. The girls and boys wear the same clothing every day and are given two meals a day with some sugared tea as a snack. By American standards this is hardly enough food, but in Nepal it seems plenty. During our time at PA Nepal, we are always fed a large lunch (their main meal of the day). This consists of an abundance of fresh stir-fried veggies, rice, and some type of Indian flatbread. I do know that the budget at PA Nepal is very tight, and to feed about 15–20 of us volunteers for many days in a row must take its toll. However, the joy on the faces of the staff and kids at being able to feed us outweighs my concerns and somehow makes all of us try even harder to be good custodians of love and care for these kids living here without parents.

REFERENCES

Braud, W.G., & Irving, W. (2001). Experiencing tears of wonder-joy: Seeing with the heart's eye. *Journal of Transpersonal Psychology*. https://www.atpweb.org/jtparchive/trps-33-01-02-099.pdf

Brown, B. (2010). *The power of vulnerability*. (Video) Ted Conference. https://www.ted.com/talks/brene_brown_the_power_of_vulnerability.

Kramer, E. (1986). The art therapist's third hand: Reflections on art, art therapy, and society at large. *American Journal of Art Therapy*, 24 (3): 71–86.

CHAPTER 13

Wisdom from Service Providers and Recipients

Interviews with Leaders, Volunteers, and Students

I wanted to include this chapter about sharing wisdom and teaching from service-learning providers and recipients, as well as community leaders, volunteers, and students. Without all the help, coordination, willingness to help and be flexible all in honor of helping those we are serving, none of the service-learning trips would be viable.

BUILDING A UNITED PLANET

Dave Santulli, founder of the nonprofit organization called United Planet, was my first entrée into service-learning from an organizational perspective. As previously shared in this book, United Planet is my preferred service-learning broker organization that has structures in place both in the United States and in more than 40 other countries, forging and maintaining relationships with service recipients and providers. In his book on relational diplomacy, Santulli (2011) wrote, "Relationships are the building blocks of a united planet," which "provides the platform of cooperation, mutual respect, and understanding needed to overcome the challenges of today's world and reach our fullest potential as a global community" (p. ix). It is this very philosophy of helping diverse folks bridge and connect across cultural boundaries that has made his organization successful and sought after as a preferred service-learning provider.

In an interview with Dave Santulli, I asked him what inspired him to do this nonprofit work. He reflected:

> My junior high school offered a Russian language program. It was a unique opportunity, especially for a public school in Maryland. My Russian teacher arranged an international exchange visit for our Russian class through a partnership with a local school. I was very fortunate to be able to visit the Soviet Union when I was 13 years old for several weeks. The most valuable part of the trip was meeting the local people, including students my own age. They expressed fear of war and a desire to build friendship and peace. I think the seed for United Planet was planted during this visit. I realized the need to bring people together and build relationships across our communities and the world. The trip also awakened my interest in seeing as much of the world as possible, given that it is very hard to understand a place unless you see it with your own eyes and meet the people there. So often, we have images of places based on what we hear in the news or on certain stereotypes. When we expand our horizons and visit the world, we form our own impressions based on direct experience. My faith in humanity is always restored when I travel in this way. Throughout my life, this seed grew. I continued to travel, live overseas, learn languages, and meet friends from different cultures, including right in my own community. I went on to live in Japan for quite a few years. When I returned to the US, I wanted to devote myself to building cross-cultural and global understanding, bringing people together, and encouraging people to work together to make a positive difference.
>
> (*Personal communication*, June 30, 2025)

Through these powerful experiences of traveling and later living abroad, Dave was able to see the world differently, and to get a sense of himself as just a cog in a bigger wheel. Because of his connection and friendship with others, he felt drawn to make the world a smaller place, where we each can know and care about each other.

I then asked Dave: How did you get started? Do you have a story to share? He responded with the following:

> When I returned to the U.S. after quite a few years overseas, I reflected on my life, experiences, and friendships. I realized that some of the most fulfilling experiences in my life had come from my cross-cultural friendships and global experiences. I wanted to help bring these transformative experiences to others while building a closer global community. I started working on some small projects even before founding the organization. People loved these small projects. They expressed that there should be more. As I reflected on them, the words "United Planet" came to me. They were the only words that ever did. It made sense—an organization that implements diverse programs and projects to build a more peaceful, sustainable, and united planet.
>
> (*Personal communication*, June 30, 2025)

I was amazed that Dave happened upon the name "United Planet" and that it stuck, because the name is perfect for what Dave believes and stands for. By the very name itself, it expresses peace, connection, and unity with all people. What better way to promote this than to have high school, college, and community volunteers travel to other countries bringing with them a sense of peacekeeping, openness, curiosity, and relationship building. I always share with my students, my friends, family, and clients that when an event happens in another country, it will eventually affect us, whether we recognize this consciously or not. We are all interconnected, and as Martin Luther King is attributed to saying, "Whatever affects one directly, affects all indirectly" (jccany.org, 2024).

Further inquiring into Dave's story, I asked, what are your biggest challenges? He replied:

> The early days were challenging. There were many doubters who questioned why we were doing this work. Some scoffed at the mission. I worked for several years as a volunteer and then at a greatly reduced wage. All that being said, I feel very grateful that I had great belief and resolve to continue. I was willing to sacrifice and work hard. I felt blessed to work with amazing team members, partners, and volunteers. The rewards have been beyond measure. In the early days there were also so many people who expressed the importance and need for the mission. It was their support and encouragement that helped fuel us to continue even though it felt hard at times.
> (*Personal communication*, June 30, 2025)

I asked, what are your biggest successes? He said:

> I hope that, in ways big and small, we achieved our mission of bringing people together, exposing them to new cultures, communities, and the world. We enabled them to expand their horizons, skills, and even aspirations for the future. I hope that the world is a tiny bit more united because of our work.
> (*Personal communication*, June 30, 2025)

I was humbled by Dave's admission that he faced many doubters and naysayers along the way. Promoting peace and collectivism is not a popular topic in the current American political landscape. Even doing small things that provide connection with others is contributing to a new way of relating with fellow humans. Dave's beliefs are similar to Hindu and Buddhist philosophy of practicing no harm (*Ahimsa* in the Sanskrit language).

Moving on to the next question, I asked, what are the benefits of volunteer groups? Are there any drawbacks? He said

> Volunteers learn and grow through their partnerships and friendships with local communities. They gain a grasp of local challenges and an

> understanding of the incredible work being done by organizations on the ground to address these challenges. They expand their horizons and have opportunities to develop their skills and grow as people. As one of my favorite educators (referring to the author Katherine Jackson) says, they learn to "lean into the discomfort." United Planet has developed a model of Global Citizen Leadership. Through it, we say our volunteers become better communicators and leaders. They develop cross-cultural and global understanding. They build awareness of sustainable development and become more civically engaged. They learn through service. They develop career and academic skills as well as socio-emotional competencies. Perhaps most importantly, they develop trust, respect, understanding, and empathy. In a way, they become relational diplomats—unifying with local people in common cause. Professionals and students share their practices with local practitioners and host organizations. Their service can play a meaningful role. Local communities also benefit from these exchanges—whether through capacity-building, skill-sharing, increased visibility for local initiatives, or simply the energy and encouragement that come from working side by side with someone from another part of the world. At its best, the experience is mutually enriching and rooted in reciprocity and respect.
>
> *(Personal communication*, June 30, 2025)

What about any negatives or drawbacks to volunteering globally, I asked. Dave responded:

> I don't see many drawbacks. I believe they occur when people are not prepared—when they don't have the right outlook or expectations. It is important to approach communities in a humble, respectful way—as a guest, a learner, and a partner. It is essential to work closely with host organizations to ensure responsible and meaningful engagement with their communities.
>
> *(Personal communication*, June 30, 2025)

Lastly, I asked, if you could change or grow your nonprofit, what would you dream for? He replied:

> I wish everyone across the world could have a global or cross-cultural experience—one that fosters friendship, partnership, and leadership. I dream that everyone might step up and take responsibility for their communities, recognize that we are one human family despite our differences, and realize that our diversity is our greatest wealth. I believe that expressive arts therapy is a powerful way to uplift and unify people. I hope that we can encourage and engage more students and practitioners in expressive arts therapy to participate in service-learning opportunities.
>
> *(Personal communication*, June 30, 2025)

Interesting that Dave is hoping for more use of expressive therapies as a viable service-learning mental health wellness delivery model. Expressive art therapy and/or art therapy are actually hard to translate to others, who may not have an abundance of creative arts therapists in their culture. Once the expressive arts are seen in action or explained, a light bulb goes on and members of other cultures get it and usually enthusiastically want these creative services. Our first trip brokered by United Planet was to Quito, Ecuador, where we worked in a school setting. Our host on the ground was a bright and engaging man named Pablo. After many conversations, over delicious tamales and coffee, he began to understand the concept of art therapy, but it was apparent that the school system that we were working with thought of us as art teachers. Of course, this did not stop us. We still utilized art as therapy and seemed to make inroads with the teaching staff, awakening their knowledge of expressive arts.

SOCIAL TOURS

We were introduced to Social Tours through United Planet. Social Tours is one of the many "boots on the ground" companies/service providers that carry the baton to the non-profit or organization where help is needed and provide the coordination for groups like ours to be able to help. In Nepal, Social Tours has relationships with PA Nepal and Antardristi, and thus all players are connected, ensuring seamless logistics. Because of the care that goes into setting the stage for good delivery of service, the Ursuline College group only has to show up and focus on the individuals who have requested help. Raj Gyawali runs the company called Social Tours. We have had a relationship with Raj for over ten years now. He has been instrumental in facilitating a connection between our group and the needs of those being served. In my talk with Raj, he said:

> Ever since I started social tours and social treks, I had one principle that stays in the back of my mind. Business only survives because of society, so one must give back to society, as we can only survive because of it. This is a constant reminder for me to do social work, and nonprofit work. Social Tours itself is a for-profit company, but one in which we are slowly moving to a concept of sustainability—and not overdoing anything—balancing a way of life, with what's required but not more than that. This helps to give time to do non-profit work and pro-bono work etc.
>
> (*Personal communication*, 6/1/25)

Raj Gyawali started his sustainable tourism company in 1998, bringing in English students to do some tourism. With the funds he built a hostel in the mountains of Nepal. Later he brought in another group, and used the profits to aid in a cataract center for those in need of eye surgery. From these humble first experiences, he began to put together other sustainable tourist ventures that showcased Nepal and at the same time gave back to the community. He has core tenants that he believes in when doing his voluntourism projects. These are, respect for every individual, in that every individual deserves respect and each and every issue that a person has requires special attention. Next, honesty and integrity, continued excellence in delivery, social responsibility of business, in that every business has a commitment toward society as a whole. Next, Raj's view on money is unique to a more collectivist culture, he says, with money never the only goal. Profits have to be made, but never by means that go against personal and humanitarian values. Making a business successful is a Dharma (a spiritual good) for society and results in a good Karma. Finally, Raj looks at the importance of environmental conservation. The environment is our greatest asset and needs preservation. Exploiting nature is short-term and yields unsustainable dividends, whereas protecting nature is long-term and yields sustainable dividends. All these ideologies seem to be a blend of a collectivist mindset integrated within a capitalist framework, but not capitalism at the expense of others, but to have just enough for oneself while giving back to the community or society one lives in.

Raj spoke of challenges. He said:

> sometimes when you work in a realm that we are in, where we believe in deep sustainability, immersion, showcasing Nepal as a learning destination, doing social work, and ensuring businesses affect development, we forget that the whole world does not think that way, and so matching what we offer to what people have a demand for is challenging. How do we find the right people to travel with us? People that also want to give back and honor and respect people and the environment. Of course, we have learned to adapt and over time we have begun to be known for our unique stance on tourism.
>
> (*Personal communication*, 6/1/25)

Raj explained what he feels his successes are in his social tours company. He said:

> I always dreamed of creating a company that would actually work differently from others and would be known for what we do. I think we have achieved this in Nepal—the industry believes we are different, so are always watching us to see what we do next—this is a nice position to be in, to have created a company image that is unique. We aim to showcase Nepal in a certain way, and get travelers to learn from it, to learn from Nepali culture, from a country mired in collectivist mindset. Every time new learning, or insights about culture happen, with groups or individuals, it's a joy, a real joy. These immersive insight moments happen all the time with the Ursuline Group, as it's such relevant work.

We are lucky to attract many groups like these that are so amazing and feel like success every time.

(Personal communication, 6/1/25)

I asked Raj what benefits and drawbacks occurred with volunteer groups. He said:

The benefits and drawback of volunteering really boils down to some key factors—skill sets, correct placement, intent, and amount of time spent doing the volunteering. So, the more the correct match between skill set and placement, the shorter and the more beneficial volunteering can be. This is especially true for high skills like therapy, massage techniques, learning through play, and many other skill sets. Match it to the right project and need, and immediately positive results can be seen within the project. Now to the volunteer with the right intent and mindset, the benefits are always there, as it opens up the mind, and allows internal reflection that grows the volunteer.

The drawback can be that with vulnerable groups, there could be separation anxiety for the beneficiaries, and for the volunteer, there could be a sense of being the knight in shining armor, so it can shift the learning balance, and that's not effective at all.

(Personal communication, 6/1/25)

Raj speaks about rightness of fit and the ability to understand the needs of the population served without swooping in as a savior. I think this is important to help volunteers understand what service-learning is about. I later asked him what he might want to change or grow within the service-learning framework. He said, in the most confident way:

I am totally happy with what we do at the moment. However, I could see us doing more to use what Nepal has to offer in terms of teaching, to help the world understand and learn how to live in a more cooperative way. I believe that getting more groups to come who would love to learn from Nepal would be a dream - that part of the travel work is very fulfilling, and an angle I would be honored to pursue more and more.

(Personal communication, 6/1/25)

Raj has created a special brand of for-profit in a collectivist mindset that gives back to the community and the environment as much as possible. This more democratic brand of capitalism within a collectivist culture is a trademark of a valuable tenant that people of Nepal can teach others across the world. There is a reciprocity in having an ethical business practice that does not rely on overconsumption or greed. Raj talks his talk and walks his walk in many ways, in that he does not own a home or a car, gives of himself to others, and values his collectivist roots. He utilizes just what he needs to live comfortably and maintain a vibrant full lifestyle.

ANTARDRISTI

Binita Adhikari is the founder of Antardristi, a safe house for girls who have been sexually abused. Her mission is to provide social justice and action for sexually abused girls, by providing education and awareness within the Nepalese patriarchal society. In my interview with her, she explained how and why she started this nonprofit. Binita said first that her vision was born of empathy. She then said:

> People frequently ignore the suffering of the victims in favor of the idea that justice consists of punishing the guilty. The story begins when I visited the Nepal Police's Women and Children Cell back in 2003. I saw that everyone's attention was on punishing the individual who had sexually abused a two-year-old girl. The traumatized, broken, quivering, terrified infant was in her mother's protective grasp, yet no one appeared to notice. As a psychology student, I could relate to the baby's anguish as well as the girl's mournful glance and nonverbal clues. I made the decision right then and there: Who else, if not me? If not now, when will it be?
>
> (*Personal communication*, 7/3/25)

As I heard this story, with tears in my eyes, I thought to myself, yes, "Right on, Binita, if not you than who?" I wondered what would have happened if Binita had not answered the call to help sexually abused girls? It is hard for me to imagine a student in psychology deciding to open a safe house, based on a visit to the police station to see a mother and her abused child, but I am sure glad Binita did just that.

I asked Binita to talk about her startup of Antardristi. She said:

> As a result of this experience, I founded Antardristi Nepal (AN) in 2003 while I was still a student, driven by a strong desire to help the defenseless victims of horrible crimes like rape and incest. *Antar* (inner) and *dristi* (sight) are the Nepali words for "*antardristi*," which means "inner sight." We must have the inner sight to feel the victims because we cannot see them with the physical eye. With few resources and little expertise, AN brought a novel approach by recognizing that helping survivors entails not only punishing wrongdoers but also attending to the psychological harm that the victim has suffered. While creating peer groups, AN set out on a mission to increase awareness of sexual abuse in schools and communities. Breaking the taboo of silence, providing a safe location for survivors to come forward, and creating a supportive atmosphere were all made possible by this project. In order to provide a wide range of services, such as trauma counseling, educational support, life skills, vocational education, empowerment building, and assistance in reintegrating survivors into their families and communities, the survivors and helpers of AN built a safe center.
>
> (*Personal communication*, 7/3/25)

She went on to add:

> A shared desire to change and a calculated approach to tackling the issues of sexual abused were necessary for the plan to become a reality. The tale of AN is one of kindness, tenacity, and a commitment to building a community that supports Nepalese survivors of sexual abuse.
>
> (*Personal communication*, 7/3/25)

As noted earlier in this book, we have spent a good deal of time over many years with the girls at Antardristi. Upon entering the doors of this safe house, there is love, care, and support in abundance. The girls have decorated the space with drawings and other creative knickknacks. There is a sense of community of "found family" here. Anyone serving these girls immediately has a sense of protection and care for the trauma they have endured. Every measure is taken to ensure privacy and anonymity. No photos are posted with faces of the girls; social media is highly monitored.

Binita shared that she does have challenges that come along with her work as founder and leader of Antardristi. She spoke of the intricate and multilayered problems that she and the survivors face:

> Working with sexual abuse issues is incredibly complex and challenging due to the sensitive, traumatic, and multifaceted nature of the problem.
>
> 1. Many survivors struggle to speak up due to shame, fear, guilt, or societal stigma.
> 2. Cases often rely on survivor testimony, which can be retraumatizing, and many cases are dropped due to lack of evidence.
> 3. Organizations (e.g., religious institutions, schools, workplaces) may cover up abuse to protect their reputation.
> 4. Victim-blaming & shame, cultural attitudes may silence survivors or protect perpetrators. There is a "Boys will be boys" attitude that prevails in this patriarchal society.
> 5. Gender and Power Dynamics can be problematic. In today's world, women are still the lesser sex, where women are seen as less valuable than men, and thus the problem of sexual abuse or incest is swept "under the rug" or suppressed.
> 6. Low reporting and more hidden cases continue to be problematic. In many of the hill tribes, there is great shame associated with sexual abuse and thus cases are hidden and not reported.
>
> (*Personal communication*, 7/3/25)

In her recounting all the challenges, I reflected that the prevalence of sexual abuse and rape have similar outcomes and challenges in the United States. She went on to say that there are just so many challenges, all the time. In March when I was visiting Nepal and Antardristi, Binita shared that just keeping the safe house operating from a financial perspective is difficult as well. She relies on grants, fundraising, and generous benefactors.

Binita gladly shared a story to help me understand the life-changing impact that Antardristi's loving staff and helpers have facilitated. She recalled a story about a 15-year-old girl named Aadhya (pseudonym) who had endured severe hardships before she arrived at Antardristi. Binita said:

> Aadhya dropped out of school to care for her siblings, as her father had left for India to work. A boy in her village took advantage of her vulnerable situation, resulting in a pregnancy. He gave her abortion medicine and promised to marry her. The villagers came to know about this and tried to reconcile the matter within the family but were unsuccessful. One of the organizations advocating for women's welfare knew about this and referred her to Antardristi Nepal.
>
> Upon arriving in Kathmandu, she learned of more tragedies, that her sister was poisoned, and her father had taken her younger brother to India. During her stay with us, we came to know that her physical health was also not good. Doctors discovered a lump in her breast that required urgent surgery to prevent the risk of cancer. Despite initial delays in treatment with father's consent delayed, we did the operation. Now, she is in good health and rebuilding her life. She has resumed her education, is learning sewing skills, and remains in contact with her younger brother and grandparents.
>
> *(Personal communication, 7/3/25)*

The story of Aadhya is just one of many stories that have brought the girls to Antardristi. There is such trauma and hardship with all the girls. They have found respite in the safe house of Antardristi, but still have to face the shame and social stigma that comes from living in a safe house and leaving their families and village communities.

Binita reflected on her biggest accomplishments to date in her life, in regard to her passion project of Antardristi. She said:

> My greatest accomplishment is helping young women and girls who are struggling. To assist them in living a lovely life following a terrible life catastrophe. We welcome those who wind up in the middle of nowhere to our facilities so they can appreciate the beauty of life.
>
> *(Personal communication, 7/3/25)*

Binita also shared of her experiences having volunteer groups help out at Antardristi. She conveyed that having volunteers can help the girls feel less lonely and happier that there are people who want to spend time with them. She also believes that having volunteers can expand professional networking and can be particularly helpful for career development and exploration. There is a downside to volunteer groups in that it takes time and also takes away from the girls everyday routine. At times more money is spent on feeding volunteers and possible traveling to sites with volunteers. Lastly, working with volunteers can be stressful for the girls, in that they are sharing with new people. I appreciated Binita's candid report on volunteers, and how at times it is hard. One of the reasons, we continue to return to Antardristi year after year is to form those relationships with the girls, to make it easier to be with us, because we have formed a lasting relationship.

Binita has a dream for Antardristi—it is not just to grow in helping girls who are survivors of sexual abuse, but to add depth. She wants to change systems of governance and views on sexual abuse. She wants more justice seeded, and more lives changed. Most of all she wants to see more love in action. Many theorists believe that love is an action verb, and I believe that Binita is onto something in her wish. If you love, do something to end the suffering of girls who are sexually abused and traumatized by others.

CHEYENNE RIVER YOUTH PROJECT

Julie Garreau is the founder of the Cheyenne River Youth Project, and the creator of the RedCan Graffiti Jam in which we volunteer every summer. I interviewed Julie Garreau to garner her wisdom on her nonprofit work and also a little of her story of how she got started doing this work. I first asked what inspired her to do this nonprofit work. She said:

> This work is part of who I am. I was raised by public servants. My father was a law enforcement officer, and my mother was the executive director of the Cheyenne River Sioux Tribe's Elderly Nutrition Center—this is the example they set for me. I also think that public service is part of being a good relative, a principle deeply rooted in our traditional Lakota values. That belief has guided me throughout my life and work.
>
> *(Personal communication, 8/15/25)*

Being part of good relations is key to the Lakota and many other Native American tribes across the United States. I found Julie's parents were important role models that set the stage for her to do this work. She added:

> Knowing that our community lacks infrastructure and opportunity, my parents worked hard to create that, and they didn't just do the basics. For example, my mother did not want the Elderly Nutrition Center to just serve meals. Instead, she created a safe gathering place for our elders providing games, special activities and other services.
>
> I learned that lesson very well: When you don't have something you need, you have to make it happen.
>
> *(Personal communication, 8/15/25)*

Making things happen is exactly what Julie did as she began the Cheyenne River Youth Project (CRYP). She shared further about how she got started serving Lakota youth, and how the program evolved over time. Julie said:

> I first got involved with the kids in this community when I was in my early 20s. In October 1988, I had the opportunity to develop a little drop-in youth center on Eagle Butte's Main Street that we called "The Main."
>
> "The Main" was the first iteration of the Cheyenne River Youth Project. It would be run exclusively by volunteers—myself included—for more than ten years.
>
> I was really passionate about the work and believed in it so much. That conviction enabled CRYP to overcome so many obstacles. For example, we didn't have people, so I started a volunteer program. We didn't have resources, so I learned how to fundraise. I didn't have the skill set necessary for something like this, so I learned.
>
> I didn't do this alone, however. I had people behind me, pulling for me and engaging with me. My biggest teachers were the kids.
>
> (*Personal communication*, 8/15/25)

Julie and Binita, who founded Antardristi, have a similar passion in that they thought if they did not start their nonprofits, then who would. Julie is a prime example of stepping up to do the work needed to help heal the Lakota youth and provide different opportunities for them. This work also comes with many challenges and Julie shared the following:

> There are so many. A big challenge has always been a lack of resources, and it can be difficult to ask for funding. We are an impoverished nation, and I am aware of the attitude many people have toward Native communities and our situation, particularly in remote, rural areas like Cheyenne River. In order to do this work, I learned we have to build respectful, mutually beneficial relationships—enduring partnerships that lift us all. I am proud of our culture and our community, and I want the people with whom we engage to really get to know who we are. We are rich in culture and ceremony, yet we also are navigating a situation not of our making.
>
> That situation is colonization. Its lasting impact affects us on a daily basis at CRYP. Intergenerational, historical trauma leads to many social ills as well as significant workforce issues. Our staff works hard to navigate these ongoing challenges with compassion and a healing mindset. We often say "the work we do here is medicine," and we believe that wholeheartedly And, as it turns out, our lack of resources has directly led to our greatest successes: creativity, adaptability, and innovative approach to youth programming.
>
> (*Personal communication*, 8/15/25)

Julie speaks of colonization and the lasting impact this has had on the Native American community. As I have mentioned earlier in this book, the effects of trauma and oppression have had devastating consequences for our Indigenous family. Because of all the time I have spent at CRYP, I agree with Julie when she says the "work we do here is medicine." There is a positive energy that permeates CRYP and the ripple effect stretches far and wide.

I wanted to know about successes at CRYP and Julie shared:

> At CRYP, we constantly find creative ways to overcome adversity. We are resourceful, and we are excellent stewards of every dollar. Without that, our organization could not have survived for 37 years.
>
> I also am proud of our innovative programming. This is not a top-down organization the kids lead the way. We pay attention so we can meet them where they are, and design programs that will be interesting and engaging for them. Every day, we provide new opportunities to learn and grow in safe spaces. CRYP has been really good at that, and several of our programs have been recognized nationally, such as the RedCan Invitational Graffiti Jam, Midnight Basketball, and Main University.
>
> Our greatest success is that we continue to adapt and thrive, always guided by our children.
>
> *(Personal communication, 8/15/25)*

I asked Julie: What are the benefits of volunteer groups? What are the drawbacks? She said:

> CRYP is a small nonprofit organization, and we do not have all the resources that other organizations might have. I couldn't hire staff in the beginning, so I created a volunteer program that became active nationally and then internationally. Some volunteers came to us as individuals for terms that ranged from a few weeks to a year or more. Others came with service groups from schools, churches and other community organizations.
>
> Volunteerism requires investment—in relationships, trust, and long-term connection. For CRYP, volunteerism is a two-way street. Volunteers give their time and energy, and we give back. We want them to have opportunities to engage in meaningful cultural exchange, so they become lifelong allies and ambassadors—not just for CRYP or even the Cheyenne River reservation, but for all of Indian Country.
>
> This is important, because often volunteers do not have an existing knowledge base regarding Native peoples. After a few unfortunate episodes involving cultural misunderstandings and, sadly, outright racism, I came to view our volunteer program as a nationwide education initiative—and then a global one. Simply sharing who we are has a ripple effect that has spread farther than any of us could have imagined.
>
> We simply couldn't do what we do without our volunteers. The work is too big, and our local team is too small to carry it alone. Volunteers help run our youth and teen programs, they provide support for special events and distributions, they help us care for our 3-acre garden, and they play a critical role in facilities maintenance and repair.
>
> *(Personal communication, 8/15/25)*

I am testament to the work that Julie does, befriending, educating, and "adopting" volunteers into the extended family that makes up the Cheyenne River Youth Project community. Volunteers come from all over the United Sates and many times abroad to help with youth programming, and other special events. Julie shared some drawbacks related to resources. She said:

> The only drawbacks involve limited resources, as always. We always wish we could do even more for our volunteers, because we value them so much. But we do everything we can, and we welcome every opportunity to build new relationships with the extraordinary people who are willing to travel to our remote, rural reservation and spend time working alongside us.
>
> (*Personal communication*, 8/15/25)

Getting to Cheyenne River Reservation in Eagle Butte, South Dakota is a labor of love And incredulity at the remote and rural nature of this reservation. The volunteer groups that return year after year, like our group, will share the feelings of collective efficacy that permeates the reservation. There is real love here and care for fellow humans. This warmth of spirit and sharing of culture is what attracts and keeps volunteers coming over and over again to help in whatever way is needed.

I asked Julie what she might imagine if she could grow CRYP in bigger ways, what would she dream of? She said:

> We are a rural Native nation. We are capable of doing the work, but we need allies and consistent resources, because this work will take decades. While some might see colonization as an historical event, it is not. For us, history is not behind us—we are still living it, every single day. The damage to our cultures and communities unfolded over centuries, and healing that damage will take a long time, as well.
>
> (*Personal communication*, 8/15/25)

The intergenerational trauma at the hands of colonizers is apparent and current on the reservation. What Julie speaks about is true, and sad. However, the Lakota tribe of Cheyenne River are incredibly resourceful and resilient and, under Julie's charge, have managed to be uplifted. She worries about the continued work as she prepares for her retirement. She added:

> We are currently in a season of transition at CRYP as I make my initial preparations for retirement in a few years. CRYP has grown and evolved so much over the last 37 years, and it has become an institution for the community. I don't want that to end. I dream of CRYP continuing for another 37 years, and far beyond. My wish is to find the resources for that to happen.

> In the nonprofit world, you have to work so hard to raise money, which takes away from the real work: serving our people. I dream of having a sustainable source of funding so CRYP can just *be*. I would like our staff to be able to focus on their work and to not have to struggle quite so hard for resources.
> That's the dream. The infrastructure is here. Now we must ensure it endures for generations to come.
>
> (*Personal communication*, 8/15/25)

As Julie prepares for the transition away from the helm of CRYP, she faces the grave reality of funding and continuing to find resources to keep this good work going. As Julie mentioned earlier, the work of CRYP is vast in its ability to help the youth as well as their families.

STUDENT GROWTH

As part of the service-learning course that students enroll in to attend the trip, there are several concepts of learning that are important to consider. The students reflect on their strengths and skills, struggles and challenges, global view, and growth as mental health creative arts provider. This next section focuses on a few exemplary reflections of these topics.

STRENGTHS AND SKILLS

Joey (pseudonym) had never been out of the country before and had been wanting to attend a service trip before she graduated with her master's in counseling and art therapy. She stated:

> I really struggled at first to work with the kids due to my fears of messing up. I also have bad anxiety trying to understand accents, so this really scared me when working with people whom I cannot understand. As I continued working with the kids, however, I realized that there were other ways to understand other than through a typical conversation. Facial expressions, movements, actions—they all came together in helping understand the bigger picture. Finally feeling more confident in myself, I found my best experiences to be with working closely with particular kids, in a more one-on-one sort of way.
>
> (*Personal communication*, 3/20/25)

Joey found that just focusing on one kid at a time helped mitigate her fear and discomfort about language barriers. She learned that staying in the present moment, and just enjoying the relational aspects of one-on-one communication, was all it took for her to feel confident in her interactions.

Another student, Emily (pseudonym), an experienced traveler and non-traditional graduate student, said the following:

> I definitely would say that my open heart and my open mind are two of my biggest strengths. I look at the world from a spiritual lens, and this allows me to be open to whatever experiences come my way. This was no different during this trip. Using the mantra "I am water, I am going with the flow" throughout the trip was truly the way I was living the experience. I think had I gone into this experience being more rigid or feeling the need to control the things around me, I would have been miserable. So, I was grateful for being able to be in the moment throughout the experience.
> *(Personal communication, 4/1/25)*

Emily had traveled before on service trips and had learned that being flexible and open-hearted were important strengths that served her well. Her mantra of "water" was a phrase that many of us, including me, used throughout the trip. Emily's spiritual lens helped her see others with more openness. She also recognized that being flexible instead of rigid was a winning strategy to help her stay in the flow of things.

STRUGGLES AND CHALLENGES

Dealing with fears of making mistakes and also getting sick or having some type of injury usually weigh heavy on a student's mind. Service-learning can be an all-encompassing process, requiring students to let go and trust.

Joey said in response to her fears:

> I struggled a lot with my fear of messing things up and misunderstanding due to the language barrier. I was terrified of making a fool of myself or accidentally offending someone. Over time, I was able to work through these fears, as I saw my peers also overcoming struggles.
> *(Personal communication, 3/21/25)*

Joey also had a bad fall on the rough roads of Kathmandu. She said:

> A few days into the trip, while walking back to the hostel, I looked up from where I was walking and accidentally fell. I twisted my ankle and slammed my knee hard into the ground. My friends who were walking with me stopped to help me, as did many of the locals. I sincerely appreciated everyone's kindness at the time, and it is something that stood out to me in the Nepali culture. While I managed to get through the rest of the trip, it was very difficult the following days as I felt a lot of pain. This was a test of my perseverance, in that

I had to try and be present with the kids even though I was in pain, and worried about a sprained ankle.

(*Personal communication*, 3/21/25)

What Joey is dealing with is not only worries about language barriers, but also physical discomfort due to a fall. Although Joey did not sprain her ankle, the worry and negative "head space" affected her ability to be present. This over-thinking and worry mindset are part of the transformation process and are worked through by every student in different capacities. For students, facing the unknown is challenging and life changing, in that everything is foreign, including medical care, medicines, food, hotels, transportation, and people.

Other types of challenges, some of which I have mentioned in prior chapters include difficulty with food choice, dealing with air quality and pollution levels, issues of cleanliness, disagreements with fellow volunteers, feelings of isolation and a general discomfort. Another student volunteer, whom I will name Terri, struggled with homesickness and feeling isolated by others. Terri was a quiet shy young woman, who tended to be nonverbal much of the time. After Terri had feelings of panic, and sought me out to confide in, I had no idea she was dealing with this much discomfort. After a quick check-in and processing of her emotions, she was able to be more open with a fellow student, and became more social and able to join more with the group. There is never a time when some kind of trauma, drama, or issue manifests itself while on a service-trip. I have learned to totally expect each person to have their own "aha" or awakening moment; even if it is a small event, or a massive explosion, we hold space for it all. I have put in place a reflective art and writing journal to help the students express their angst and/or joys of the experience.

VIEW ON GLOBAL ISSUES

Students change their outlook and frame of reference once they have provided service for folks who are mostly underrepresented in developing countries. There are two areas that seem to resonate with students, the collectivist culture and the absence of a strong capitalist view. Many students return to the United States, searching for community that can be more supportive and cooperative while others create a self-imposed "shopping ban" trying to not buy any new clothing or item that is not absolutely needed. Irene (pseudonym) was a young graduate student, who was naive in many ways about the world. She said:

Seeing how the people interacted in Nepal was one of the most wonderful parts of the experience. There was such a strong sense of community,

> and everyone seemed to be looking out for each other. I even saw this through driving, which to me seemed very chaotic, yet they were all on the road collectively, looking out for each other, so accidents could be avoided. Given the vast number of struggles that many people face, being able to rely on one another is so important. It is something that I wish we had more of within the United States. When people are struggling, it is so common in the United States to see people get ignored, yet it felt like in Nepal, people would go out of their way to help each other. I really want to embrace this mindset and encourage the same behavior here in the United States.
>
> (*Personal communication*, 3/29/25)

Irene's openness and candor about her thoughts of the Nepalese collectivist culture vs. the individualistic culture of the United States are poignant and give pause to reflect on differing worldviews and how this is seen in human behavior in various countries around the globe. Because Nepal, for example, has a collectivist worldview, where good karma and practicing non-harm are commended, looking out for your neighbor or fellow driver makes sense.

CHANGES AS A MENTAL HEALTH CREATIVE ARTS THERAPIST

One of my greatest hopes is that the service-learning experience can be a transferrable skill and make an impact within clinical placement sites. If student volunteers can learn to lean into their discomfort, be more flexible and open-minded, as well as learn to pivot quickly as needed, then their newly acquired skill set will ultimately benefit their clinical placement and career. Another student, Mark (pseudonym), said:

> Coming back from South Africa, and settling back in at my internship, I have already noticed growth in myself. I have had a much easier time fully focusing on my clients. I feel like I have connected much more deeply with my clients as well. As my clients are children, it showed me how most children still act the same and want the same things, despite being on opposite sides of the world. As I gained confidence in interacting with the South African kids, I have seen this confidence continue to grow with my young clients in the United States as well. I also appreciated working with the kids in South Africa, as they have such a different background than my own clients. The traumas they experienced, I have not come across in my own work yet; however, I can take what I learned and apply it to these situations as I inevitably come across them. This, among all the other things I learned during this trip, I will hold on to forever and use it to shape my work and who I am as a counselor and art therapist.
>
> (*Personal communication*, 9/1/24)

Mark is "right on" in his assessment here. First, he says, kids are similar, and all want the same types of things, like play, love, learning, etc. Next, he says, that in seeing trauma in the South African kids, he can apply these lessons learned to future clients who might be experiencing trauma. Once one has worked with a person who has experienced trauma or other hard things, an "emotional muscle" of sorts is created allowing for a better therapeutic relationship, and this type of learning and awareness becomes a transferrable skill-set.

ALL YOU NEED IS LOVE: THOUGHTS FROM A COMMUNITY VOLUNTEER

Kathy, a community member and daycare provider, after years of wanting to attend our trip to Nepal, finally decided it was time. She had recently undergone chemotherapy for a chronic type of cancer and had been cleared by her doctor to attend this trip. As a daycare provider and mother to two daughters, her strength was in working with the kids at PA Nepal and Antardristi. In a heartfelt soliloquy, she described her thoughts and feelings about the service-learning trip. Kathy wrote:

> It is difficult to recognize our own strengths and gifts we are quick to judge ourselves, However, leaving for Nepal gave me the opportunity to reflect on what I can offer as well as receive from those I meet. I have a deep curiosity in people and their story, their culture and what brings life to them. I wanted to learn as much as I could about these "neighbors" living 8,000 miles away.
>
> As a daycare provider, I was not afraid to get down on the floor and hug, play clapping games, jump, and toss a ball, answer curious questions, and just be in their presence. It felt natural, good, and most of all it felt loving.
>
> I tried to keep myself open to challenges which would undoubtedly come, and there were some in the mountainous terrain of Nepal. Growing up in Ohio, which is relatively flat, this was a challenge for sure. There were other challenges of squat toilets with no toilet paper, and little water or soap to wash one's hands. I recognized that there was a lack of refrigeration, and no dryers to dry clothes. These challenges, which were just part of daily living, made me consider how fortunate I am in my life in the USA. We are all born under the same stars, the same sun lights our day, the same moon puts us to sleep. In contemplating all of this, I return to joy. The joy that the children and I shared together was contagious. My heart was continually opened by one kid at a time, until I was overflowing with love. My epiphany was, all that really matters is love.
>
> It was important for me to spend time just talking and being with the people of Nepal. Immersing myself in a spice tour, walking around the city, hearing the language, the temple bells, the motorbikes, seeing the colors of prayer flags and laundry on rooftops drying in the sunshine. All of this

completed my reciprocal learning of Nepal and her people. I am forever changed and humbled by this trip, and hold the kids and people of Nepal in a space of love.

(*Personal communication*, 8/8/25)

My hope in including interviews, testimonials, and wisdom from leaders, volunteers, and students is to help the reader understand the back story or behind the curtain experiences of service-learning. Each person, whether a leader, volunteer, or student, has their own unique story and perspective on helping. It is my hope and goal to see the interconnectedness of all people and how we can work together to create a more untied planet, as founder of United Planet, David Santulli, suggests.

REFERENCE

Santulli, D. (2011). Relational diplomacy: Innovations in Peacebuilding: A study of Cyprus. Washington, DC: Arlington Street Press.

CHAPTER 14

Epilogue

Gratitude, Humility, and Love

I cannot begin to extol my gratitude, humility, and love for serving others by providing service-learning experiences for students/volunteers as well as the people we have served. Many times, providing service feels hard, with little acknowledgment of the difficulties that volunteers go through to be able to provide loving care and service for others. However, I believe that most often providing service is pure joy, in that we the servers take away far more than what we gave. This reciprocal relationship of service-learning is at the core of this type of pedagogy.

It is an honor and a privilege to work with others who have trusted us enough to let us help or serve in some way. Sometimes the smallest tiny act of service means the most to one of the people we have helped. The truth is we never know, but learn to trust the process. Just like the young woman in Nepal who kept the picture of her and me all these years, to remind her of our relationship, the service and pay it forward mentality continues.

This past summer while volunteering at the Cheyenne River Youth Project in Eagle Butte, South Dakota, my colleague and co-leader Dr. Megan Seaman and I were honored for our ten years of service to the reservation and project. We were told that the elders/leaders were going to say a few words about our tenure of service and hence were totally unprepared for the beautiful ceremony that began to unfold. We were honored as veterans of CRYP and then brought into the midst of the sacred drum circle on the last day of the RedCan Graffiti Jam. It is a Lakota tradition, to honor people by wrapping them in a traditional star-pattern Lakota quilt.

Once wrapped in this homemade gorgeous quilt, we were honored and praised. Next, every member of the tribe who was present as well as the volunteers came up and shook our hands and/or gave us a hug. We were

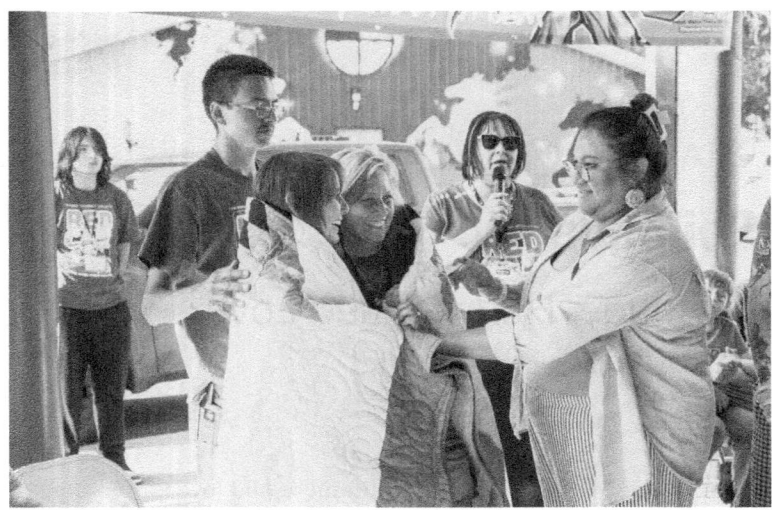

Figure 14.1 Megan Seaman and Katherine Jackson star-quilt honoring ceremony

smudged and purified and held in the highest regard. This ceremony, impromptu and surprising, felt like a wonderful way to share the joy of reciprocal service-learning. The unexpected gifts that keep giving, long after the experience has ended. I am most humbly honored to do this work, and to have the fortitude to keep it going.

My gratitude and heartfelt love to all those who I have served and who have intentionally, and at times unintentionally, given me back all the love tenfold. I remain deeply moved and transformed by the goodness of humanity and the ability of many to see that we are all each other's relations.

Index

Note: Page references in *italics* denote figures, in **bold** tables.

3-Marker Challenge 94
9/11 attack 168

abundance 175–176
accepting invitation, best practice 164–165
Adhikari, Binita 17, 174, 184–188
Adichie, C. 138
adult learners 78, 80, 81, 83, 85, 88, 90; *see also* learning
advanced placement (AP) classes 145
Afghan community center 149–151
Africentrism 96
Afrikaans language 45, 46, 131
AIDS/HIV 10–11, 67, 175
All About Me Book 90
American Art Therapy Association (AATA) 113, 151
American Counseling Association 113
Antardristi 62–63, 106, 117–118, 161, 184–187; founded by 184, 188; and PA Nepal 117–118; relationship building 62–63; safe house 127
Antardristi Nepal (AN) 184, 186
Arnett, J.J. 145, 147
art creation 54, 83, 93, 123
arts-based expressive therapy 7–22; hand images 15–16; history 8–9; Nepal 17–20; overview 7; paper heart strings 20–22; service-learning with 9–10 Zimbabwe 10–15

Art Therapy in Asia: To the Bone or Wrapped in Silk (Kalmanowitz) 10
authenticity 59, 60, 62, 65, 66

Baakens River 46
Bagmati River 5, 35, 36
beading 122
Bennett, Milton 3
best practices/logistics/wisdom 159–174; abundance 175–176; accepting invitations 164–165; breaking bones and sickness 169–170; emotional breakdown 171–172; garnered 172; human experiences 173–174; join in with locals 162–164; nonprofit volunteer group 168–169; overview 159–160; utilize resources 162; waiting for invitation 160–161. see and be seen 165–166
Block, P. 104
Boer Wars 45
Braud, William 173
breaking bones and sickness 169–170
Brown, Brene 171
buddhist site 36–37
Burke, Kathleen 30
Butler, Lyn Liao 68

Cady, S. 61
calligraphy 122, 125
Camacho, Jorge 115–116
Cane, Florence 8
Cape Town 164

Catholic Charities 101, 102, 160
Champa Devi 42–44, 72, 170
Chan, S.M. 9
Cheyenne River Reservation 16, 31–34, 53, 56, 86, 91, 93, 104, 109, 114–117, 159, 165; graffiti painting at *34*, 123; horse graffiti piece at *55*; social justice 114–117
Cheyenne River Sioux Tribe's Elderly Nutrition Center 187
Cheyenne River Youth Project (CRYP) 31–34, 54–56, 87, 92, 93, 94, 105, 114, 115, 187–191
Chilcote, Rebecca 11, 28, *29*, 167, 172
Chishamba, Gideon 13, 175, 176
Chitwan National Park 37–39
Christian religion 28, 159
Coca-Cola 42, 163
coffee filter mandala *127*
Coll, C.G. 60
collaborative drawing 142
College Board 145
Collins, D. 113
colonization 4–5, 33, 60, 122, 188
colorful moments 74–75
communicative learning 80–81; *see also* learning
community: Afghan 149–151; based experiential education 142; collaboration 88; dialogues 92; kitchen 163; meals 104; members 93, 156; Native American 31–32, 88; oppression 114; volunteer 195–196; volunteers 16, *16*
community-based research (CBR) 143
Congo 25–26
contextual border crossing 24, 88–89, 91–92, 95, 98
cooking with a Russian teen *141*
Cook-Nobles, R. 60
counseling and art therapy 8, 77–79, 82, 160; careers in 78; expression 98; program 28, 65, 85; service-learning trips 93; trainees 77, 79, 85
course connection 152–153
Covid crisis 169, 174
creating dialogues/expression 98
Creative and Mental Growth (Lowenfeld) 8
creative arts 115–116
creative/expressive arts practices 132–138, 181; play as therapy 134–138; South Africa 132–133; yoga 133–134

critical social theory 96; *see also* theories
Csepanyi, Zsuzsa 120
cultural competence 101–111, 142; Lakota Sioux 104–105; multicultural counseling inventory 107–111; Nepal 105–107; overview 101; Sudanese boys 101–103
cultural exchange 41–57; boy story and 51–52; Champa Devi 42–44; defined 41; graffiti arts 54–56; Lakota 53–54; South Africa 45–51; Taiwan 41–42; tipi 56–57
cultural humility 59, 81, 142, 152, 153, 166
cultural immersion 23–39; Cheyenne River Youth Program (CRYP) 31–34; Congo 25–26; elephant sanctuary 37–39; El Salvador 29–31; hindu and buddhist site 36–37; hindu sacred site 35–36; overview 23; perspective transformation theory 24–25; Rapti River 39; thatched roof 26–29; via sacred sites 34

dance 49–51, *51*
deep breathing 134
Democratic Republic of Congo (DRC) 159
Developmental Model of Intercultural Sensitivity (DMIS) 3
developmental theory 143; *see also* theories
Dias, Bartolomeu 45
Dinka and Nuer tribes 101
discourse 26, 82–83, 96–99
dissonance 24, 44, 79, 89–91, 95, 97, 98
dual enrollment 145

Eagle Butte 31–33, 65, 116, 119, 188, 190, 197
early emerging adulthood 147
Ecuador 118
educator/education: community 142; experiential 1, 2, 28, 142; higher 145, 146; role 153–155; undergraduate 139–156; vocational 184; volunteers 170; *see also* learning; school; students
Einfeld, A. 113
elephant sanctuary 37–39
El Salvador 29–31, 119, 159–160, 162, 164–165
Elwood, S.A. 27

emerging adulthood 145–146
Emerson 133
emotional breakdown 171–172
English language 45, 46, 47, 52, 67, 120, 130, 181
ethnorelativism 3, 26, 71
exceptional human experiences (EHEs) 173
"Experiencing Tears of Wonder Joy" (Braud) 173
experiential education 1, 2, 28, 142; see also educator/education
expressive therapies 74, 119–120, 143, 144, 153, 155, 180

Family Educational and Privacy Act (FERPA) 146
Frankl, Viktor 52
Freire, P. 5, 85, 97
friendship bracelet 28, 63, *64*, 93, 142, 174
Furco, A. 1–2

Ganges River 35
Garreau, Julie 33, 105, 114, 187, 188
George, C.L. 144
Gilmore, K.J. 147, 155
girls' empowerment program 50
Global Alliance for Africa (GAA) 10
Global Citizen Leadership 180
global issues 193–194
Goodman, G. 9
Gorbachev, Mikhail 139
Gossen, Katie 50
Gqeberha 45–49, 75, 129–131, 163–164
graduate student experiences 143–145
graffiti arts 54–56
graffiti painting *34*
gum boot dancing 133
Gyawali, Raj 169, 181–183

Handbook of Expressive Therapy (Malchiodi) 8
hand-painted mandalas 125
hand stencils 15–16, *16*
hiking experience 42–44, 70
Himalayan range 17, 43, 44, 171
Hindu: and buddhist site 36–37; deities of 35; origin of 44; practice of Yoga 133–134; sacred site 35–36; Vedic text 137
hip hop dance 49–50, *51*
Hladek, Melissa 65, *70*

Holi celebration 70, 72, 75, 119, 135, 136
human experiences 173–174
Hungary 65, 119–120, 159, 164

Illeris, K. 24, 25
immersion process 23; see also cultural immersion
indigenous art-making practices 122–131; Gqeberha 129–131; Lakota Sioux Art practices 122–124; Nepalese 125–128
In Search of Self in India and Japan (Roland) 61
instrumental learning 80
internal review board (IRB) 107
The Invisible String (Karst) 68–69
"Invisible Strings" (Swift) 68
Isaac Booi Primary School 71, *87*

Jackson, Katherine 92, 94, 156
Jacobs, R. 142
Jacoby, B. 1
Jim Crow laws 46
Johnson-Bailey, J. 97
joining with locals, best practice 162–164
Jordan, J. 59–61, 66

K-12 International Baccalaureate curriculum 72
Kalmanowitz, D. 9, 10
Kapitan, L. 9–11
Karst, Patrice 68
Kasl, E. 97
Kathmandu 18, 43, *90*, 136, 169, 171, 174, 186, 192
Kazel, Dorothy 29–31
Keya Café 33
kid-oriented yoga 134
Kiely, R. 24–25, 43, 78, 86–91, 98
Kim, P.Y. 153
Kitayama, S. 156
Kramer, E. 8, 9, 18, 49, 166

Ladysmith Black Mambazo 137
Lakota Sioux tribe 53, *53*, 53–54, 91, 114, 190; art practices 122–124; cultural competence 104–105; elders at a drum circle *53*; hoisting tipi poles *57*; working amongst 104–105
Lawrence, R.L. 97
leadership skills 153, 155

learning: adult 78, 80, 81, 83, 85, 88, 90; communicative 80–81; service-learning 1–5; transformative 77–99; *see also* educator/education; school; students
leeches on foot 65–67
Leitson, Jordan 50
liberation theory 5; *see also* theories
logistics 166–168
Lowenfeld, Viktor 8–9
Luther King, Martin 179

Malchiodi, C. 8, 9
mandalas 125–126, *126*, *127*
Mandela, Nelson 45–47
Man's Search for Meaning (Frankl) 52
Markus, H.R. 153
mask making 48, *48*, 49
McDonald's restaurant 41
McNiff, Shaun 9
Meersand, P. 147, 155
mental health 91, 107, 113, 153, 174, 180, 191, 194–195
Mezirow, J. 24–26, 78, 79, 97
Miller, J. 59, 62
Monkey Temple *see* Swayambhunath Temple
Moon, C. 9–11
Mount Everest 43
Mugabe, Robert 175
Multicultural Awareness Subscale scores 107
Multicultural Counseling Inventory (MCI) 107–111
Murray-Garcia, J. 101
mutual empathy 59–60
mutual empowerment 59, 60, 63, 65

National Endowment for the Arts (NEA) 114
Native American Community 31–32, 88, 188
Naumburg, Margaret 8
Ndebele language 46
Nepal: cultural competence 105–107; drumming 137; girl drawing on a clay pot *19*; government 39; indigenous art-making practices 125–128; mountains and hill towns of 106; safe house for girls 62–63; student volunteers planting *20*; style modern music 173; traditions and norms of culture 106; yoga in 133–134

Nepal Police's Women and Children Cell 184
Nonna Roma 148–149
nonprofit volunteer group 168–169

Onosu, G. 23
origami boxes *129*, 129–131

Palliative Care Center 41
paper heart strings 20–22
Pashupatinath temple 35–36
Pasquarelli, S. L. 155
Pedagogy of the Oppressed (Freire) 5
Peniel Center 10–11, 13, 27, 67, 109, 163, 171, 175
personalization of work 91–92
perspective transformation theory 24–25; *see also* theories
piggyback races 135, *136*
plant painting 125
play therapy 134–138
Polaroid camera 174
Pollock, M. 25
"pop-up" art station 124
Port Elizabeth *see* Gqeberha
postcolonial theory 1, 4–5; *see also* theories
Potash, J. 4
practical considerations 152–155
Prema elephant 38, *38*
pre-trip score 107–108
Prinzhorn, Hans 8
Prisoner Assistance Nepal (PA Nepal) 17, *21*, 22, 63, 65, 70, 106, 117–118, 176; and Antardristi 117–118; celebrating Holi at *70*; heart doilies at *21*, *69*; Social Tours and 181–183
privilege/power 84–86
processing/connecting 92–96

raksi 106, 163
Ranamagar, Indira 18
Rapti River 39
RedCan Graffiti Jam 33, 54, 93, 94, 114, 119, 123, 187, 189
Red Thread of Fate (Butler) 68
Reik, Theodore 18
Reken, Van 25
relational-cultural theory (RCT) 59, 62
relationship(s): and caring 83–84; formation and transformation 84; microskills 84; in self-growth, role of 62; therapeutic 82, 84, 85

relationship building 59–75; across years 63–64; Antardristi 62–63; Cactus 67–68; colorful moments 74–75; consensus 83–84; cultural differences in 60–62; invisible string theory 68–69; relational-cultural theory 59–60; in service-learning 65; story 69–71; sustained family impact 71–73
Roland, A. 61
Romani people 119–120
Roysircar-Sodowsky, G. 107
Russian Orthodox church 173
Russian youth *140*

sacred sites 34–35
Samata School 70, 166, 167
Sanskrit language 138
Santulli, D. 168, 169, 177–179, 196
Sapana Village 37
Satoro, Ryunosuke 168
school: attending 18, 105; colorist perspective in 45–47; fees 118; high 145, 148; leaders 130; mandala painting 125; township 89; *see also* educator/education; learning; students
Schroder, D. 140
Seaman, Megan 19, 27, 87, 114, 134, 171, 172, 197, *198*
see and be seen, best practice 165–166
self-in-relation theory 59; *see also* theories
servant leadership 104
service-learning 1–5; alumnus 108; with arts-based expressive therapy 5–10; DMIS 3–4; experiences 77, 89, 160, 194; liberation theory 5; overview 1–3; postcolonial theory 4–5; providers 42, 104, 106, 113; social justice and 113–120; transformative 86–88; trip 147, 162; types of 2; undergraduate education 147–151
Service-Learning Art Directive/Activities Planning Guide 154
service providers/recipients 177–196; Antardristi 184–187; Cheyenne River Youth Project 187–191; community volunteer 195–196; mental health creative arts therapist 194–195; Social Tours 181–183; strengths and skills 191–193; student growth 191; United Planet 177–181; view on global issues 193–194

sex trafficking 106, 124
sexual abuse 17–18, 161, 184, 185, 187
Sigmon, R. 2
Simon, Paul 137
Skenandore, Hoka 55–56
snake medicine 124, *125*
Snyder, M.J. 96
social change ideology 118
social justice 88, 91, 113–120; Antardristi and PA Nepal 117–118; Cheyenne River Reservation 114–117; Ecuador 118; expressive therapies 119; Hungary 119–120; introduction 113–114; and social change 120
social media 68, 71, 174, 185
Social Tours 69, 169, 181–183
Soto, Angelina Villalobos 54 *55*
South Africa 45–51; creative and expressive arts practices 132–133; dance 49–51, *51*, 132–133 education system 46; kids 195; languages 45; yoga in 133–134
Soviet Union 139, 156, 178
spiritual awakening 171–172
Staniunas-Hopper, Jodi 156
St. Dominics school 119
stick-jumping game *12*
Stiver, I. 59, 62
Stoecker, R. 113, 114
Stories for the Third Ear (Wallas) 18
Student Learning Outcomes Survey of Community Based Research 144
students 191; anxiety 149; counseling 95, *96*; preparing food for distribution *148*; undergraduate and graduate **151**; volunteer 36, 54, 129, 168, 193; *see also* educator/education learning; school
Sudanese boys 101–103
Surrey, J. 60
sustained family impact 71–73
Swayambhunath Temple 36–37, *37*
Swift, Taylor 68

Tai Pai Hospital 41
Taiwan 41–42
TammiJo 124
Taylor, E.W. 96
Taylor, K.B. 86
Tervalon, M. 101
Tharu people 39, 74
thatched roof 26–29

theories: critical social 96; of developmental model of intercultural sensitivity 3–4; invisible string 68–69; perspective transformation 24–25; postcolonial 1, 4–5; self-in-relation 59; transformational learning 80–81
Therapeutic Arts Program (TAP) 10
"third hand" technique 9
Thoreau 133
tipi 56–57; canvas 56; hoisting 57; raising 56, 104; sacred 57
Tissue Paper Hair Ornament *128*
tourist-curated activities 162
transformation, defined 78–80
transformative learning 77–99; contextual border crossing 88–89; critique 96–97; defined 80; discourse 82–83; dissonance 89–90; integrating 98; overview 77–78; personalizing 91–92; privilege and power 84–86; processing and connecting 92–96; relationships and caring 83–84; theory 80–81
transformative service-learning 24, 78, 86–88, 96; *see also* service-learning
Tucker, Earl 49

undergraduate education 139–156; and graduate student experiences 143–147; overview 139–143; practical considerations 152–155; service-learning 147–151; *see also* educator/education
United Planet 118, 152, 168, 177–181, 196

Ursuline College 7, 29, 30, 33, 53, 107, 159, 169
utilize resources, best practice 162

Vietnam War 26
volunteers 43, 92, 124, 171, 196; community 195–196; group 168–169; at Nonna Roma 149; piggyback races *136*; service-learning 4, 63, *64*, 114, 161; student 36, 54, 129, 193; touching prayer wheel *37*

waiting for invitation, best practice 160–161
Wallas, L. 18
watercolor paintings 122, 125
Watson, Lilla 5
white bull *103*
wisdom garnered 172
women preparing vegetables *14*
wood carving 122
World War I 160

Xhosa language 46, 47, 52

yoga: asanas/postures 134; marathon 117; in Nepal and South Africa 133–134; sessions 134
Yorks, L. 97
Youth Ambassadors of America 139
Youth Summit 139
Youth with a Mission (YWAM) 167

Zimbabwe 10–15, 27, 73, 167, 172
Zimbabwean National Guard 73
Zulu culture 132

For Product Safety Concerns and Information please contact our EU representative GPSR@taylorandfrancis.com Taylor & Francis Verlag GmbH, Kaufingerstraße 24, 80331 München, Germany

Printed and bound by CPI Group (UK) Ltd, Croydon, CR0 4YY

14/04/2026

02089738-0007